FAMILY THEMES AND HAWTHORNE'S FICTION

Gloria C. Erlich

FAMILY THEMES AND HAWTHORNE'S FICTION

The Tenacious Web

RUTGERS UNIVERSITY PRESS

New Brunswick, New Jersey

Library of Congress Cataloging in Publication Data
Erlich, Gloria C.
Family Themes and Hawthorne's Fiction
Bibliography: p.
Includes index.
1. Hawthorne, Nathaniel, 1804–1864—Biography—
Youth.   2. Hawthorne, Nathaniel, 1804–1864.   Doctor
Grimshawe's secret.   3. Family in literature.
4. Novelists, American—19th century—Biography.
I. Title.
PS1882.E74   1984   813'.3 [B]   83–13989
ISBN 0–8135–1028–7

43,391

To my families—

BLANCHE AND DANIEL M. CHASSON

PHILIP, JULIE, AND AUSTIN ERLICH

And my mentors—

OLA ELIZABETH WINSLOW

YVOR WINTERS

"If you know anything of me, you know how I sprang out of the elements, without visible agency—how, all through my boyhood, I was alone; how I grew up without a root, yet continually longing for one—longing to be connected with somebody—and never feeling myself so. . . . I have tried to keep down this yearning, to stifle it, annihilate it, with making a position for myself, with being my own past, but I cannot overcome this natural horror of being a creature floating in the air, attached to nothing; nor this feeling that there is no reality in the life and fortunes of a being so unconnected. There is not even a grave, not a heap of dry bones, not a pinch of dust, with which I can claim connection, unless I find it here."

Ned Etherege in *Doctor Grimshawe's Secret*

Contents

CONTENTS

Chronology

1780	Hawthorne's mother, Elizabeth Clarke Manning, born; died 1849.
1801	August 2, marriage of Hawthorne's parents.
1802	Hawthorne's sister Elizabeth (Ebe) born; died 1883.
1804	Nathaniel Hawthorne born on July 4 in Union Street house, Salem, Massachusetts.
1808	Death of father, Captain Nathaniel Hathorne, en route to Surinam, Dutch Guiana.
	Hawthorne's sister Maria Louisa born; died 1852.
1809	Removal of the Hawthorne family to the Manning home on Herbert Street, Salem.
1811	Attended school of Joseph Worcester and had opportunity to associate with boys of his own age.
1813	Injury to foot, lasting several years, took him out of school and made possible solitary reading along with home tutoring.
	Last communication from Uncle John Manning, who had left to fight in the War of 1812.
	Grandfather Manning died en route to family lands in Raymond, Maine.
	Uncle Richard Manning moved to Raymond to oversee sale of family lands and never returned to Salem.

1816	Summer, Mother took up residence with children in Raymond.
1818	Mother and three children visited family in Salem, but returned to Raymond.
	Brought back to Salem for study, mother and sisters remaining in Raymond.
1820	Tutored by Benjamin Lynde Oliver to prepare for college entrance.
1821–1825	Attended Bowdoin College, Brunswick, Maine.
1822	Mother gave up residence in Raymond and returned to Herbert Street house, Salem.
1824	Uncle Robert Manning married Elizabeth Dodge Burnham.
1825–1837	"Long seclusion" in attic of mother's home.
1828	*Fanshawe: A Tale* published anonymously at author's expense.
1828–1832	Family lived at 16 Dearborn Street, North Salem, in house built for Madame Hawthorne next to his own by Robert Manning.
1830–1837	Many tales and sketches published anonymously or pseudonymously in periodicals.
1836	Edited the *American Magazine of Useful and Entertaining Knowledge*.
1837	Publication of *Peter Parley's Universal History* as one of Samuel Goodrich's *Peter Parley* series of children's books. Publication of *Twice-told Tales*.
1838	Engagement to Sophia Peabody.
1839–1840	Measurer of coal and salt at the Boston Custom House.
1841	Publication of *Grandfather's Chair*.
1841	April to November, member of Brook Farm Community.
1842	July 9, married Sophia Peabody in Boston.
	October 10, death of Uncle Robert Manning. Second and enlarged edition of *Twice-told Tales*.
1842–1845	Lived at the Old Manse, Concord, Massachusetts.
1844	Daughter Una born.
1845	Edited Horatio Bridge's *Journal of an African Cruiser*.

1846   Son Julian born.
             Publication of *Mosses from an Old Manse*.
1846–1849   Surveyor of the port of Salem.
1849   Death of mother.
1850   Publication of *The Scarlet Letter*.
1850–1851   Lived in Lenox, Massachusetts, and came to know
             Herman Melville.
1851   Daughter Rose born.
             Publication of *The House of the Seven Gables*, *The Snow-
             Image*, and *True Stories from History and Biography*.
1851–1852   Lived in West Newton, Massachusetts.
1852   Franklin Pierce elected president of the United States.
             Publication of *Life of Franklin Pierce*, *The Blithedale
             Romance*, and *A Wonder-Book for Girls and Boys*.
1852–1853   Lived at The Wayside, Concord, Massachusetts.
1853   Death of sister Maria Louisa following explosion of a
             Hudson River steamer.
             Publication of *Tanglewood Tales for Girls and Boys*.
1853–1857   Served as United States Consul at Liverpool,
             England, appointed by Franklin Pierce.
1857–1859   Lived in Rome and Florence.
             Illness of daughter Una.
1859   Returned to England and completed *The Marble Faun*,
             published 1860.
1863   Publication of *Our Old Home*, dedicated to Franklin
             Pierce.
1864   Died May 19 at Plymouth, New Hampshire, in
             company of Franklin Pierce. Buried May 23 in
             Concord, Massachusetts.
             Left manuscripts of four unfinished romances.

Preface

I should say a few words about the genre of this book, what it is and what it is not. It is not a literary biography or a psychobiography or a work of literary criticism, although it has elements of all three. Perhaps we should call it a thematic study of the continuities between Hawthorne's life and his art, the psychological and experiential sources of his fiction. The material flows freely between the biographical and the fictional poles, moved less by chronological sequence than by the movement from lived experience to imaginative expression. As a natural history of Hawthorne's imagination, the account is mindful of sequence but subordinates narrative to theme.

Biographies of Hawthorne tend to be factual, and literary studies tend to be interpretive without sufficient regard to historical fact. I have attempted to base interpretation on fact, that is, to place biographical research in the service of critical understanding. For this reason, I have restricted my focus to the major aspects of Hawthorne's formative years, reconstructed these from primary sources, and presented my findings in the light of what followed in Hawthorne's life, both experiential and creative.

The result is an interpretive structure resting on a factual foundation. There is speculation here, but informed speculation, which readers can easily separate from fact and weigh for themselves, testing it for coherence and explanatory value. This statement, placed here at the beginning, can be understood as hovering over the speculative sections in lieu of qualifiers, which tend to clog the prose.

Unlike a standard literary biography, this book does not move serenely from birth to death, treating literary works as they occur among other events in the author's life. Such orderly biographies are necessary, and the 1980s have produced two substantial ones, *Nathaniel Hawthorne: A Biography* by Arlin Turner and *Nathaniel Hawthorne in His Times* by James R. Mellow, which greatly amplify our knowledge of Hawthorne as a man in the world.[1]

My purpose is not to replicate such works but to portray Hawthorne's inner life, scanting when necessary the picture of him as man of affairs—citizen, politician, or wage earner—in order to isolate the organizing principles of that inner life. To do this, I had to recreate the "seedtime of his soul," the childhood period that most biographers find too ordinary for detailed examination. Randall Stewart's biography of 1948 covers both boyhood and ancestry in twelve pages.[2] The recent biographies mentioned above make some attempt to characterize Hawthorne's maternal relatives, but neither tries to view this family constellation as it might have affected the personality and imagination of a fatherless young boy with a passive mother and a powerful father-surrogate.

Neglect of the family that surrounded Hawthorne in his youth is most surprising in the most thoroughly psychoanalytic of all Hawthorne studies, *The Sins of the Fathers* by Frederick C. Crews. This work announces that "Hawthorne's interest in history is only a special case of his interest in fathers and sons, guilt and retribution, instinct and inhibition," and that his "sense of the past is nothing other than the sense of symbolic family conflict writ large."[3] Emphasizing "filial aggression" and intensely alert to Hawthorne's frequent displacement of fathers with surrogate figures and his ambivalent, often hostile, depictions of older men, Crews yet fails to seek a biographical explanation for these patterns. He attributes them to unresolved Oedipal conflicts but does not consider the fact that Hawthorne had no living father who could have occasioned the particular kind of resentment observable in his fiction. Hawthorne's recurring pictures of tyrannical older men who dominate, even enthrall, younger ones was more likely generated by a living father-surrogate than by a father who vanished when the child was only four years old.

This substitution of uncle for father surely affected the quality and character of Hawthorne's Oedipal experiences and shaped his attitude toward older men. Crews derives his evidence for Hawthorne's neurosis from his fiction without examination of the actual conditions of his childhood and without recognizing the significance of his troubled relationship to his maternal uncle, Robert Manning. Both before and since Crews's landmark study critics have observed the presence of Oedipal themes in Hawthorne's work, but without reference to their biographical roots.

In this study I try to identify the genesis and particular qualities of these motifs. If incestuous longings and Oedipal hostilities are as universal as Freud believed, identification of them in an imaginative product does not tell us very much. We must try to understand these archetypal experiences as they occurred in a particular person in a particular family situation, and as they expressed themselves in particular literary structures. Beyond merely identifying psychological themes, we must try to reconstruct the quality and energy of the affect they engaged, the longevity of this engagement, and the ways in which these themes found expression, whether devious or overt.

Identification of common psychological themes without differentiation of their specific qualities homogenizes our impressions of writers whose work is marked in varying ways by similar motifs. I am thinking, for example, of Eric J. Sundquist's dazzling study of four American authors—Cooper, Thoreau, Hawthorne, and Melville—in *Home as Found*. Although Sundquist states that Hawthorne's historical sense "belongs equally to his personal life and to the historical tradition,"[4] he follows Crews in ignoring the personal life and deriving his evidence from the fiction. Sundquist concentrates on a cluster of psychological themes common to these authors—primal scene speculation, search for origins, genealogy, home, incest, repetitions of and atonement for ritual murders of the father—and relates these themes to the virginal American landscape but not to their experiential origins. This treatment causes the authors and their works to sound rather too much alike. As much as Melville and Hawthorne had in common, including strikingly similar features of their family constellations, they differed significantly in the ways they handled experience. Even when writing out of common autobiographical motives, these authors differed from each other in the personality and in the levels of feeling that they chose to express.

It does not suffice merely to identify preoccupation with incest, for example, without determining the quality and duration of the provocation, the resistance or complicity of the subject, the capacity for sublimation—in other words, the layer of self engaged with this theme—as well as the urgency of the need to communicate it and the kind of communication (devious or direct) that would satisfy this need. I do not pretend to have done all this with Hawthorne, but I believe these are the kinds of questions to ask. We should ask not only whether the theme was near the surface or deeply buried, but what degree of transformation or disguise the author's personality required.

Psychological themes will inform literary works differently according to whether they are overt or covert, latent or manifest. Although I cannot ascertain how consciously Hawthorne used autobiographical materials in his fiction, my investigation shows that he transformed them so greatly that even critical awareness of recurrent plots and character types has not heretofore aroused great curiosity about the author's formative experiences.

To redress this neglect, I have used family documents to recreate his first images of human personality in its various family roles. His creative imagination as well as his experiences in the world were influenced by his childish perception of family figures, which was not always identical with their factual reality. Where possible I have tried to distinguish between the historical reality of the family and his mythicized versions of it. In so doing I have been able to test against surviving documents many family myths generated by biographers over the past century—for example, those dealing with Hawthorne's and his mother's reclusiveness. Doubtless, I have generated a few myths of my own that will in turn have to be debunked by others.

One source of error in studies of Hawthorne's childhood has been biographers' reliance on a purported "first diary," allegedly transmitted by a childhood acquaintance and edited by Samuel T. Pickard in various versions starting in 1870, less than ten years after Hawthorne's death. Given the sparsity of evidence about Hawthorne's early years, even biographers aware of the dubious provenance of this diary have been unwilling to dispense with what appears to be an autobiographical record of the boyhood years. I have not used this diary in reconstructing Hawthorne's childhood because I regard it as fraudulent. Evidence for my conclusion and a detailed history of the diary and Pickard's correspondence about it are collected in "Who Wrote Hawthorne's First Diary?" and published in the 1977 issue of the *Nathaniel Hawthorne Journal.*[5]

In keeping with my focus on the inner life, I have chosen to treat Hawthorne's books as events in the author's life rather than as events in the literary world. Of course they were literary events, though often depressingly minor ones, but the critical reception has been superbly covered by Donald Crowley in *Hawthorne: The Critical Heritage* and by others.[6] I treat the works as products of the author's developing vocation, the vicissitudes of which shaped his sense of identity. Insofar as these works grafted his private imagery onto existing literary conventions, they established successful continuity between inner and outer, between private life and culture, and helped solidify his relationship to the world. Thus fictional works deriving from inner life processes and serving as validations of the author's vocation became internalized within his evolving sense of self, a process that in turn issued in further works reflecting this new consolidation. The continuous flow between inner and outer is the subtle process I have tried to capture.

Because the continuities I trace are incremental repetitions, my structure follows a somewhat musical pattern of theme and variation. Accordingly, I begin with an overture introducing the major themes of Hawthorne's life: maternal deprivation, paternal loss, and avuncular domination. These forces retarded his artistic development until two major losses precipitated his creative breakthrough at age forty-five. My first chapter, "The Access of Power," begins with Hawthorne at his creative peak, the period of *The Scarlet Letter*.

The second chapter steps back to reconstruct the circumstances of Hawthorne's childhood and the personalities of his maternal relatives, the Mannings, with whom the Hawthornes lived after the death of his father. His adult figures were not, as he wished us to think, grim Puritan hanging judges, but generous and energetic business people who tried to instill mercantile values into an indolent artistic boy. Despite his resistance, Hawthorne internalized their values so thoroughly that he was always to distrust his chosen vocation as artist and to incorporate the tension between artist and merchant into much of his fiction. With the larger family pattern established, the next two chapters close in on the central figures, female and male, of his earliest experience. The family experience provided material that his mythicizing imagination was later to transform into literary structures. My search was not for the "originals" of literary characters in any mechanical or superficial sense but for the materials and processes of imaginative transformation. Seeking the deeper levels of continuity between life and literature, I found lifelong variations of the author's "identity theme."* The primary roles and relationships evolved continuously over the course of his life, generating mythic magnifications that his imagination played out in fictional form.

When we understand the meaning for Hawthorne of these archetypal relationships we perceive that their inner workings generated not only character types but narrative structures. His way of perceiving experience and adapting it to literary conventions, his way of introducing, plotting, and closing narratives, were just as closely influenced by these familial imprints as was his repertory of characters. This shaping influence was not uniformly beneficial, as can be seen by contrasting his successes with his failures. At the period of *The Scarlet Letter*, when Hawthorne felt a sense of coherence and power, the family drama issued in an almost perfectly harmonious narrative structure. At a time of fragmentation, during Hawthorne's old age, the same forces virtually disabled his narrative control.

My last chapter, the fifth, brings together the entire constellation of themes where they appear most compulsively, in *Doctor Grimshawe's Secret*, a late unfinished romance. My lengthy chapter on such a fragmented and rarely read book perhaps needs some justification. This fascinating failure allows a privileged view of the author in the process of struggling to devise a narrative structure to embody violently inchoate psychological forces. In this record of struggle we glimpse the transformative process by which personal myths enter literature. While observing Hawthorne strain to embody his own life themes in fictive forms, we see that his primary family drama not

---

*I use the term "identity theme" in the sense defined by Norman N. Holland in *5 Readers Reading* (New Haven and London: Yale University Press, 1975, pp. 56–62), which he in turn relates to the theories of Heinz Lichtenstein and Charles Mauron. In brief, Holland defines the "identity theme" as the "one theme or style permeating all aspects of an individual's life. In that sense, we have an unchanging self, but nevertheless reality and one's own inner drives demand that that self reach out to new experiences. It then grows by adding these experiences as new variations to this unchanging central theme. An 'identity theme' is determined by past events, yet paradoxically it is the only basis for future growth and, therefore, freedom. It is the foundation for every personal and human synthesis of new experience, be it falling in love or simply reading a book" (p. 61).

only remained with him until the end of his life but became more active and destructive than ever. The central motif of *Doctor Grimshawe's Secret* is an all encompassing spider web, and this study testifies to the persistence of such silken traps.

Acknowledgments

This study was greatly aided by the use of correspondence donated in 1975 and 1976 by Nathaniel Hawthorne's great-grandson, Manning Hawthorne, to the Essex Institute of Salem, Massachusetts, and to Bowdoin College, Brunswick, Maine. I wish to thank Mr. Hawthorne for the generous, informative letters he wrote to me about the location and provenance of documents and for his kind permission to quote from Hawthorne and Manning family letters and records. I have tried to reproduce these letters as written, retaining their spelling and punctuation with a minimum of interpolation. Where terminal punctuation and initial capitalization are omitted in the originals, I use triple spaces to indicate sentence division.

Although Hawthorne restored the "w" to his family name in the 1820s, I have spelled "Hawthorne" with the "w" for the author's name at all ages and for that of his mother and sisters, using "Hathorne" only for the author's father and other paternal forebears.

Gratitude is due to the Essex Institute for allowing me to use and quote from its incomparable Hawthorne-Manning Collection. I particularly want to thank Irene Norton for the personal interest she took in helping me locate materials and feel at home in Salem.

The Bowdoin College Library generously allowed me to quote from its extensive Nathaniel Hawthorne Collection. Mary Hughes was especially helpful in making the time I spent at Hawthorne's college pleasant and productive.

I thank David E. Schoonover, Curator of the Collection of American Literature at the Beinecke Rare Book Room of Yale University Library for permission to quote from this collection and Donald Gallup, former curator, for allowing me access to the Hawthorne files of the late Norman Holmes Pearson at a time when it was not particularly convenient for him or the library. Professor Pearson's transcripts of Manning family correspondence are cited in my notes as "Pearson Transcript." Photocopied transcripts of Elizabeth M. Hawthorne's letters from Montserrat survive in two copies, one in the Pearson collection and another divided between the Essex Institute and Bowdoin College Library. Because these transcripts were made by Richard Clarke Manning, they are cited as "Manning Transcript."

Quotations from Hawthorne's works are taken from *The Centenary Edition of the Works of Nathaniel Hawthorne*, edited by William Charvat, Roy Harvey Pearce, Claude M. Simpson, et al. (Columbus: Ohio State University Press, 1962 –). Quotations from this edition are cited parenthetically within the text by volume and page number. Quotations from Hawthorne's letters correspond as closely as possible to the texts of the Centenary Edition of the letters, which was in press simultaneously with this book. Professor Thomas Woodson has generously checked my transcriptions against those of the Centenary Edition and patiently answered my many queries. My quotations from the Centenary volume XV, *The Letters, 1813–1853*, are cited by letter number. Quotations from the forthcoming volume XVI, *The Letters, 1853–1864*, are identified in the notes by date only because letter and page numbers are not yet available. For the few Hawthorne letters not quoted from the Centenary texts I use other methods of citation.*

I thank Joel Myerson for permission to reprint material in chapter two that was first published as "Hawthorne and the Mannings," in *Studies in the American Renaissance* (1980). A short version of chapter five, "Doctor Grimshawe and Other Secrets," appeared in the *Essex Institute Historical Collections* in January 1982 and is included here with permission from the editor.

For many constructive suggestions at early stages of the manuscript, I wish to thank William L. Howarth, Richard M. Ludwig, and Carlos Baker, all of Princeton University. At an intermediate stage Annette Kolodny volunteered encouragement without which I might have abandoned the project. For astute criticisms of the first chapter, I thank Kathleen Neuer, Mary Oates of Rider College, and

---

*On pages 109, 120, 123, and 124, quotations cited to Volume VIII, *The American Notebooks*, have been altered to conform to the transcripts made by Barbara S. Mouffe in *Hawthorne's Lost Notebook: 1835–1841* (University Park: Pennsylvania State University Press, 1978).

members of the Work in Progress seminar of the Princeton Research Forum. At the concluding stage, Suzanne K. Hyman made a valued contribution. I owe a special debt of gratitude to Aileen Ward and members of the Biography Seminar of the New York Institute for the Humanities for illuminating discussions on the art of biography and for a sense of colleagueship in this difficult endeavor.

Excellent suggestions came also from Rita Gollin, State University of New York at Geneseo, and David Leverenz of Rutgers University. For encouragement and for generous consultations I thank Rae Carlson of Rutgers University and Silvan S. Tomkins, a professor emeritus of Rutgers University.

I am grateful for the intuitive and tactful copy editing done by Emily Wheeler for Rutgers University Press. For professional integrity and years of devotion to this book, I thank Carolyn Kappes, a typist and computer impressario who understands the humanistic uses of technology.

I hope that the members of my family who have had to live with this book over so many years will find that their sacrifices were justified. Special appreciation goes to Austin Reade Erlich, who provided essential resources otherwise difficult to obtain, and Philip Erlich, who supported the project in manifold ways.

FAMILY THEMES AND HAWTHORNE'S FICTION

ONE

The Access of Power

"But I cannot die till I have achieved my destiny. Then, let Death come! I shall have built my monument!"

"The Ambitious Guest"

IN MEDIAS RES

Hawthorne's life was shaped by the contours of his career—a long, slow ascent, a brief period of mastery, a painful decline much swifter than the ascent. One way of understanding both life and career is to begin in the middle, the high point of his achievements as man and writer. Approaching his life at its peak, when he broke through to his first major work, provides a reference point for his life before and after, revealing the forces that retarded his artistic development from the perspective of his brief but exhilarating mastery of those forces. Without pretending to explain the mystery of Hawthorne's creativity, we *can* try to identify both the circumstances that delayed its flowering and the inner and outer events that enabled him to break free in an access of creative power.[1] Recent studies of adult development that clarify the interrelationships between life and career help explain the remarkable burst of creative energy that occurred at a most surprising time in Hawthorne's life.

In 1849, the year before Hawthorne published *The Scarlet Letter*, he was forty-five years old, had been married seven years, was the father of two young children, and had published collections of tales and sketches and several volumes of children's books; however, he had not yet produced the work that would validate his identity as an author.

Having learned during his first married years at the Old Manse that the proceeds from his writing were too meager and too uncertain for his family's needs, he sought and in 1846 accepted a political appointment to the Salem Custom House. He had expected that this sinecure on which he had relied to support his family was to be his indefinitely, but on June 8, 1849, he learned that the newly elected Whig government intended to replace him. While absorbing this blow, he was a daily witness to his mother's terminal illness. Throughout the following month she lay dying in an upstairs room of his home in Salem. She died on July 31 and was buried August 2.

Yet within a month, and despite a fit of "brain fever," this normally slow and indolent author was writing nine hours a day, more than twice his usual stint. The intensity of his concentration so astonished his wife Sophia that she wrote to her mother on September 2, "Mr. Hawthorne writes *immensely*."[2] By February 3, 1850, he had completed *The Scarlet Letter* and its introductory essay, "The Custom-House." The book was printed rapidly and released on March 16.

Within six months of two shattering losses, Hawthorne produced his first full length work and undisputed masterpiece. The linkage in this familiar but remarkable chain of events is more than sequential. Hawthorne's breakthrough into his mature achievement was causally related to these very losses. His confrontation with death, directly in the loss of his mother and symbolically in the stagnant "death-in-life" of the Custom House experience, apparently potentiated his sudden access of power. Death in its real and its symbolic forms came at him at an age when he was peculiarly receptive to its message, that is, at the natural turning point known today as the midlife crisis.

Both events contributed to closing the Salem era in Hawthorne's life. "The Custom-House" preface discusses the personal significance of the "natal soil" of Salem and reasons for terminating his physical relationship to it. But "The Custom-House" is a misleading specimen of autobiography, concealing as much as it reveals. Hawthorne offers to establish a "true relation with his audience" and then pretends to be only the editor of *The Scarlet Letter*. In exposing his ties to Salem he artfully selects only *some* of those ties, the picturesque ones of his Puritan ancestors on the paternal side. The main reason he gives for remaining in a town he finds drab is his link to the bones of his paternal ancestors, "the sensuous sympathy of dust for dust"; hence one might expect that the most recent addition to his family graves, that of his mother, would *bind* him to Salem rather than free him to leave it.

But he makes no mention of the death of his mother, and he presents the Custom House essay as his valediction to all that Salem meant to him as well as announcement of a new beginning. The entire essay speaks of transition, of moving from past and present into the future, of recapitulating past attachments and allegiances in order to separate from them. This farewell to his prolonged professional apprenticeship, to a life of uncertainty and preparation, to influences that made him feel trivial and unmanly, is also a salute to his new sense of mastery. For an author so closely bound to his "natal soil," this heralded change of place signals a change of status.

Salem was his "natal soil" as well as his ancestral burying ground. These unsettled maternal and paternal influences had to be integrated and transcended before he could accomplish his mature work. In departing Salem, he was marking the end of his literal sonhood, saying farewell to the mother from whom he had been too often separated as a child, and farewell to the graves of rather intimidating paternal ancestors. Most of all, he was turning away from father substitutes who had unintentionally fostered attitudes of dependency threatening to his manhood. In announcing his departure, he was renouncing all that had delayed his personal and artistic maturation—overpowering ancestors, patriarchal figures of many kinds, and dependence on "Uncle Sam's gold."

In the two years following this departure he published *The House of the Seven Gables*, *The Blithedale Romance*, *The Snow-Image*, *True Stories from History and Biography*, *A Wonder-Book for Girls and Boys*, and a biography of Franklin Pierce, that is, the bulk of his completed works. In other words, between beginning *The Scarlet Letter* in late 1849 and completing *The Blithedale Romance* in April 1852, Hawthorne wrote three of his four full-length works of fiction and prepared another collection of tales, a biography, and several books for children. Of the children's books, his most popular, *Tanglewood Tales*, appeared in 1853.

The losses of 1849 that precipitated this burst of creative activity appear to have been the culminating events of a crisis that had been

3

developing during his long years of apprenticeship followed by failure to establish himself as a successful and self-supporting author. Hawthorne's struggle with problems of delayed creativity and vocational identity can be illuminated by the work of Erik Erikson and by a recent study of adult development by Daniel J. Levinson (and others), *The Seasons of a Man's Life*. These studies are keenly attuned to the role of work in shaping a man's life and are especially attentive to the psychological meaning of time. Erikson's biographical studies emphasize the peculiar strains that creative people experience if they have to wait through prolonged periods of preparation before attaining professional maturity. However, his eight-stage division of the life cycle emphasizes youth and adolescence, whereas Levinson's schema of four overlapping major eras (childhood and adolescence, early, middle, and late adulthood) is more oriented toward adult development. In defining clearly and examining closely the periods of adult development and in focusing attention on the pivotal function of the midlife transition, Levinson reveals the creative potential of this period, a useful concept for studying Hawthorne's artistic breakthrough.

Levinson's study clarifies mechanisms of change and development by viewing them as a continuous process of building and modifying the life structure, which he defines as "the basic pattern or design of a person's life at a given time." The components of this structure are occupation, love, family, a man's "relationship to himself, his use of solitude, his roles in various social contexts—all the relationships with individuals, groups and institutions that have significance for him."[3] At any given time, only those components that cohere can be accommodated by the structure. Of the elements that must be subordinated or suppressed for the sake of cohesion, those too important to endure permanent exclusion will eventually demand recognition.

The success of a life structure is measurable by its ability to conserve and do justice to as many important aspects of the self as possible while maintaining the harmonious functioning of the whole. It can be as complex or as ingenious as its creator. Those who, like Hawthorne, feel it to be "the best definition of happiness to live throughout the whole range of [one's] faculties and sensibilities" (I, 40) will fight harder than others to ward off any hint of "death-in-life" such as he experienced in the Custom House. The stronger the

4

life force, the more creative are the possible responses to stagnation or to suppression of any urgent aspects of the self. Creative also is the ability to redefine important but neglected aspects of the self so as to harmonize them with the dominant elements.* The concept of the adult life course pictures life as a journey with an inner timetable, a patterned sense of where one ought to be at a given age. The timetable operates in us like a standard with which we need to feel that our actual achievements are in synchrony. Should we fail to pass at or near the expected times the milestones of intimacy, vocational identity, "settling down,"⁴ and attainment of seniority, we feel dissatisfied with life and ourselves. Normally, we feel ourselves to be timely or belated insofar as our own position on the time scale accords with the schedule or standard of the timetable. The milestones we pass mark our approach to the destination, which is the termination of life.

*For example, one may have potentialities as both a painter and a scholar in life circumstances that favor the choice of scholarship as a career. If one gives up painting for scholarship, total denial of this talent may cause frustration or dissatisfaction. If strong enough, the suppressed desire to be a painter can demand satisfaction in various ways. It can be reduced to a hobby, it could be so urgent as to lead one to abandon the first choice and build a new structure around painting, or it may go underground and influence the direction of the scholarship in such a way as to redefine both capacities. The original interest in portraiture may, for example, re-emerge as a scholarly interest in biography.

Although Levinson does not say so, this conception of life structures always in need of adaptation suggests the further thought that the life of the self may be like an evolving artistic creation. One creates a self by selecting from potential capacities those elements that cohere into a satisfying structure and subordinating those that do not. An almost aesthetic sense of fitness may govern the structuring process and guide the selecting, coordinating, and harmonizing of the parts. Moreover, the adaptive capacity to reshape components of the self so as to include as much as possible into the life structure resembles the artist's gift of invention.

Ideally, one who ripens into the stage Erikson calls Integrity may be able to view his completed life cycle as a wholly satisfying artifact the parts of which cohere with an inevitability that could be termed "aesthetic." According to Erikson's definition, Integrity seems comparable to the final chord of a symphony that sums up all that precedes it: "It is the ego's accrued assurance of its proclivity for order and meaning. . . . It is the acceptance of one's one and only life cycle and of the people who have become significant to it as something that had to be and that, by necessity, permitted of no substitutions." Erik H. Erickson, *Identity: Youth and Crisis* (New York: Norton, 1968), p. 139.

5

Awareness of death evolves along with the developing organism. As many psychologists, among them Robert Jay Lifton, make clear, even the infant has anticipatory knowledge of death through its experience of separation, beginning with the separation caused by birth itself, and enhanced by subsequent degrees of separation from the mother. Every act of individuation, every putting away of childish things and outgrown relationships, every advance involves a concomitant loss that anticipates the ultimate loss of self.

Gifted people who feel an unfulfilled destiny gestating within are especially attuned to the ticking of this inner clock. Fearing that they may not live to bring forth the work that they consider their special trust, they may feel prematurely old or expect to die young. Erik Erikson speaks thus of Sigmund Freud, interpreting his railroad phobia, associated with fears of premature death, as dread of "'coming too late' . . . 'missing the train,' that he would perish miserably before reaching some promised land . . . [or] creative destination."[5] Similarly, Hawthorne, who also had a protracted period of preparation, felt hounded by the passage of time that withheld fulfillment. Late in rising into the dominant generation, he feared he might die before arriving at his full powers.

When young, Hawthorne confided to his sister Ebe a fear of early death that should not be dismissed as mere romantic affectation. He later attributed premature death and unfulfilled destinies to many of his characters along with self-referential markers distinguishing them from other literary figures of the doomed artist. In his first novel he created Fanshawe, a poetic idealist who dies with gifts unrealized, followed by the young wayfarer of "The Ambitious Guest," a tale of the apprentice years of Hawthorne's late twenties. Based on his own trip through New Hampshire as described in letters home,[6] the story presents, however awkwardly, Hawthorne's own existential themes. Against the wintry mountain pass and threats of death he places the radiant hearth of a wayside inn at which the lone traveler takes refuge. This solitary guest of high ambitions is welcomed by a contented, loving family that spans the generations from grandparents to parents to children with enviable completeness. Mutual prescience of a common danger creates an immediate bond of sympathy between the aristocratic youth and this humble group.

The traveler's desire to achieve some monument to his own life

6

before he dies evokes from his hosts unexpected expressions of their own ultimate wishes. The father is willing to settle for a common slate gravestone to record his identity for posterity. The grandmother asks that a mirror be held over her coffin that she may make a final postmortem check on her appearance. Concerning such wishes for continuity after death the wayfarer concludes, "There now! . . . it is our nature to desire a monument, be it slate, or marble, or a pillar of granite, or a glorious memory in the universal heart of man" (IX, 329).

That night an avalanche destroys them all, ambitious guest along with humble hosts. Personal tokens left behind at the inn evoke tears for the modest family, but the ambitious guest left no record of his life or death except, of course, Hawthorne's tale, which ironically records the traveler's words: "As yet, I have done nothing. . . . I cannot die till I have achieved my destiny. Then, let Death come! I shall have built my monument!" (IX, 328). Hawthorne's words were to be the monument of this youth's ambition as they were eventually to be his own. His fear of premature death, like his periodic depressions, derived from a persistent sense of stagnation.[7]

His lifelong sense of belatedness emerged in a recurrent dream of twenty to thirty years' duration, persisting even after he had become an internationally acclaimed author. At a particularly mellow period of reflection and contentment following Christmas of 1854, he recorded in his notebook: "For a long, long while, I have occasionally been visited with a singular dream; and I have an impression that I have dreamed it, even since I have been in England. It is, that I am still at college—or, sometimes, even at School—and there is a sense that I have been there unconscionably long, and have quite failed to make such progress in life as my contemporaries have; and I seem to meet some of them with a feeling of shame and depression that broods over me, when I think of it, even at this moment. . . . How strange that it should come now, when I may call myself famous, and prosperous!—when I am happy, too!—still that same dream of life hopelessly a failure!" He attributes the persistence of this sense of failure beyond and despite the reality of success to "that heavy seclusion in which I shut myself up, for twelve years, after leaving college, when everybody moved onward and left me behind."[8] His twelve-year period of literary apprenticeship throughout the years when others establish themselves so magnified the ticking of his inner clock that he was always to be haunted by it.

In fortuitous circumstances, such an urgent sense of belatedness can spur torpid creative powers. At midlife, especially, the realization that there is more life behind than ahead, that this may be one's last chance to make a distinctive contribution, may generate a major reorganization of priorities and energies. The concept of the ages of man, pivoting on a radical reorientation somewhere near the midpoint, is not merely a modern phenomenon or perception. Familiar from anthropological, mythological, and cross-cultural investigation, the idea is as old as wisdom literature.

Potentially the most balanced of all the periods, midlife tempers energy with experience. At this time even the average person, according to Levinson, can have a "firmer structure with which to use his considerable energy, imagination and capacity for change."[9] For an artist like Hawthorne, who felt delayed in bringing forth what was stirring within him and was beginning to doubt that it would ever come forth alive, the particular losses that occurred at this pivotal point in his life provided the needed impetus.

<hr />

ALTERNATIONS

To understand how the events of 1849, Hawthorne's forty-fifth year, transformed this leisurely author of tales into the furious creator of *The Scarlet Letter*, we need to review the development of his vocation and career.[10] He had decided to be a writer while still a Bowdoin undergraduate. Even though his family put up no obstacles, their distinctly mercantile values had lodged securely in his psyche and always undermined for him the seriousness and manliness of the writer's trade. The Manning family, which took in the Hawthornes after the death of Captain Hathorne, was prosperous, hard working, and enterprising. Confident of their own values, they transmitted their emphasis on money and diligence to the insecure young artist. Even though he adhered to his own preference, he was always to feel ambivalent about it. The full flowering of his artistic powers was delayed by a sense of triviality, a conviction that serious masculinity was reserved for the "man of affairs." The model of the man of affairs closest to him was his maternal uncle, Robert Manning.

Hawthorne's early statement that he "could not be a Poet and a Bookkeeper at the same time" expresses his inability to incorporate simultaneously the two values that dominated his life. Unable to discard either or to harmonize the polarities, he tended throughout life to alternate between these two roles.[11] This vacillation delayed the ripening of his talent despite his early start. Both Hawthorne's self-doubts and his tendency to vacillate originated within the family situation.

Immediately after college Hawthorne set about developing himself as an artist and devoted more than ten secluded years to working at his craft. He started by aiming directly and probably prematurely at his ultimate goal, becoming a novelist. In 1828 he privately published *Fanshawe*, a Gothic novel, and then recalled it. During this period he returned to shorter literary forms, the tale and sketch, reaching a level in these genres that he was never to surpass. Some of these early pieces would probably have secured him a permanent reputation, but short works did not satisfy his own standard for a serious literary vocation. He published some of these early pieces in periodicals and annuals, but always anonymously or pseudonymously.

After *Fanshawe* he would not appear before the public under his own name until it could be on the title page of a volume. When he was almost thirty-four years old, he allowed his college friend Horatio Bridge to lure him out of hiding with a collection of enough pieces to make up the volume *Twice-told Tales*. In 1837, then, he had his name on a book, but not yet on a substantial, complex piece of long fiction.

For a brief and unrewarding period just prior to the publication of *Twice-told Tales*, Hawthorne tried to combine the man of letters with the man of affairs by becoming an editor of *The American Magazine of Useful and Entertaining Knowledge* and doing other literary hackwork. After falling in love and determining to marry Sophia Peabody, he swung over to the "bookkeeper" or "affairs" side of his nature by working at the Boston Custom House. He hoped to be able to write in his spare time. After two years of this unsatisfactory effort to become self-supporting, he tried the rather desperate gamble of joining the utopian community of Brook Farm, hoping thereby to make a home so that he could marry Sophia. This was no way to unite the ideal and the actual; he found farming uncongenial and so exhausting that he could not write. The experiment left him completely disillusioned with utopian schemes.

After marrying Sophia in 1842 at the age of thirty-eight, he took his bride to the Old Manse in Concord, Massachusetts, and devoted another three years exclusively to writing. During this very happy period (Edenic, he called it), Hawthorne again tested the "Poet" identity and wrote enough to make up his next volume of collected tales and sketches, *Mosses from an Old Manse*. Three years of full-time writing produced more tales and sketches but not a major work. As we shall see later, the preface to *Mosses* gives clear signs that Hawthorne felt he had failed both to establish a serious identity as an author and to meet his family responsibilities by writing. He left the Manse, evicted by its owner and impoverished. He moved back to Salem and returned to the manly "responsible bookkeeper" identity by accepting political appointment as Surveyor of the port of Salem. During the surveyorship he produced little writing. Not until his "decapitation" as Surveyor alleviated his need to be a man of affairs was he able to harness his full imaginative powers and "achieve a novel that should evolve some deep lesson, and should possess physical substance enough to stand alone" (X, 5).

Despite the genuine achievements of his early tales, between the ages of forty-one and forty-five, Hawthorne was weighing his literary accomplishment and finding it insubstantial. Critics like to dismiss his self-deprecations as a pose, an artfully constructed persona of the prefaces with little or no biographical significance. But even a persona is related to the self; it is a selection from and a heightening of genuine personality traits. Even when Hawthorne whimsically exaggerates his trifling, he refers to genuine concerns about himself. Moreover, the author as idle trifler is not a notion peculiar to the prefaces; it was a figure of long-standing concern in Hawthorne's fiction as well. The literary expressions of Hawthorne's misgivings about his manliness, his seriousness, and the value of his profession are rooted in life experience.

He depicts the fiction creator as socially marginal at least as early as "The Story Teller" sequence, a product of his late twenties. This fragmentary collection of framed tales was one of his attempts to fuse a solid literary work out of separate stories after the fashion of Washington Irving. Failure to get the frame and stories published together was a great setback to his ambition to produce a substantial work. The extant parts of the frame narrative reveal a storyteller who feels vocationally diminished by contrast to the more manly and imposing figure of his guardian, Parson Thumpcushion, as well as by other substantial men of affairs.

In "Passages from a Relinquished Work," probably intended as the opening of the frame narrative, we can see the author's sincere attempt to do justice to a very troubling presence in the life of an orphaned young artist. The narrator conveys, in addition to the Parson's emphatic personality and oppressive presence, a balancing sense of his decency, good intentions, and generosity, trying to attribute to the difficulties of a guardian-ward relationship the conflicts that each experienced with the other. Although the Parson's firm convictions about the proper vocation for a young man did not prevail over the young artist's intentions, they effectively undermined his valuation of his own talents. The Parson insisted on the young man's "adopting a particular profession," whereas the future Story Teller was determined to "keep aloof from the regular business of life."

Although the Story Teller leaves home for life on the road, he is unable to escape the Parson's image of the artist as an idler, a word associated with fiction-mongering even up to the time of "The Custom-House." He felt ranked with libertines and paupers, "with the drunken poet, who hawked his own fourth of July odes" (X, 407). The negative image inculcated by his guardian pursues the young man who fled home in order to escape it. The narrator's first friend on the road, his fellow traveler and later competitor for audience attention, is a young divine who combines the Story Teller's alter ego with a youthful incarnation of the Parson. In high spirits and full of confidence that his "idle trade" demands the highest mental and emotional capacities, the Story Teller learns that his first performance is to be with a British company entertaining at a tavern. In this liberated atmosphere, his fellow performers turn out to be "of doubtful sex," and the Story Teller enjoys the unnerving success of being appreciated for the wrong reasons.

After the performance, the Story Teller receives a letter from Parson Thumpcushion that he burns without reading, but by which he is profoundly affected. "I seemed to see the Puritanic figure of my guardian, standing among the fripperies of the theatre, and pointing to the players,—the fantastic and effeminate men, the painted women, the giddy girl in boy's clothes, merrier than modest,—pointing to these with solemn ridicule, and eyeing me with stern rebuke. His image was a type of the austere duty, and they of the vanities of life" (X, 421). Needless to say, the licentious image spoiled the Story Teller's taste for his chosen profession.

"Passages" attempts levity but clearly wrestles with a young writer's genuine feelings about his stern but benevolent father-surrogate. In implying that such a guardian can become a *Doppelgänger*, an internalized figure whose memory converts artistic endeavor into vanity if not depravity, Hawthorne was coming dangerously close to private experience. Little wonder that he relinquished the work.

In *The Shape of Hawthorne's Career*, critic Nina Baym asserts repeatedly that much of Hawthorne's writing before *The Scarlet Letter* tamely follows what he conceived to be audience expectations and therefore deprecates imagination and extolls the common destiny of ordinary mankind. In contrast to those who attribute biographical significance to "Passages," she denies that it could represent more than a minor aspect of Hawthorne's personality. But in discussing the *Twice-told Tales* period, she declares, "Hawthorne's sketches represent a voluntary repression of a powerful talent that is astonishing in its perversity. No audience would have demanded from him the concessions that he made in advance. . . . We cannot wonder that he always wrote with an audience in mind; but we have to wonder at the severity of his conception of that audience." She attributes to Hawthorne's inexperience of the world his imperfect understanding of his audience, and then explains his repression of the imagination by saying that in ignorance of his real audience, he invented a readership "composed of rational teachers and stern ministers—a readership of Parson Thumpcushions!"[12]

Such repression of the imagination as we find in Hawthorne is more likely due to involuntary forces than to concessions to audience expectations. Indeed, his repressive Puritans who make the fiction writer feel trivial are probably transformed images of his own guardian, Robert Manning, rather than of an inaccurately perceived audience of readers. Robert Manning was not in fact unimaginative or even opposed to imagination, but with his artistic nephew he took a stern and puritanical line.

As later chapters will show, the Mannings were known for their "sensibility" as well as for their business acumen, and Robert Manning exemplified both. He was an extremely capable and prudent businessman, but he also devoted both money and energy to the cultivation of fruit trees. A person who readily and naturally assumed responsibility, he directed the Manning family business after the death of his father, and, although not the oldest son, he became the man in the lives of his sister's young family after Captain Hathorne's death. Robert Manning made the essential decisions in the lives of the Hawthorne children and is well known as the uncle who sent Hawthorne to college. We shall see that he also assumed responsibility for Hawthorne's early education and often came between the boy and his mother. Robert Manning tended to be playful and loving with his Hawthorne nieces but was quite strict with young Nathaniel.

Although Hawthorne respected the motives of his Uncle Robert, he often longed to be free of his tyranny and his values. For such a dreamy boy, an uncle who was always keeping him to the grindstone must have seemed very puritanical indeed. Young Hawthorne felt more kinship with the renegade Uncle Samuel, much closer to his own age, who liked taverns, story swapping, the irregular life of the road. In fact, the Manning family plotted regularly to bring Samuel into line. They tried in vain to keep him employed in Uncle Richard's general store in Maine in the hope that he would settle down.

Often accompanying Samuel on his horse-buying trips, young Nathaniel formed a strong bond with him against the strict Manning code of hard work, sobriety, and religion. The dream of being a vagabond storyteller derives from this happy association, which terminated with Samuel's early death. Samuel was never tamed by Manning values and did not live to pay the price of living outside them. Internalized as a joyful figure of vagabond irresponsibility, this uncle remained part of his nephew's psyche as an impulse toward rootlessness. Continually changing residences, Hawthorne called the only home he ever owned "The Wayside" and was eventually to die in a wayside hotel. "The Story Teller" dramatizes the influence of both uncles in the form of joyous digressions from the bourgeois ideal shadowed by figures representing the puritan conscience.

Also a part of "The Story Teller" sequence, "The Seven Vagabonds" depicts another version of the same polarity. The narrator is a young man "in the spring of [his] life and the summer of the year" at a crossroad of three directions. He is drawn toward a caravan, a house on wheels, operated by a traveling showman and an itinerant bookseller, and shortly thereafter joined by a con man, a fiddler, operators of a showbox, all of them aspects of the artist. Attracted by their gay, spontaneous way of life, and by the notion of a home on wheels, he wishes to join this carefree band. The old showman questions his fitness for the role of roving entertainer; he finds the narrator merely a "strolling gentleman" in contrast with respectable vagabonds who get their "bread in some creditable way. Every honest man should have his livelihood" (IX, 365). On the spot, the wanderer invents the vocation of traveling storyteller in order to establish respectability with this motley crew. Only with the aid of an advocate among them is he accepted by the band headed for a camp meeting. Joyful at having joined a society of outsiders, the narrator feels at one with their world until he spies a horseman approaching from the direction of the camp meeting. A Methodist minister sitting his horse with "rigid perpendicularity, a tall thin figure in rusty black" (IX, 368), this priestly spoilsport brings word that the camp meeting has broken up. The merry group disbands, blasted by the Methodist's grim visage.

Even among vagabonds, the Story Teller feels trivial and suspect. He lacks a "creditable" livelihood and seems not entirely one of them. This youth choosing a direction in the spring of his life reminds one of another divided artist figure, Thomas Mann's Tonio Kröger, whose honesty is suspected even on a visit to his home town, and who is always associated with a gypsy in a green wagon. Neither others nor he himself can quite believe in his respectability. This divided artist is rejected by both communities, the bourgeois and the bohemian.

Mann attributed his own and his protagonists' guilty identities as artists to the split inherited from burgher fathers and bohemian mothers. In Hawthorne a similar mentality obtained, but in the case of this fatherless boy, it is more likely derived from the influence of two important uncles—the carefree Samuel and the eminently respectable Robert. If Uncle Samuel fostered the rootless vagabond tendency, Uncle Robert, with the values of the whole Manning clan behind him, could well have been transformed into the censoring puritanical figures who, under various guises, often ministerial, make the impecunious artist feel like an idler, a mere "fiddler," a lightweight, and a man of uncertain masculinity.

In a sense Hawthorne was transmuting his two uncles into psychic symbols of an archetypal polarity—the Dionysian and the Apollonian, primitivism and civilization, self and society. These opposing forces meet in full panoply in "The Maypole of Merrymount," another early work. In the contest for empire between jollity and gloom, "jollity" manages in the course of description to incorporate the decorative arts (as opposed to the functional), carnival, masquerade, fantasy, and, above all, sexual license with the unmistakable implication of sexual ambiguity. Indulgence runs amok, allowing the author license to revel in the pleasures of unrestraint before closing in with the forces of repression. When, after pages of inventive revelry, Governor Endicott finally enters the circle, "no fantastic foolery could look him in the face. So stern was the energy of his aspect, that the whole man, visage, frame, and soul, seemed wrought of iron, gifted with life and thought, yet all of one substance with his head-piece and breast-plate. It was the Puritan of Puritans" (IX, 63).

The triumph of discipline was inevitable; few can imagine adult human life as endless play. Revelry must end, children must grow up, Edens must be forfeited for a world of sober work. And, because the polarities do represent two genuine aspects of human nature, neither of which can be totally denied, even Endicott of the armored head and heart and soul of iron softened his strictures to bring them within tolerable human limits. Even the "severest Puritan of all" knew enough to garland the heads of the newlyweds with "roses from the ruin of the Maypole." Perhaps only the truly disciplined, like Governor Endicott, Hawthorne, and Thomas Mann, know how to value the sensuality that is restrained by iron bands of control.

Toadying to an unimaginative audience was not the reason Hawthorne's earlier tales conclude with control of the forces of extravagance, ambition, or imagination and advocate settling for the normal course of human existence within social boundaries. On the contrary, he let his more extravagant characters test the unlimited for him and sadly concluded that it was unlivable.

Moreover, like most of us, Hawthorne had within him an image of restraint and responsibility that made it impossible for him to give free rein to the Byronic impulses that he personified in Oberon, hero of "The Devil in Manuscript." Not only was Hawthorne a descendant of founders of New England society, he was also reared in the very middle-class home of the Mannings. He could safely play with the fantasy of vagabondage just as he could safely play with the fantasy of Oberon, the doomed poet, whose early death and touching literary remains would wrench the hearts of his unappreciative family. He could entertain these identities imaginatively, *because* he was safely anchored in the bourgeois tradition, had "some slender means" inherited from these bourgeois earnings, and had received enough discipline from his unappreciated Uncle Robert that he could earn his own living when necessary.

Hawthorne's harsh portrait of Endicott in "The Maypole of Merrymount" is tempered by recognition that such iron men form the basis of social structures. Such disciplinarians seem most like iron men, most repressive, to those driven by urgent impulses. Note, therefore, the description of Governor Endicott—his sternness, his energy, his iron soul, and the unity of his armored personality. So forceful that fantastic foolery could not confront it, this personality is the prototype of the iron men who appear in various guises throughout Hawthorne's work. Whether merchants, blacksmiths, monomaniac philanthropists, ministers or Puritan fathers, they invariably make artisans of the imagination feel trivial, unworthy, and unmanly.

THE OLD MANSE:
AUTUMN WITHOUT HARVEST

Viewing the preface to *Mosses from an Old Manse* in the context of Hawthorne's preoccupation with older, more substantial guardian figures, we see that even this highly esteemed essay reflects a sense of professional failure. A feeling of mastery and the accompanying professional identity were not to come until several years later when *The Scarlet Letter* was under way. "The Custom-House" acknowledges and responds consciously to self-denigrating statements of "The Old Manse." Indeed, the Manse preface was composed after the Hawthornes had been evicted from the parsonage and returned to Salem to begin the surveyorship. The narrator of "The Old Manse" is awed by his predecessors in the Manse just as the narrator of "The Custom-House" is awed by his stern and manly Puritan ancestors. He says that the Old Manse was profaned by his occupancy, for "a priest had built it; a priest had dwelt in it. . . . It was awful to reflect how many sermons must have been written there" (X, 4). In this context of the profundity and solemnity of the priestly vocation, the narrator expresses inadequacy: "I took shame to myself for having been so long a writer of idle stories, and ventured to hope that wisdom should descend upon me . . . and that I should light upon an intellectual treasure in the Old Manse." Profound studies should have been expected from such solemn influences; "In the humblest event I resolved at least to achieve a novel that should evolve some deep lesson, and should possess physical substance enough to stand alone" (X, 5).

> The treasure of intellectual gold, which I hoped to find in our secluded dwelling, had never come to light. No profound treatise of ethics—no philosophic history—no novel, even, that could stand, unsupported, on its edges. All that I had to show, as a man of letters, were these few tales and essays, which had blossomed out like flowers in the calm summer of my heart and mind. . . . These fitful sketches, with so little of external life about them, yet claiming no profundity of purpose . . . such trifles, I truly feel, afford no solid basis for a literary reputation. (X, 34)

The priestly predecessors inspire no profound treatises of philosophy or ethics, but they do inspire in the author of tales a feeling of inadequacy before such forceful men.

The mellow tone of "The Old Manse," the newlyweds' Edenic happiness, the rich associations of the dwelling and the natural beauty of the setting, may obscure the artist's bitter disappointment. A sense of failed imagination pervades the essay. Although the

Manse is recalled amidst summer beauty and bounty, its tenant had been evicted in the autumn without having brought his resolve to fruition. He had burrowed among the books and sermons of the garret "in search of any living thought, which should burn like a coal of fire, or glow like an inextinguishable gem" (foreshadowing the scarlet letter, inflamer of living thought to be found in the attic of the Custom House), but his imagination never really caught fire at the Manse. Even this widely appreciated preface strains hard to set the imagination aflame. The author leads the reader around the premises, into the garret, up the Assabeth River, onto the historic battleground, trying to associate, moralize, reconstruct the Indian and Revolutionary past, all associative methods productive of fine writing in the style of Washington Irving, but not yet of the living coal of fire.

The breast-scorching letter had to await yet another eviction than this one from the Eden of Hawthorne's first married years. Viewing the three-year idyll as one prolonged summer, a season made melancholy by the foretaste of coming decay, the forty-one-year-old Hawthorne was banished from paradise without having tasted the fruit for which he came—the book that would "afford a solid basis for a literary reputation." Using the metaphor of the seasons, an age-old symbol for the eras of man's life, Hawthorne expresses how anticipatory knowledge of seasonal change taints the present: "How early in the summer, too, the prophecy of autumn comes!" (X, 26). But summer without autumn is promise without fruit, and the narrator draws the inevitable parallel of midlife to the change from full summer to the decline of autumn. "Ah, but there is a half-acknowledged melancholy . . . when we stand in the perfected vigor of our life, and feel that Time has now given us all his flowers, and that the next work of his never idle fingers—must be to steal them, one by one, away" (X, 26).

Although his fruit would eventually ripen, Hawthorne thought he had withered as a creative artist. He left the Old Manse with a loving wife and a baby girl, but penniless and without plans for income. Worst of all, he left the Manse without the professional accomplishment that would justify or validate him in accord with his own high ambitions. The penultimate paragraph of "The Old Manse" expresses disappointment gracefully, without apparent bitterness:

These fitful sketches, with so little of external life about them, yet claiming no profundity of purpose . . . such trifles, I truly feel, afford no solid basis for a literary reputation. Nevertheless, the public . . . will receive them the more kindly, as the last offering, the last collection of this nature, which it is my purpose ever to put forth. Unless I could do better, I have done enough in this kind. (X, 34)

Lest anyone dismiss this modesty as merely a literary pose, we should compare it with a letter Hawthorne wrote to Evert Duyckinck just before *Mosses* was issued:

It is rather a sad idea—not that I am to write no more in this kind, but that I cannot better justify myself for having written at all. As the first essays and tentatives of a young author, they would be well enough—but it seems to me absurd to look upon them as conveying any claim to a settled literary reputation. . . . If they were merely spring blossoms, we might look for good fruit hereafter; but I have done nothing but blossom all through the summer. I am ashamed—and there's an end.[13]

In the metaphor of the seasons of life, the forty-one year old Hawthorne admits to his editor shame for work that would be good enough as the "tentatives" of a young author but falls short of what would "justify [him] for having written at all." Knowing that this was the season to produce ripe fruit, he is ashamed of spring blossoms.

Three years of devotion to writing at the Old Manse were followed by three years in the Custom House, a professional moratorium during which Hawthorne lived out the other side of his divided nature—the man of affairs. He had hoped that the light duties required of the Surveyor would allow time for writing, and he did produce some minor pieces, but ultimately he reaffirmed what he already knew and had tested at the Boston Custom House, that he could not be a poet and bookkeeper at the same time. As "The Custom-House" tells us, his "imagination was a tarnished mirror," and the torpor of life among the living dead deprived him of "an entire class of susceptibilities, and a gift connected with them" (I, 36). Not the mandate from Mr. Surveyor Pue, not moonlight nor firelight, were of any avail. He endured a sleep of the imagination believing it to be not sleep, but living death.

LOSS AND RESTITUTION

This foretaste of death was like the mythical visit to the under-world that privileges rare souls to return as persons twice-born, enabled by contact with death to realize their destined work. The golden bough in Hawthorne's case was the gift of the sibyl Time, which gave him at this moment of optimal balance the impetus needed for fusing the themes of his entire life into two powerful forms, the mythicized autobiography of "The Custom-House," and the fictive projections of his own life themes in *The Scarlet Letter*.

For such an antithetical writer as Hawthorne, Daniel Levinson's use of Jung's polarities works especially well. The Jungian polarity that Levinson considers central to all periods of developmental change is the Puer/Senex or Young/Old antithesis, because at every stage of life we are both young and old. Insofar as Young represents growth, energy, and potentiality, it is present in all hopeful begin-nings and is symbolized by seed, blossom, or spring. Insofar as Old represents termination, separation, completion, it anticipates death and is symbolized by fruition and winter.[14] At midlife, when Young and Old are in optimal balance, the major developmental task is the reintegration of this and other related polarities.

Destruction/Creation is a variant of Young/Old that is particularly appropriate for our study of Hawthorne's period of mastery. Says Levinson, "in reappraising his life during the Mid-Life Transition, a man must come to a new understanding of his grievances against others for the real or imagined damage they have done him. . . . he must come to terms with his guilts,—his grievances against him-self—for the destructive effects he has had on others and himself. . . . What is involved, above all, is the reworking of painful feelings and experiences."[15] Levinson adds that the reworking of destruction at midlife can result in development of a "tragic sense." He cites the research of Elliot Jaques, whose examination of the lives of hundreds of artists affirms that in the midlife crisis artists face their own mor-tality and destructiveness, often in ways that markedly enhance creativity.[16]

Hawthorne's loss of his mother little more than a month after the loss of his government sinecure sharpened his sense that life was passing without his having established himself either financially or professionally. Such a realization might easily have been depressing, even paralyzing, had he not turned the juxtaposition of losses to creative use. Although loss of the surveyorship was first chronologically, his written account of it followed the death of his mother. On the assumption that the mother's death retrospectively altered his perception of the Custom House experience, let us consider the maternal loss first.

While gentle Elizabeth Hawthorne lay dying in the upstairs room of the Mall Street house in her sixty-eighth year, her son became sharply aware that he stood "in the dusty midst" of human existence. Overcome by unexpectedly strong feelings after taking farewell of his dying mother, he stood grief-stricken at the window of her room and heard the shouts and laughter of his two children playing outdoors, enacting the death of their grandmother. He recorded in his journal: "And now, through the crevice of the curtain, I saw my little Una of the golden locks, looking very beautiful; and so full of spirit and life, that she was life itself. And then I looked at my poor dying mother; and seemed to see the whole of human existence at once, standing in the dusty midst of it" (XIII, 429).

Standing literally between his dying mother in the darkened room and his children play-acting the death of their grandmother in the summer sunshine below, Hawthorne had a powerful perception of his place in the cycle of life. At the very last moment that he was both son and father, he knew himself as the middle term between two generations. Pivoted on this transient moment, acutely poised in the midst but about to fall into the exposed position of father who is no longer son, he took in the meaning of the middle station. As the middle term he had enjoyed approximate maturity as a father but not full vulnerability as long as he still had someone between himself and death. With the passage of his sole remaining parent, there would be no buffer before him.

Moreover, because he loved and identified with his children, he had to share their initiation into the knowledge of mortality as they tried to encompass this first loss by enacting it in play. Their new vulnerability also became his. Standing in the dusty midst, imaginatively experiencing death with his mother and the knowledge of death with his children, he embraced in his own stricken soul the entirety of the life course and the true meaning of time.

Midlife carries its own message of time, but such an empathic experience of death can help release the creative potential of this period, the time of "optimal Young/Old balance." Hawthorne's acute experience of time and mortality may have facilitated also the reintegration of the Destruction/Creation polarity, the reworking of old animosities into the tenuous balances of "The Custom-House" and *The Scarlet Letter.* The preface was composed when the novel was well under way, when Hawthorne knew that the death of the Surveyor had truly liberated the literary man. Thus the revival of his creativity retroactively reinterpreted those Custom House years into a living death that precedes rebirth.

Like many a man in his forties, Hawthorne as Surveyor found himself with a seemingly assured income that he did not dare relinquish, but trapped in a life structure that suppressed the most valued part of his personality, "that one talent which is death to hide." As a conscientious husband and father who had known poverty, he was unlikely ever to have resigned his Custom House post. It is little wonder, then, that eventually he came to regard loss of this sinecure as an act of Providence, an act, that is, of an ironic Providence comparable to that afforded a "person who should entertain an idea of committing suicide, and, altogether beyond his hopes, meet with the good hap to be murdered" (I, 42).

A major difference between the essays "Mosses from an Old Manse" and "The Custom-House" lies in the energy released by Hawthorne's knowledge of having arrived at his mature powers. No longer a gentlemanly reviver of faded pictures of the past, he is, in his major phase, a knowing master of the past in its dynamic relation to the present. "The Custom-House" is energetic not only in its prose but in its dynamic balance of opposing forces.

Instead of a genial guided tour of Salem and its port, we get a picture bristling with contrarieties. The town is drab and ugly, about as attractive "as a disarranged checkerboard," but the author is deeply attached to it. The wharf, once a scene of vigorous traffic, now is dilapidated and overgrown with grass. The American eagle poised over the Custom House entrance is a figure electric with the central polarities of the essay itself. This symbol of government is fierce, truculent, and threatening, but many seek to shelter themselves under its wing. Her bosom may appear to have "all the softness and snugness of an eider-down pillow," but she will very likely "fling off her nestling with a scratch of her claw, a dab of her beak, or a rankling wound from her barbed arrows" (I, 5). We shall return to this symbol of unreliable protection, for its paradoxes are not yet exhausted.

The first view of the Custom House itself does more than evoke a colorful picture of past activity in contrast to present decline. Instead, the author presents figures of the past, the shipmaster, the owner, the merchant, and the young clerk in relationship to each other and to time. He shows the young clerk evolving into the merchant by prematurely buying shares in his master's cargo, and the homebound and the outwardbound sailors as emblems of a continuing cycle of life.

Because Hawthorne's mother communicated to him her dread that he might be lost at sea like his father, he was the first male Hawthorne in many generations not to become a sailor. In becoming a writer rather than a sailor he not only failed his ancestors, he also broke the chain of generational continuity: "From father to son, for above a hundred years, they followed the sea; a gray-headed shipmaster, in each generation, retiring from the quarter-deck to the homestead, while a boy of fourteen took the hereditary place before the mast, confronting the salt spray and the gale, which had blustered against his sire and grandsire. The boy, also, in due time, passed from the forecastle to the cabin, spent a tempestuous manhood, and returned from his world-wanderings, to grow old, and die, and mingle his dust with the natal earth" (I, 11). By failing to share his father's vocation, Hawthorne lost an opportunity for identifying with the father who left so little positive trace on his life. Surveying the port of Salem was as close as he ever came to commanding a ship. Perhaps presiding over an important scene of his father's life helped close the rift between the generations and returned to him some portion of his father's power.

The authority he exercised over sea captains may have provided some small sense of having surpassed his father. Surely the narrator of "The Custom-House" expresses a curious pride in having under his orders such a "patriarchal body of veterans." This Nathaniel Hawthorne who himself so feared the contempt of his virile Puritan ancestors was amused "to behold the terrors that attended my advent; to see a furrowed cheek, weather-beaten by half a century of storm, turn ashy pale at the glance of so harmless an individual as myself" (I, 14).

Authority over patriarchal figures very much like his father serves to remedy Hawthorne's sense of triviality. He enjoys the exercise of power, a feeling of having arrived at seniority, of being of the dominant generation. "The Custom-House" traces a process of integration of past selves, a drawing together of "identity fragments," and marks the forging for a time at least of a unified, independent, and powerful self that can safely comprehend both the dreaded Surveyor and the "harmless individual."

As the master of patriarchal elders, the Surveyor assumes a benign paternalism; he becomes the protector of childish old men as well as the judge of their worth. He experiences himself as a dominant adult by shielding elderly father figures from their own weakness. In perceiving and rendering various ways of growing old as epitomized by the Inspector and the Collector, the narrator anticipates his own coming decline and takes note of better and worse ways of aging. This close study of aging men has great import for one who is on the slippery peak of middle age. He derives from it not only a warning about time but a poignant picture of death-in-life, or stagnation, which makes the passing moment all the more precious. Figures of old men wallowing in torpid dependency are warnings to himself, fearful negative identities to him who enjoys a similar dependent relationship to Uncle Sam. *Carpe Diem!*

Hawthorne's transformation of this experience corroborates Levinson's view that experiencing stagnation is essential to development and not entirely negative. Stagnation can be redirected by an understanding of one's own weaknesses and destructive impulses.

> To become generative, a man must know how it feels to stagnate—to have the sense of not growing, of being static, stuck, drying, bogged down in a life full of obligation and devoid of self-fulfillment. He must know the experience of dying, of living in the shadow of death. The capacity to experience, endure, and fight against stagnation is an intrinsic aspect of the struggle toward generativity in middle adulthood.[17]

Hawthorne may have felt destructive toward the gourmand Inspector, but he turned the energy of this anger to creative use by subtly relating the cruel picture of squandered life to his own temptation toward self-indulgence. Having truly depicted stagnation, he roused himself into a fury of creativity. He directed his portrait of the Inspector against his own tendency to indolence. With caricatures of enervated civil servants no longer capable of self-reliance, he combated his own attraction toward and fear of dependency. Instead of sketching characters for picturesque local color, he directed them toward energizing himself as narrator.[18]

In contrast to that of the vapid Inspector, the reverent portrait of the Collector is an idealization of old age as a brooding, inward Tiresias figure apparently based less on observation than on imaginative projection. Already unapproachable because turned inward on his own memory, the Collector lends himself to affectionate contemplation and idealization. The narrator imputes to him ideal manliness, bravery, endurance, integrity, kindness, elegance, as well as "a young girl's appreciation of the floral tribe" (IX, 23). Attributed to this inaccessible, slumbrous old idol are all the contrary traits that if harmonized would make up a complete human being. The combination of military ferocity with feminine elegance and love of flowers suggests the integration of masculine and feminine traits that students of adult development believe takes place in middle and late adulthood.[19] Because of the totally imputed rather than observed characterization of the Collector, this sketch stands out from the realistic portion of the essay and prepares us for the coming sketch of the narrator's spiritual father, Mr. Surveyor Pue.

Both the Inspector and the Collector spend their time in recollection of their pasts, one of past dinners, the other of past heroic deeds. The attic of the Custom House is full of dreary records of the past on which the author tries "exerting [his] fancy, sluggish with little use, to raise up from these dry bones an image" of Salem's brighter days. The gift of a usable vision of the past comes from the ghost of Hawthorne's predecessor, Mr. Surveyor Pue, an historic figure whom he adopts as his "official ancestor." Reminiscent of the ghost of Hamlet's father, the ghost of the former Surveyor charges his successor to complete his untold story of Hester Prynne and to give Mr. Pue his rightful credit. Surveyor Hawthorne accepts the commission in a spirit of filial duty and reverence.

In pledging filial obedience to Mr. Surveyor Pue, Hawthorne ignores his own father and bypasses his forefathers and guardian, to create the ghostly father he needs. This former Surveyor of customs who could also value and preserve in writing the story of Hester Prynne incorporates the author's own hitherto unresolved antitheses, the man of affairs who is also a man of letters. In creating this paternal source of his own invention, Hawthorne engenders himself as master of his own talent, an author finally capable of producing a major, life-justifying work.

This essay so charged with a sense of time, of past recapitulated and laid to rest, of valediction to all that was prelude as Hawthorne looked forward to the future as an author in full possession of his powers, this autobiographical address to the reader of what bound him to a Salem he neither liked nor enjoyed, makes no mention of Hawthorne's truest links to his "natal spot." With exquisite tact and evasion he speaks neither of father nor mother, any more than he does of sisters, uncles, and aunts. He talks of forefathers and generations of fathers and sons, of patriarchal veterans in the Custom House, and of a filial duty to Mr. Pue, but of no actual father.

Nor does he mention the mother whose recent death nevertheless pervades the work. Instead, the residue of his grief emerges from the language: "the sensuous sympathy of dust for dust," dry bones, rigid corpses, decapitation, murder, ghosts. When the narrator, exploring the debris of the past in the Custom House attic, is about to discover Surveyor Pue's parchment, the language of death and stagnation gathers and condenses:

> . . . the names of vessels that had long ago *foundered at sea* or *rotted at the wharves*, and those of merchants, *never heard of* now on 'Change, nor very readily decipherable on their mossy *tombstones;* glancing at such matters with the saddened, weary, half-reluctant interest which we bestow on the *corpse of dead activity,* —and exerting my fancy, sluggish with little use, to *raise up from these dry bones* an image of the old town's brighter aspect. . . . I chanced to lay my hands on a small package. (I, 29; italics added)

"The Custom-House" is death and ghost-ridden, but real parents are notably absent from the text. Parents and children are left for symbolic treatment in *The Scarlet Letter.*

Nevertheless, parents real and surrogate leave their traces in "The Custom-House" in indirect but powerful ways. The presence of Hawthorne's mother emerges in his preference for the word "natal" over "native" in such phrases as "natal spot" or "as if the natal soil were an earthly paradise." In saying that drab Salem was for him "the inevitable center of the universe," the navel, as it were, of his emotional world, he fuses the natal and the native aspects of his birthplace. Thus separation from Salem marks a late stage of his individuation, the completion of a major transition.

Although such mothers as Hawthorne depicted in his works are clearly mothers, fathers are represented in diffuse and fragmented ways. Hester Prynne is established early and prominently as a solitary mother, but the novel depicts father-figures instead of fathers. We have Roger Chillingworth, Puritan elders and divines, a plurality of authority figures. Pearl's search among these figures for her true father may well be a major subtext of *The Scarlet Letter.*

Maternal presence and paternal absence are the positive and negative poles that generate this historical romance. With Hester standing on the scaffold like an image of the virgin mother, or "Divine Maternity" as the narrator terms it, the absence of a father becomes the dominant question for the community, the clergy, the governor, and most of all for the child. In response to the paternity question posed in the marketplace by the clergy, Hester refuses to assign Pearl an earthly father but consigns her instead to a greater one: "My child must seek a heavenly Father; she shall never know an earthly one!" (I, 68). By suggesting the paradoxical notion that the illegitimate child may be of divine origin, both Hester and the narrator raise the factual issue of paternity to social, psychological, and metaphysical dimensions.

The tricky question of who "made" Pearl is played out on all three levels. In chapter six the perennial childish question of "where Pearl comes from" becomes a serious challenge when the evasive mother hesitates before providing the catechetically correct answer, "Thy Heavenly Father sent thee!" (I, 98). Hester's evasion causes Pearl to deny that she has a heavenly father and to demand an answer more satisfying to her estranged reality.

Her steadfast refusal of a heavenly father without an earthly one generates her recalcitrant behavior when the town fathers test Pearl's knowledge of catechism to determine Hester's fitness to raise the child. To the first question, "Who art thou?" Pearl answers significantly, "I am mother's child . . . and my name is Pearl" (I, 110), a response embodying the reality of her experience, the child of a mother only, no last name. To the question "Who made thee?", resonant enough for any child but especially so for a bastard, she perversely asserts that she has not been made but plucked from the wild rose tree by the prison door. This confirmation that Hester is not properly educating Pearl raises the danger of losing custody of the child. Fearing this, Hester demands menacingly that Dimmesdale "look to it" that mother and child not be parted, thus rousing the biological father to behave protectively.

Pearl's perverse refusal to acknowledge a heavenly father without being acknowledged by an earthly one thus provokes what she has been yearning for all along, a paternal response. Her behavior also activates her biological family, compelling intense interaction between mother and father and between father and daughter. Dimmesdale's protective act subdues Pearl's wildness and impels her gently to lay her cheek against his hand. His hesitation before responding to this tenderness is observed not only by the hyper-acute child but by ever-vigilant Chillingworth, who immediately revives the dormant question of the identity of Pearl's father.

This chapter, which connects the mystery of creation to the unsolved paternity question, is taut with multiple meanings. Three years later than the marketplace scene, it reassembles all the principal characters to reenact the earlier events with the difference that Pearl is now not an infant but a conscious agent. In a heightened version of their first public interview, her mother and father communicate directly to each other in a double language designed to deceive the world. Thus in Hester's charge that the minister defend her claim to the child, she iterates three times in one paragraph, "Thou knowest me better than these men can. . . . Thou knowest. . . . Thou knowest" (I, 113), apparently referring to pastoral familiarity but meaning also carnal knowledge.

Every irony is wrung out of the catechetical question of who "made" Pearl, but now Pearl's unconscious needs are stage-managing the scene, bringing the parents into relationship, stimulating a renewed inquiry into paternity, evoking responses to her deepest needs. This uncanny infant manipulates the script from here on and so manages events that the narrative concludes with acknowledgment by her father. Hester never seeks to stand up publicly with the minister and finally does so only reluctantly, whereas Pearl, who seeks this persistently throughout the book, flies to his embrace. The grand finale of both the surface plot of adult actions and the underlying plot directed by the child is the public restoration on the scaffold at noonday of the true biological family.

Pearl's eldritch quality stems directly from the intensity of her search for paternal recognition. Lacking overt clues, she developed uncanny intuitive gifts. She had to search through her mother to discern her father, to sift and study Hester's relationship to men, to become an observer of the slightest gestures and behaviors of her elders. Pearl, that bundle of searching intuition, is, like Hester and Dimmesdale, a projection of aspects of the author.

The world looked to Pearl much as it did to the child Nathaniel Hawthorne, who scarcely knew his father. His chaste widowed mother must have seemed to him like the virgin mother, complete within herself. Eventually seeking the father every child must have, he, like Pearl, had to search through the mother for the missing male parent. And like Pearl, he found not one man in indisputable possession, but two, one a biological father who failed to claim his wife and child, the other a man somehow related to the mother with authority of an indeterminate sort over both mother and child. This unwarranted authority was, as appears in chapter three, sufficient to separate mother and child for the sake of the boy's education—the kind of separation threatened by Governor Bellingham after Pearl's faulty response to the catechism. In Pearl's case, the true father intervened to protect the mother-child relationship from tampering by would-be surrogate fathers—a development that young Nathaniel must have wished for in vain. Viewing the action of *The Scarlet Letter* from Pearl's perspective, that of a child trying to piece together its basic family constellation, to locate its father and account for the puzzling intruder, we find her early *Umwelt* much like that of her creator.

When Pearl's quest is fulfilled by her father's public embrace, she gains a father only to lose him. She attains not a father's care or solicitude, only the knowledge of who her father *was*, essentially all that Hawthorne had—knowledge of a lost father. Release of Pearl's gender identity and humanity depends on acknowledgment from her biological father; her material fortunes, however, depend just as surely on the inheritance bequeathed her by Roger Chillingworth, her mother's shadowy former husband. Chillingworth endows Pearl with the means for a larger destiny than her mother alone could have supplied, and he thereby assumes a genuine aspect of the fatherly role, that of provider.

This fragmenting of the biological and the sustaining aspects of fatherhood was a critical feature of Hawthorne's childhood experience. We must imagine how he tried to construe his family constellation both before and after his father's death. Probably content at first to be the only male in the family, he suddenly found himself surrounded by Manning relatives. While still trying to discern his mother's relationship to her parents, sisters, and brothers, he found one brother, Robert Manning, taking over the affairs of all the Hawthornes. Robert Manning was generous with love, interest, and material benefits, but Nathaniel grew to resent benefactions that he felt to be intrusive coming from someone other than a father. He became excessively sensitive about dependency on the Mannings in general and on Uncle Robert in particular.

Sensitivity about dependency fuels the animus against civil service permeating "The Custom-House." In the early part, unreliable parenting is symbolized by a maternal eagle, which promises protection and downy warmth, but will sooner or later "fling off her nestlings with . . . a rankling wound from her barbed arrows" (I, 5). But in a long shrill paragraph leading into the "decapitation," Hawthorne symbolizes the federal government as male and an uncle. Through the agency of the civil service, Uncle Sam encourages dependency so far into the adulthood of the public servant that "his own proper strength departs from him." The debilitated officeholder is sure to be ejected eventually, having become a person who "for ever afterwards looks wistfully about him in quest of support external to himself" (I, 39). At this stage, all he can hope for is restoration to office.

Such pervasive effects does Hawthorne attribute to government employment on the character, manhood, and vitality of the civil servant, that the reader senses motivation by an uncle more influential than Uncle Sam and a dependency characteristic established far earlier than middle life. In the "devil's bargain" between the civil servant and Uncle Sam, Hawthorne depicts the seductive lure of dependency.

This faith, more than any thing else, steals the pith and availability out of whatever enterprise he may dream of undertaking. Why should he . . . be at so much trouble to pick himself out of the mud, when, in a little while hence, the strong arm of his Uncle will raise and support him? Why should he work for his living here, or go to dig gold in California, when he is so soon to be made happy, at monthly intervals, with a little pile of glittering coin out of his Uncle's pocket? It is sadly curious to observe how slight a taste of office suffices to infect a poor fellow with this singular disease. Uncle Sam's gold—meaning no disrespect to the worthy old gentleman—has, in this respect, a quality of enchantment like that of the Devil's wages. Whoever touches it should look well to himself, or he may find the bargain to go hard against him, involving, if not his soul, yet many of its better attributes; its sturdy force, its courage and constancy, its truth, its self-reliance, and all that gives the emphasis to manly character. (I, 39)

Despite this emphatic rejection of public office, in less than four years Hawthorne was again to seek and accept a government post for the third and last time, the Liverpool consulate. The habit of dependency followed by rebellious leave-taking was a recurring one. But even though Hawthorne was later to seek the support of Uncle Sam's arm, he left the Custom House in 1849 with the exhilaration of one who feels he has thrown off such support just in time to salvage his independence and manhood. Rebounding with an energy equal to the threat of entrapment, he severed his ties to Salem by offensive statements about the government and his colleagues. It felt like a rebirth, and for a while it was.

Like Freud, who entered his major phase after the death of his father (*because* of it, Freud believed), Hawthorne confronted mortality through the death of his mother at a similarly receptive age, and was able to turn this loss to creative ends. As befits a *memento mori*, his *Scarlet Letter* closes on a chord of death and reconciliation. A final spatial ordering rectifies the initial sense of irregularity—Salem viewed as a "disarranged checkerboard"—of the Custom House overture. The author's farewell to his characters distributes them in

31

a space symbolic of achieved harmony. Hester, having returned to Salem to take up voluntarily the destiny formerly imposed on her, attains by this act of free will and acceptance of her own past, a final integrity of life. Pearl, now married and a mother, lives separated from Hester by the broad Atlantic. Physically unable to reach her distant mother, Pearl sends instead tributary gifts that Hester can no longer use, gifts analogous to the posthumous memorial that is *The Scarlet Letter* itself.

Once reconciled, Hester subsides into death as easily as one already a ghost. "And, after many, many years, a new grave was delved, near an old and sunken one . . . yet with a space between, as if the dust of the two sleepers had no right to mingle. Yet one tombstone served for both" (I, 264). Having survived Pearl's father by many years, she rests next to him under a common headstone but separated by a symbolic space. The carefully specified interval between Pearl's parents is reserved for the ghost of the husband who had separated them in life yet played a definitive role in that life. Both the bracketing stone and the spatial interval help order the familial "disarrangements" that generated the romance. Pearl's parents, unlike those of the author, are in death brought side by side under a common memorial bearing a symbol that translates to a verbal legend, "On a field, sable, the letter A, gules." What life had sundered, symbolism and words have reunited.

For Hester and Hawthorne the scarlet letter had "done its office." The once alienated woman becomes a figure of guidance and counsel, turning her accrued wisdom back into society. Although unable to fulfill her grandiose early dream of becoming a prophetess, she yet is able, by sharing her wisdom with the coming generation, to leave behind a legacy that will justify her life and sufferings. This return to society of the fruits of private experience, like the publication of a fine book, forges satisfying links between self and world. Joining the chain of humanity by transmitting meaning rather than offspring is a late adult form of generativity.

On the life-enhancing effects of contact with death, a modern psychologist, Robert Jay Lifton, tells us something poets have long known: "to 'touch death' and then rejoin the living can be a source of insight and power. This is true not only for those exposed to holocaust, or to the death of a parent or lover or friend, but also for those who have permitted themselves to experience fully the 'end of an era,' personal or historical."[20] If the "end of an era" be added to the already cited experiences of death, Lifton's insight raises to a yet higher power the forces activating Hawthorne's creative breakthrough.

Of course, responses to death vary according to many circumstances, not least of which is the stage of life at which we encounter it. Even if all other elements were constant, confrontation with death would affect us differently at various ages and states of being. At age forty-five, when Hawthorne lived through his mother's death, he was still capable physically and emotionally of growing from this anguish, of being revitalized. But ten years later, when his fifteen-year-old daughter Una came close to death from malaria in Rome, he himself was unwell and professionally almost spent. He was, in fact, only five years from his own death. He had not written a novel for seven years and his only literary work during the Liverpool consulate had been notebook entries and the outline of an English romance.

While the Hawthornes lived for months pent up in a Roman apartment fighting off the expected death of their lovely first-born child, Hawthorne wrote daily and completed a draft of *The Marble Faun*. He wrote regularly because having left the consulate he needed money, and because he could make good use of his time while housebound. Perhaps, also, he hoped to recapture his earlier artistic rebirth in proximity to death. Una survived, although she never recovered completely, and Hawthorne finished his last romance, a rich though not a great one.

Una's brush with death did not place her father in "the dusty midst of life" but rather pushed him closer to the end of it. This man still suffering the loss of his own father was terrified of losing the child whose existence returned him to the chain of generations. His own hold on generational continuity was inherently too fragile for him ever to recover from this threat, even though loss of a child was far from uncommon in his day.

At fifty-five Hawthorne was too ill, too tired and dislocated, too frightened, to weld together the fragments of his identity as he once did to produce his first book. With discipline and extensive use of notebooks, he completed his Italian romance, which resumes all his

33

old themes, but lacks the economy and passion of *The Scarlet Letter*. A marble faun endowed with life represents only a clever allegorical idea, whereas Pearl, the animated scarlet letter, danced his own life theme. And of little Pearl, Una had been the original. Una, whom he never tired of observing, awakened in her father memories of the child in himself. Unable to guarantee or protect the life of this reminder of his early self, this first evidence of his own maturation into paternity, and this link with posterity, Hawthorne experienced a radical threat to his own continuity with life, a threat not canceled by Una's recovery. The lesson in human mortality was not the same one he experienced at his mother's deathbed.

Although the cohesion that Hawthorne achieved in his forty-fifth year was not to be a lifelong possession, it did make possible the solid achievement of *The Scarlet Letter* and thereby confirmed his identity as an author. The death of his mother could not have been thus influential had his life with her not been equally so. In an early tale, "The Threefold Destiny," Ralph Cranfield's worldwide search for his special destiny is concluded with the imperative sign, "Effode—Dig!" which tells him that in order to find the treasure he had been seeking so long "he was to till the earth around his mother's dwelling, and reap its products!" (IX, 481). Ralph Cranfield's threefold destiny, "the maid, the treasure, and the venerable sage with his gift of extended empire" (IX, 475), resembles critical stages in adult development as described by Erik Erikson—the stages of intimacy, capacity to earn a living, and attainment of identity through significant work. Indeed, "The Threefold Destiny" might stand for those aspects of adult life that Hawthorne was notably slow in achieving— marriage, reliable income, and identity as an author.

Reliable income was always a problem for him, but marriage and professional identity did grow out of the natal soil. Like Ralph Cranfield, Hawthorne scholars have searched far and wide for exotic explanations of Hawthorne's personal mystery and his fictional preoccupations. Let us try looking closer to home, digging deeper in the "natal soil" around his mother's dwelling, and see if it might yield the treasure we have long been seeking.

TWO

The Hawthornes among the Mannings[1]

"The boy has been baptized in blood; will ye keep the mark
fresh and ruddy upon his forehead?"

"The Gentle Boy"

THE MATERNAL LINE

Most biographies of Hawthorne begin just where Hawthorne,
had he wanted a biography, would have wished them to begin—
with the first generation of Puritan ancestors on the Hawthorne side.
These stern, authoritarian ancestors were the remote paternal forebears who were chosen for attention by an author who never publicly mentioned his father or his equally long maternal lineage. It is a
rare biographer who does not follow Hawthorne's lead and ignore
the maternal ancestor, Nicholas Manning, who reached the shores of
Massachusetts only thirty years later than the better-known William
Hathorne. Dramatic events were also associated with the first American Manning, but Hawthorne does not mention them. However, in
the family chronicle by Vernon Loggins we learn of an event just as
likely to affect an author's imagination as having an ancestor who
presided over witch trials.[2]

In 1680 the wife of Nicholas Manning accused him of incest with
his two sisters, Anstiss and Margaret. Nicholas Manning fled into
the forest, but his sisters were tried, convicted, and sentenced "to be
imprisoned a night, whipped, or pay £5, and to sit, during the services of next lecture day, on a high stool, in the middle alley of
Salem meeting-house, having a paper on their heads with their crime

written in capital letters."[3] The two sisters, Anstiss Manning, a spinster of thirty, and Margaret Palfray, a pregnant married woman of thirty-three, sat on repentance stools throughout the service with the horrifying word INCEST on their caps before the eyes of their family and the entire congregation. This event was described in Felt's *Annals of Salem* with the names withheld, and Loggins believes that so keen an antiquarian as Hawthorne would have known the identity of the brother and two sisters.[4]

These Mannings, too, were ancestors of the author of *The Scarlet Letter*, which opens with a scene remarkably like that of the disgrace of the two Manning women, a place of public assembly where the whole town is gathered to witness the exposure of a sexual sin. But in tracing his ties to the past in the autobiographical "Custom-House," Hawthorne does not mention a familial precedent for a man who escapes punishment for sexual transgression and a woman who endures public humiliation. Instead, his autobiographical statements link him to the persecutors of such transgressors, the stern William and the persecuting John Hathorne, that is, to the judgmental and punitive paternal heritage.

Guided by the author, biographers traditionally have selected from the available facts, finding the historically prominent Hawthornes a more suitable lineage for a romancer than the mercantile Mannings, who came to be regarded as mere providers for the widow and her children. Recent biographers try not to "discount the Manning influence," but none have given it detailed consideration.[5] In fact, the Manning family provided a good deal more than financial security and a dramatic history of incest. Their cultural aspirations and sensibility helped stimulate Hawthorne's imagination. Their mercantile values implanted a firm respect for actualities. Moreover, in the form of many uncles, they supplied the fatherless boy with models of masculinity that may have been too imposing but were sorely needed.

The Manning family had been in New England just about as long as the Hawthornes but had made a less dramatic mark on its history. Originally gunsmiths and blacksmiths, by Hawthorne's time they had acquired large land holdings in Maine, a Salem-based stage-coach company, and other profitable ventures. Although thoroughly business-minded, even in dealings within the family, they were generous, concerned with one another, interested in books, and very pious.

THE BLENDING OF TWO FAMILIES

The family that both Hawthorne and his biographers tend to minimize is the very one that provided the atmosphere of his childhood and youth. On the death in Surinam of his sailor father whom he scarcely knew, his mother returned to the home and family of her childhood. Only a block away from the Union Street house that she had shared with her husband and his mother, the Herbert Street house of the Manning family was yet far from the home that young Nathaniel and his sisters would have known had their father lived. Madame Hawthorne, as she was called after the death of her husband, lost the status of wife and potential mistress of her own home and returned to the dependent position of daughter and sister in a large family of strong personalities. She maintained few ties with her husband's relatives, some of them quite wealthy and influential. Although Nathaniel knew and occasionally visited his paternal aunts and grandmother, he was effectively cut off from their influence and financial help. Like his mother and sisters, he reverted to the influence and domination of the large, affectionate Manning family, which at that time contained two strong-minded parents and nine children, the youngest of whom was only thirteen years older than Nathaniel.

The Mannings were a varied cast of characters surrounding and sometimes dominating the Hawthorne children. This change in constellation from a paternally supported and dominated family to a dependent one engulfed by strong-minded grandparents, aunts, and uncles must have had far-reaching effects on the children's basic concepts. Imagery of self and family, of authority and parents, of the very meaning of providing and nurturing, had to be radically altered.

In order to understand the role that the Mannings were to play in the psychology and creative life of Nathaniel Hawthorne, we must see them both realistically and as they were projected in his personal mythology. First, a factual picture must be drawn based on surviving records such as account books and correspondence. Then we must try to view these Mannings as they appeared to the children—a multiplicity of female and male authority figures who appropriated parental functions, albeit of necessity and with good intentions. The three orphans beheld their needy and submissive mother surrender maternal authority to her own mother and sisters. Although the children loyally tried to shore up her role, Aunts Mary and Priscilla took it over decisively. The children saw the providing function belonging naturally to their father preempted by Manning family resources. Nathaniel in particular grieved to see paternal authority move gradually to his Uncle Robert.

To the proud Nathaniel, his uncle's assumption of responsibility and authority seemed a usurpation of power. The boy's reported penchant for declaiming "My lord, stand back, and let the coffin pass" may indicate precocious recognition of his own theme in *Richard The Third*, a drama of displaced authority, disinherited princes, and usurpation of power.

Of the personalities of the Manning grandparents, there is little extant evidence. Richard Manning senior was an energetic businessman with wide holdings in real estate. Starting out as a blacksmith, he founded the Boston and Salem Stagecoach Line and amassed considerable property before his death in 1813. Income from these properties supported his family for many years after his death. Among the items inventoried in his estate, along with mahogany furniture, china, and silver plate, were fourteen books valued at fourteen dollars, the first library to which Nathaniel had access.

Miriam Lord Manning, seven years older than her husband, was strong-willed and self-righteous. Her granddaughter recalls her passion for cleanliness: "I have been told that grandmother used to take the back of the Franklin stove down into the yard and *wash* it."[6] She was also parsimonious and domineering. In a vein of humorous complaint, Nathaniel wrote to his Uncle Robert shortly after he was forced to leave Raymond, Maine, and return to Salem for schooling:

I have nobody to talk to but Grandmother, Aunt Mary & Hannah and it seems very lonesome here. there is a pot of excellent guaver jelly now in the house and one of preserved limes and I am afraid they will mould if you do not come soon for it's esteemed sacrilege by Grandmother to eat any of them now because she is keeping them against somebody is sick and I suppose she would be very much disappointed if everybody was to continue well and they were to spoil. we have some oranges too which Isaac Burnham gave Gmother which are rotting as fast as possible and we stand a very fair chance of not having any good of them because we have to eat the bad ones first as the good are to be kept till they are spoilt also.[7]

As the wife of a prosperous and hard-working man, the grandmother was intolerant of requests for charity. When aid was requested for the needy children of her sister, she asked Ebe Hawthorne to make the following reply:

Grandmother requests me to say to you, that she hopes none of her children will be troubled as she has been, with the company of distant relations, and that if Mr Giddings' children are in want, let them work as she did at his father's, and if they cannot maintain themselves so, let them go to the poor-house.[8]

Mrs. Manning did not distribute until 1823 monies that her daughter Maria Miriam bequeathed in 1814 to various religious societies.

Despite these negative implications, the senior Mannings were held in honored esteem by their children. A charming letter from twenty-two-year-old Mary shows family cohesion and aspiration to culture.

Dear & Honered Parents,
With Pleasure I write to you & the Idea of addressing such Invaluable Friends In some measure Consoles me for your absence. I assure you we make a tolerable Figure. William & Richard fill their Stations with Dignity. the Children all behave very well, John & Samuel go to school every day at the stated hours wich is more than I expected. . . . where wee all called to subscribe to my Letter, Nine Promising Children might be seen Greeting their Parents, wich no doubt you deem your Greatest Riches. Pray Heaven not one of them may be unworthy of you.
I have no particular news to write May this find you injoying Health and Happiness, Is the wish of your Affectionate Daughter
Mary Manning[9]

Of the nine Manning children only three, in addition to Elizabeth C. Hawthorne, ever married. Richard married Susannah Dingley in 1815, Priscilla Miriam married John Dike, a widower with two children, in 1817, nine years after the Hawthornes moved in, and Robert Manning did not marry until 1824 at the age of forty, shortly before Hawthorne's graduation from college. Of the Manning aunts, Maria Miriam died at twenty-eight. Mary, the eldest of the Manning children, who remained in the Herbert Street house until her death in 1841, was a puritanical and sharp-tongued spinster. An inveterate and acidulous letter writer, she kept a sharp eye on the children, especially while their mother was living in Maine. Mary was of keen intelligence and high principles, very outspoken, and provided a lively contrast to Elizabeth Hawthorne's passivity. All the parental feelings of these eight aunts and uncles were focused on the Hawthorne children during their formative years, an overwhelming substitution for the one lost parent.

Elizabeth Hawthorne had five brothers. In order of age they were William, Richard, Robert, John, and Samuel. John was part of the joint Manning-Hawthorne household for five years before his disappearance during the War of 1812. William and Samuel, the oldest and youngest of the brothers, remained unsettled and rather improvident, a cause of concern to other members of the family, who wished to see them productively employed. William, the first born, outlived all the others. He gave young Nathaniel paid employment as clerk and bookkeeper for the stagecoach lines, often slipped him additional money, and generously offered more when needed, more than Nathaniel felt willing to accept.

Closest to Nathaniel in age, Samuel was like an older brother or mentor in the ways of masculine behavior. The cavalier Samuel often took his nephew along on horse buying trips for the family business. These journeys with the carousing, story-swapping, popular young uncle were a refreshing alternative to life in the Manning household, providing varied experiences and opportunities to socialize with farmers and working people. In Sam's company and outside Salem, Nathaniel loosened his inhibitions, talked more freely, and felt exhilarated by the variety and freedom of anonymous social intercourse. Liberated from his customary identity, he wrote letters from these trips of rare humor and joyousness. Unfortunately, Samuel's death from tuberculosis at age forty-one deprived Hawthorne of another significant male figure. At the time of Samuel's death in 1833, Nathaniel was twenty-nine and still in his mother's home.

With his soberer and more industrious Uncle Richard, Nathaniel had a different kind of bond. They shared a love of books (many of Richard's books passed into Nathaniel's possession) and the disability of lameness. Richard's lifelong lameness, further exacerbated by a chaise accident in Raymond, caused hypochondria and occasional melancholia. But Nathaniel thought him plucky, saying "though he is lame, yet he outstrips all of his Brothers." [10] The fruitful contact of the early years was chilled by what Nathaniel perceived as such a frigid reception after college graduation that he determined never again to return to the Eden of his youth. In fact, he made only one further visit to Richard, who felt himself to be unfairly exiled in Raymond.

John Manning, born in 1788, was a mysterious figure who dominated the Manning home by his absence. He enlisted as a sailor during the War of 1812 and was last heard from in 1813. His death was never reported and his mother always expected his return. This mysterious disappearance of a sailor resonated in the boy's mind to the failure of his own father to return from a voyage. The grandmother's faith in her son's return probably encouraged a similar hope and fear in Nathaniel, who often meditated on the horror of unconfirmed deaths.

From the age of four to nine, Nathaniel lived in the same household with all six of the Manning men. The year 1813 marked a turning point, for in that year Grandfather Manning died on his way to "the land of promise" (such was the family term for Raymond), Richard Manning took up permanent residence there, and John left to fight in the war, never to return. After 1813 the men left in Herbert Street were only three in number—William, Samuel, who was often away traveling, and Robert. The following year, young Aunt Maria Miriam died. Richard and Robert divided up the work of settling their father's estate. Richard handled the Maine land sales in addition to buying and selling thousands of additional acres; Robert managed the stagecoach lines with the rather ineffective help of William and took over from their mother the complex task of administering the estate. So well did he manage family affairs that even his brief absences from Salem caused panic in the others. Samuel wrote: "Mr Tucker sends it as his opinion that we shall all go to Hell to gether without you return soon."[11] All the brothers soon became accountable to Robert, who also had other business interests of his own.

UNCLE ROBERT

Strength is incomprehensible by weakness, and therefore the more terrible. There is no greater bugbear than a strong-willed relative, in the circle of his own connections.
The House of the Seven Gables

We see the most capable and influential of the Manning clan first in the context of his family; his role in the inner life of Nathaniel Hawthorne will emerge in later chapters. After Grandfather Manning's death in 1813, Robert Manning became virtual head of the household and manager of all the family business affairs except the land sales delegated to Richard in Maine, and on these, too, Robert kept a close supervisory eye. In addition he was a successful broker and later became the most famous pomologist in America. He is still sufficiently regarded as a horticulturist to rate a lengthy article in *The Dictionary of American Biography*. Starting with the gardens that he planned for his intended home in Maine, Manning conducted experiments for twenty-five years to ascertain the varieties of fruit trees best suited to New England climatic conditions. In 1822, the year that his sister returned permanently to Salem, he realized that he would never make his home in Maine and bought approximately three acres in North Salem, then called Northfield, and began his orchards in earnest. He imported fruit tree stocks from all over the world, a costly enterprise because many specimens perished in transit. Frederick C. Sears writes in *The Dictionary of American Biography* that

> his interest and enthusiasm led him also to give away both scions and trees with a liberality that did more for the fruit interests of the country than for his own fortune. At the time of his death he possessed by far the finest collection of fruits in America and one of the best in the world, consisting of over one thousand varieties of pears alone, and nearly as

many more of the other fruits combined. . . . While modest and unassuming, he was always delighted to give the best information he had regarding fruits to all comers. In 1838 he published the *Book of Fruits* — "Being a descriptive catalogue of the most valuable varieties of the Pear, Apple, Peach, Plums, and Cherry for New England culture". . . . To Manning, more than to any other man of his time, and perhaps more than to all others combined, the fruit growers were indebted for the introduction of new and choice fruits, for correcting the nomenclature of fruits— at that time in a state of great confusion—and for identifying varieties.[12]

Even from this encyclopedia article Manning's public personality emerges—enthusiastic yet modest, altruistic, orderly, and order creating. His daughter Rebecca adds to this picture a sense of Manning's enthusiasm and informality.

Robert Manning was an enthusiast in regard to trees—especially fruit trees—and pear trees most of all. . . . He had a large correspondence with horticulturists, both in this country and in Europe. He was a charter member of the Massachusetts Horticultural Society in 1829, and the beginning of its library was made by his gift of some of his own books. . . . His garden did not have any formal laying out—rather it "growed" like Topsy. . . . An elm tree in front of the house on the street, set out in 1825 still is flourishing. [Shades of the Pyncheon elm!] Robert Manning received a silver pitcher from the Massachusetts Horticultural society "for his meritorious exertions in advancing the cause of pomological science, and for procuring and distributing new varieties of fruits from Europe."[13]

Over the years Manning contributed to horticultural journals articles that were frequently edited and polished in style by Nathaniel. Ebe, too, helped Robert overcome those educational deficiencies that hampered him in his chosen work; she translated a French horticultural book, *Bon Jardinière*, into a leather-bound notebook, showing that this girl who scorned all mundane chores would do a careful, patient piece of work for her Uncle Robert. The preface to his *Book of Fruits* (1838) tells us how Robert felt about his own work in language so formally Augustan that one detects the editorial hand of his college-trained nephew:

But to a young man with the advantages of fortune and a familiarity with the modern languages, researches of this nature would open an inexhaustible source of enjoyment. He could scarcely be more honorably and usefully occupied than in collecting and identifying fruits, and introducing them to the notice of his countrymen; nor better rewarded than in witnessing his anticipation, from year to year, continually realized and continually renewed.[14]

This advice was later accepted by Manning's own first son, who, though only fifteen years old at his father's death, proceeded immediately to carry on the horticultural work for which he had been trained and eventually became a distinguished pomologist in his own right. Robert Manning had a far different effect on his son than he had on his nephew. Nevertheless, Hawthorne's long contact with professional horticulture stimulated and refined his interest in plant symbolism.

Although younger than William and Richard and four years younger than his widowed sister Elizabeth, Robert Manning was a person who readily and naturally assumed responsibility. More fully than any of his brothers he took over guardianship of his sister and her children. Although Madame Hawthorne had her own small income from her father's estate, Robert contributed toward the children's education and made the essential decisions in their lives. Occasionally Mary or Priscilla Manning made sharp comments about Robert's domineering nature, but apparently Elizabeth Hawthorne never demurred. So fully did she submit to his will and sometimes that of her sisters that we often find the children wanting their mother to remain in Raymond where she could at least be mistress of herself, even though this meant they would be separated from her.

Even with the mother present, Robert seemed to be his nephew's keeper, as shown by Priscilla's letter to Robert during Nathaniel's exemption from school because of a foot injury.

He amuses himself with playing about the yard, and in Herbert St. nearly all day. be so good, Robert, as to favour him with your advice (which I think will not fail to be influential) with regard to attending to writing, and some of his lessons, regularly, the benefits he will *derive*, will *amply repay* him for the *exertion* it will *require*. however rich the soil, we do not expect fruit, unless good seed is sown, and the plants carefully cultivated. Far be it from me to complain of him, at his age, he cannot be expected to have consideration enough, to do this, except it be required of him.[15]

Her underlinings and her attitude toward amusement when it interferes with education express a forceful personality.

The foot injury of 1813 released Nathaniel from regular school attendance, gave him freedom to read, loaf, play with his cats, and generally to escape from activities enjoined by his family. His education was not entirely suspended, since Joseph Worcester, later the compiler of a dictionary, came to hear his lessons, but he was freed to read books of his own choice from the family library. Because one foot appeared not to be growing normally, a good deal of attention was focused on it, many doctors were consulted, progress reports exchanged, and the boy was generally petted and indulged.[16] In later years he recalled having played this injury for all it was worth. Through it he learned the power of weakness, a way of manipulating his manipulators in order to create a psychic space in which to develop in his own slow way.

But even this strategy was partially frustrated by the fact that family members repeatedly invoked Uncle Robert's authority to keep the boy on the Manning track. Like Priscilla, Ebe urged Robert to insist that Nathaniel walk on the weak foot instead of pampering it: "I don't know that Nathaniel's foot will ever get well if you dont come home. He wont walk on it & the Doctor says he must; so do come soon."[17]

Despite genuine trust and respect, Priscilla, Mary, and Richard expressed irritation at Robert's censoriousness and assumption of power. Priscilla characterized his speech habits as "his usual decided manner."[18] Her responses to Robert's unilateral decision that the Hawthornes should not yet remove to Maine reveals not only her annoyance, but also the family's tendency to accept his decisions whether or not they agreed.

August 29, 1814

The candour of your reply, in answer to our inquiry, receives our acknowledgements. We were convinced, by the reason, and propriety, of what you advanced, that it would be better to defer the visit, till another season.—Do you not give us some credit, for distrusting our own judgment, and referring the case to you; it would have been quite inconsistent with our general character, had we acted with precipitation. I know you will be gratified at hearing, and I think it but justice, to the Children, to relate to you, the manner in which they received this answer, so peculiarly interesting to them; altho they had been anticipating one, the reverse of that received, yet when I informed them what you had written,   they cheerfully submitted to your decision. [19]

Ignoring this sarcasm Robert responded only to news of the children's obedience:

Priscilla's account of the behaviour of the Children is very Flattering, but I wanted no evidence to confirm my opinion, that they were all that good Children should be.   the Children here are not subjected to that order & Subordination, which is so necessary to discourage bad habits, & confirm good ones,   ours I hope will duly appreciate the advantages they enjoy, & profit by them. [20]

Even autocratic Aunt Mary feared Robert's criticism, especially of her spelling and grammar. She wrote to him, "do not look for any bad spelling or any ungrammatical sentence in my letter, but reade it as if spelt & wrote well." Another letter concludes, "Do not criticise the writeing spelling &c of your affectionate Sister/Mary Manning." [21]

Excerpts from Richard's letters over the years show him chafing under Robert's criticism of the way he conducted the Maine business affairs.

December 6, 1816
I do not think the proceedings for three years back is so bad as you have surmised and if there is any blame I am willing to take my part of it.

April 4, 1825
You say that you cannot understand the concluding part of my last letter. I will explain it to you, viz it was by your direction that I undertook the Cape Law Suit, and I did not feel very good natured about it, that was all Brother Robert, that was all, and I remain as ever your affectionate Brother

Richard Manning

February 19, 1825
[Regarding the case mentioned above] I shall have to pore over a parcell of Musty Deeds to find the conveyance from the Proprietors to Father,   if it was all my own I should be almost tempted to quit at once,   I wish

Father had disinherited me from this part of the Estate. . . . I have not
had a new Garment this two Years & had rather do without for two Years
to come & live off Roast Potatoes, then to be continually perplext with so
much business that I am not competent to attend to,   better is a Dinner
of herbs & peace therewith, than a Stalled Ox where there is Strife. . . .
Perhaps you will say Richard complains without cause   it may be so   I
charge 100 dollars a Year for my servises but if I was not lame & not concerned in the business I would not undertake it for 500. . . . You wished a
long letter and if I have performed nothing else I have done that . . . I will
try to remain your affectionate Brother

Richard Manning[22]

Richard was angry at Robert for encouraging him to enlarge his
general store in the expectation that Robert would eventually par-
ticipate in it and that the whole family would join him in Raymond.
On December 18, 1820, Richard sent Robert a long, angry letter
about his decision not to move to Raymond. Richard quotes excerpts
from five years of Robert's letters expressing his intention of moving
himself and the rest of the family to Maine. Truly angry at being left
alone in Raymond after having enlarged the business and supervised
the building of Robert's house, Richard ended the letter without his
customary complimentary close of "your affectionate brother."

Robert Manning wrote brief, functional letters to his fiancée and
wife, whereas he wrote courtly ones to his mother, affectionate teas-
ing ones to his Hawthorne nieces, and warm, solicitous ones to his
sister Elizabeth. Such differences in tone, along with the fact that he
remained a bachelor until age forty, suggest that his most intimate
feelings had been preempted by his sister and her family. For many
years he regarded the Hawthorne children as virtually his own. In
1828, after his marriage and removal to North Salem, he built next
door to his own house another for his sister Elizabeth in which she
lived for about four years. The special closeness between Nathaniel's
mother and her brother may well have been confusing to the boy
and disturbing in unconscious ways.

Both nieces received affectionate attention from their uncle and responded in kind, but with Maria Louisa he had an especially warm
relationship.

Raymond, August 13, 1813

Dear Louisa,

Do you know your Uncle wants to see & kiss you, if you dont come down in the woods & see me I beleive [*sic*] I shall come home—it appears to me I have been gone a year & I expect when I come home you will be as good & as tall as your mam & you must have a paper on your arm so that I can tell it is my little girl, do you tell Eby & Nat to be good Children & ask your Mam to put you in a Basket & let Nat wheal you down to see me in his wheel barrow Louisa this is a pleasant place in the summer & we have the pretty little fish of all kinds & wild pigeons & berries & sugar pears, but then there is no school for little Children & that is bad you know so when you grow up you must come down & keep school learn the little boys & girls to read & they want to learn but their parents cant learn them so they run almost wild in the fields picking berries & playing and are so happy in this way I almost wish I was one of them. well so Nat wont write me a letter about the war & privateers— he must look out for a lecture when Uncle John comes home. . . . then Uncle R will come home & then the good walks & talks & rides but no matter. I was going to write a short letter but what a long one so you be a good girl & that will please your uncle

Robert [23]

All three children received ample advice to be good, but the kisses and good walks, talks, and rides were reserved for Louisa. Maria Louisa wrote many letters urging her uncle to come home that they might take walks together, telling about her flowers, and, as Priscilla reported, she asked others to inquire about him: "she is very desirous of knowing every circumstance relating to you, and frequently asks when you are coming home." [24] Robert Manning's special relationship to the docile Louisa suggests that like his nephew he had a preference for undemanding, submissive females.

The differences in Robert's perception of the three Hawthorne children and in his relationship to them are revealed in a letter to Priscilla of July 1814.

I sincerely sympathize with Nathaniel in his misfortune [the foot injury] he must be patient & hope for the best, I will not say he must be a good boy for there is no need of reminding him of his duty, I intend writing him a long letter, & one to Louisa about the Lambs, & one to E[be] about the many romantic views on which she could employ her pencil. [25]

Robert's communications to and about Nathaniel were not about lambs, romantic views, good walks and talks, but about obedience, duty, and the importance of schooling. Robert wrote to the boy's mother in 1819, "I intended that Nathaniel should have wrote this week but as he would have lost one evening at school, I chose to let him write next week."[26] The uncle controlled even Nathaniel's letters to his mother.

Family members reported to Robert about Nathaniel's school performance, relying on the uncle to demand greater vigor and less self-indulgence. Robert's letters to the boy expressed dissatisfaction with the infrequency of his letters, an alternating hope and confidence in his "goodness" (by which he generally meant diligence and obedience), and concern about his future occupation. Because he took Nathaniel more seriously than he did his nieces and possibly because he sensed the boy's concealed rebelliousness, he treated him with greater severity, revealing to the nephew the more prudential aspect of his nature.

Although Uncle Robert could express to Louisa empathy with the happy Raymond children who had no schools to go to, a feeling Nathaniel might have shared readily, he communicated to the boy his inclination to "that order & Subordination, which is so necessary to discourage bad habits." Robert's passion for order is also revealed in the meticulous records he kept for his orchards and in his taxonomic services to pomology. A self-taught man this successful in scientific methodology and business management must have had innate ability to order details and considerable intellectual capacity. Despite poor health, a familial tendency to pulmonary disorders, and a lifelong problem with headaches, he had a great deal of energy, which he contrasted with his nephew's characteristic lethargy.[27] Nathaniel's passivity and indolence appeared especially unmanly in the presence of Robert Manning's energetic capabilities, not only to the uncle but to the boy himself. The resulting self-distrust was to be permanently in conflict with Hawthorne's innate pride.

Feeling diminished by proximity to Uncle Robert's worldly capabilities and by his expressed and implied criticism, Nathaniel came to fear situations in which he would be tested by others. Before taking his entrance examination for Bowdoin, he wrote to his mother, "Mr Oliver says I will get into College, therefore Uncle Robert need be under no apprehensions."[28] Robert's account of this examination underscores Nathaniel's own apprehension of failure.

> October 5, 1821
> Nathaniel immediately called on Mr. Everett with Mr. Oliver's Letter Mr. E came with him to see me & proceeded to the Presidents to introduce Nathaniel 2 o Clock was appointed for his examination. during the whole journey he was doubtful. & after he returned from the Presidents he was positive he should not pass & requested me to be ready to return Immediately. I encouraged him as much as possible. at 2 o clock he attended & in 1 hour returned, having been examined, passed & a chum appointed him.[29]

A glowing report returned by Uncle Dike after a Bowdoin visit to Nathaniel just prior to graduation was strangely displeasing to the young man who feared having to meet family expectations. His letter of complaint communicates with rare candor Uncle Robert's role in this dread of being judged.

> July 14th. 1825
> I am not very well pleased with Mr. Dike's report of me. The family had before conceived much too high an opinion of my talents, and probably formed expectations, which I shall never realize. I have thought much upon the subject and have finally come to the conclusion, that I shall never make a distinguished figure in the world, and all I hope or wish is to plod along with the multitude. I do not say this for the purpose of drawing any flattery from you, but merely to set Mother and the rest of you right, upon a point where your partiality has led you astray. I did hope that Uncle Robert's opinion of me was nearer to the truth, as his deportment toward me never expressed a very high estimation of my abilities.[30]

When this desire to hide from judgment was later to conflict with his yearning for public recognition, he compromised by publishing his stories, but anonymously or under false names.

THE MANNINGS FROM THE CHILDREN'S PERSPECTIVE

During Madame Hawthorne's residence in Maine from 1816 to 1822, the children were often away from her, living for the most part with the Manning family on Herbert Street. Nathaniel spent most of his time in Salem after 1819 when he was sent back to attend school, whereas the girls traveled back and forth. All three missed their mother desperately yet begged her to remain in Maine, where she could be mistress of herself and where they could have a refuge from Manning supervision. They recognized the good intentions of their aunts, uncles, and grandmother but felt oppressed by their constant criticism. To some degree all three children complained to their mother of "domineering" attitudes, manipulation, and a generally unpleasant atmosphere. Back in Salem preparing for college, Nathaniel complained of "eternal finding-fault":

> March 7th 1820
> Mr. Oliver thought I could enter College next commencement, but Uncle Robert is afraid I should have to study too hard. I get my lessons at home, and recite them to him at 7 o'clock in the morning. I am extremely homesick. Aunt Mary is continually scolding at me. Grandmaam hardly ever speaks a pleasant word to me. If I ever attempt to speak a word in my defense, they cry out against my impudence. However I guess I can live through a year and a half more, and then I shall leave them. One good effect results from their eternal finding-fault. It gives me some employment in retaliating, and that keeps up my spirits. Mother I wish you would let Louisa board with Mrs Dike if she comes up here to go to school. Then Aunt M. can't have her to domineer over. I hope, however, that I shall see none of you up here very soon.[31]

Aunt Mary's reward for her concern and conscientious reports to the family on Nathaniel's health and welfare and on Louisa's food, schooling, and clothing, was that in their minds she became the "bad mother" in contrast to whom the remote real mother became an idealized one. As Raymond became increasingly for Nathaniel a garden of Eden presided over solely by a loving mother, he became frantic at family efforts to return her to Salem, where, he told her, she "would have to submit to the authority of Miss Manning."[32]

True, Aunt Mary's will often prevailed over that of the mother, and Mary was indeed a powerful woman whose maternal instincts rushed into the vacuum left by Elizabeth Hawthorne's absence. But Nathaniel's anguish over the substitution rather than serious failings on Aunt Mary's part probably accounts for his reiterated complaints.

51

In casting these two mother figures into contrasting roles, he was engaging in the process of transforming reality into myth. A later step would be the further transformation of such family myths into fictional ones.

The eldest of the Hawthorne children, the imperious Elizabeth, or Ebe as she was called by the family, habitually judged people by her own standards. She gives in the following letter a full picture of the atmosphere of the Manning home as the children experienced it. Ebe's open flaunting of the Manning work ethic, her refusal to accommodate in matters of hours or chores, or to hide her contempt for such matters, may have brought down upon her an extra share of frowns and lectures, but her complaints differ from those of Nathaniel and Louisa only in their more analytical tone. Ebe was twenty when she wrote the following letter and more able than the others to recognize the Manning "solicitude for my welfare," which was unfortunately undermined by their failure to "understand the art of government" by judicious timing of their lectures and selection of issues for criticism. By scolding indiscriminately the Mannings lost the attention and respect of their charges, making them long for the peaceful atmosphere of Raymond and the governance of their own indulgent mother. "Friends," below, refers to the family.

Salem, May 14th, 1822

Dear Mother,

I received Maria's letter on Friday, and was very sorry to learn than you intend to come to Salem but I presume your determination is fixed, & I *know* that in one week after your return you will regret your present peaceful home. Not all the pleasures of society, great as they *are represented* to be, can afford the slightest compensation for the tumultuous and irregular life which one is compelled to lead in a family like this. I wish I had remained in Raymond. I am obliged to visit every day and all day, because if I am half an hour at home, my ears are assailed by long and severe lectures, which may possibly be just, but are certainly most injudicious & ill-timed. Without doubt I am wrong in many instances, but if all my errors were crimes, the remarks upon my conduct, & the language which *my friends* employ towards me, could not be more harsh than it is at present. If I attempt to converse with any one of the family, if I ask the slightest question, a reproof is invariably joined to the answer I receive. Bodily Labour comprises their only idea of intellectual and moral excellence, and an angel would fail to obtain their approbation, unless he came attired in a linsey-woolsey gown & checked apron, and assumed an *honourable* and *dignified station* at the washing tub.—If I remain at home, the whole family express their astonishment at my "moping in the house when the weather is so fine," & if I go out two days in succession, I am, with equal justice and elegance, accused of "spinning street-yarn." If I do, I am blamed for devoting my attention exclusively to one person, who unfortunately never happens to be the right one. I shall never be able to give satisfaction to them, yet I believe all this is done and said in kindness, & that they really feel a great deal of solicitude for my welfare; but they do not understand the art of government. I am perfectly willing to be ruled and managed, but it must be done dexterously, and not by open rebuke, or repulsive frowns.

I am

Your affectionate daughter,

E.M.H.[33]

PIETY AND PRUDENCE

Strong, pious, successful, and self-righteous, the Mannings mingled in their letters spiritual advice not to lay up one's treasures where moths and rust will corrupt them along with up-to-date bulletins on the cost of butter, eggs, flour, and requests to ship food staples or yard goods from Maine or Salem, wherever they were cheaper. They were fully aware of the price of everything and tried faithfully to remember the value of religious things, easily mixing piety and prudence in their advice.

Mary, whose letters delightfully blend religion with business and other practical matters, advised Richard in 1813:

Dear Brother   it gives me great pleasure to hear you are so pleasantly situated. I felt very uneasy about you, on receiving your first Letter after your arrival at Raymond. . . . let me admonish you as a first step to hapiness, to pay a strict regard to the Sabbath yourself, and discountenance every deviation in those whome your influence may affect. [Mary then asks Richard to send wool and flax if prices are reasonable, and concludes the letter] I hope you will be carefull to do business as with strangers for that is the way to keep Friends.[34]

When he grew old enough to fight back, Nathaniel liked to tease Aunt Mary about both her missionary zeal and her spinster status. From college he wrote to her about the revival of religion in Brunswick, Maine, adding that "unfortunately it has not yet extended to the college." A missionary society had been formed on campus, "but it does not meet with much encouragement. . . . I suppose you would be glad to hear that I was a member, but my regard to truth compels me to confess that I am not." Expressing regret that he would be unable to attend Uncle Robert's forthcoming wedding, Nathaniel added slyly, "I console myself with the hope that you, at least, will not neglect to give me an invitation to your wedding, which I should not be surprised to hear announced. Elizabeth says that you are very deeply in love with Mr. Upham. Is the passion reciprocal?"[35]

Affectionate concern, piety, and business reports filled the letters of the Manning women. The men generally made perfunctory inquiries about each other's health and welfare before proceeding to discussion of their complex business interests. Surviving account books show that Richard and Robert kept close track of such divergent matters as the administration of the elder Richard Manning's estate, the stagecoach lines, Robert's brokerage business and extensive traffic in fruit trees, as well as the sale and purchase of thousands of acres of land in Maine.

Every monetary exchange, outlay, or expense of the various family members was carefully recorded, accounted for, credited to or deducted from his or her share of the Richard Manning estate, all in properly notarized due bills, IOU's, and promissory notes. No gift or service was too inconsiderable for this cost-accounting treatment.

Family accounts show that Madame Hawthorne was charged board for herself and her children against her share of the estate. Robert billed his mother for transacting business for her under a power of attorney from the time of his father's death in 1813 until 1824, and for "use of my Horse-Chaise & Sleigh in Journey from Salem to Raymond & from Raymond to various parts of Cumberland & Oxford County $150." In turn Robert paid his mother rent for use of the buildings on Union Street for the stagecoach business. Samuel billed Mary three dollars for moving goods to North Salem and two dollars for gravel and repairs to the house. Mary billed the estate of her father for services to "my Mothers Family from April 19, 1823 to Dec. 19, 1826 two years at one Dollar per week Eight months at $2 per week,"[36] and complained that if Priscilla's husband received five dollars every time he carried money from Raymond to Salem, she would expect the same compensation. She billed William $2,464.47 for eight years of interest, rent, washing, mending, and making clothes. William borrowed from Richard, Robert, and Mary, and signed promissory notes on each of these loans. He was a poor business risk and had to sell some of his stock in the stagecoach lines to Robert. In 1837 Robert became liable for unpaid notes he had endorsed for William.

Family attitudes toward William, the long-lived black sheep, reveal much about Manning values. Richard, who was conscientious about responsibility and perhaps excessively scrupulous about finances, could not quite forgive his spendthrift brother. Mary, on the other hand, passed over the Hawthornes in her will and bequeathed all her assets to William, but protected in a trust. Improvident but generous William was the only Manning to whom Hawthorne was ever to make any return. For this uncle, who used to slip him extra money in his early days, Hawthorne wrote to his friend President Pierce in 1859 introducing Uncle William that he might request a job in the Salem Custom House,[37] and, indeed, a janitorship was found. Earlier Hawthorne had asked his publisher, Ticknor, to "pay the drafts of John Dike, of Salem, to the extent of $100 . . . for the benefit of W. Manning, an old and poor relation of mine."[38] Cautious even at this late date about putting money directly into the hands of Uncle William, Hawthorne nevertheless chose to repay his debt to the Mannings by kindness to the uncle who least reflected their values.

THE MANNING SENSIBILITY

The Manning preoccupation with money and business did not preclude imagination and sensibility. Richard complicated the elaborate financial accounts that he sent to Robert over the years by requesting the family to purchase for him many amenities not available in the frontier town of Raymond. In addition to patent medicines and clothes, Richard continually requested periodicals and books of fiction, history, travel, and biography. His varied interests are only partially indicated by the following extracts from letters he wrote to Robert:

May 16, 1814

You requested me to send you a list of the Books & other articles I want, all that I now recollect are the Cottage Girl a Novel   Anecdotes historical & Literary, Herriotts Travolls in Canada, and Withcraft or the art of fortune telling (dont Laugh at my whims) & Jelliffs patent Interest Table, & a bottle of sodiac powder price 50 cts at William Kidders Boston, two silver table spoons at Morgans if conveinent [*sic*], bring your Sullivans District of Maine, ask Wm to loan me his small Dictionary, and I will return it when I have done with (which will not be this many years I hope but do not tell him so).

January 28, 1823

I wish you to pay for my Boston Evening Gazette & for the Essex Register one Year each, & please to buy me a Magic Lantern at Elisha Dwelle. . . . likewise a pack of Comic Cards at Munroe & Francis, & likewise the Cooks Oracle by Dictor Kitchener, & Biography of American Heroes Revolutionary by Col Garden, & my Mind & its thoughts by Sarah Wentworth Morton, and a New England Tale, all at Munroe & Francis.

March 31, 1824

The London, Boston and Salem Papers I thank you for, they are a treat that I ought not to indulge myself with very often. I almost surfeit myself in looking them over.[39]

He even requested an "Aeolian Harp & an extra sett of strings" and "one superb imitation cashmere Shawl." To one of Richard's lists Mary appended a characteristic request, "one of those Books on Prison disipline, and Doctor Person's discorses on Temperance."[40]

The effect of Richard's "indulgence" in the delights of reading shows up in the gradual change in his letters. At first functional and businesslike, over the years they grew increasingly literary. Sometimes he would append a little poem to illustrate an aphorism of his own creation or embellish local news with literary allusions. Of the dismissal of an autocratic postmaster, he wrote to Robert in 1828, "we can say as Brutus said on the death of Cesar [*sic*] (I cannot remember the exact words but it ends with,) and Death for his Ambition." Congratulating Robert on the birth of a child, he wrote in 1829, "I wish . . . that you and Rebecca will live to see your children and grand-children grow up like Olive plants around your table."[41]

This hardheaded business family was not immune to the cult of sentiment. Priscilla's letter informing Richard of Maria's death is a gem of its kind.

May 20, 1814

The mournful task devolves on me to tell you, we have lost a beloved sister, Maria has left this world, we dought not for a better   she breathed her last in the arms of her friends, this after-noon and was enabled to give evidence to the truth of religion, and that God is the support of those who put their trust in him.   her dying words were, it is the will of God. let God be praised. My Redeemer, his precious Blood, is the foundation of my hope. My every wish is satisfied, God is good and I am his own child, the world is *nothing, nothing* to me. she kissed us, and bade us Live to the Glory of God. O that we may all be enabled to do so. may we hear this warning Voice, which bids us be ready—   I could not send this distressing intelligence without imparting to you the consolation, which the peace in which she died has afforded   May the God of all consolation support you in these hours of affliction   May we all have grace, to lay it to heart.   pray for us.

Your affectionate Sister
Priscilla Manning[42]

With the possible exception of Maria, Priscilla was the most literate and literary of the Mannings. Her letters display self-conscious flourishes, an eye for details, and ability to imagine scenes from which she was absent. Regarding a severe winter, she wrote to Elizabeth Hawthorne: "The trees have the last week exhibited the most beautiful appearance, the branches were covered with ice, and bent almost to the ground with the weight of it, some hung in such a manner as to resemble Chandeliers. twigs and weeds not larger than a straw, were covered an inch in thickness   I thought Elizabeth would [have] enjoyed it very much."

In 1816 Priscilla wrote to Robert, visualizing the Hawthorne family at Raymond, "Betsy solicitously enquiring if she shall there fix her abode, Elizabeth surveying those scenes, with which her imagination has been so charmed, that she has quitted, without regret, friends who have not parted from her with indifference; Nathaniel and Louisa, visiting the Lambs, admiring the streams, and—with you, discovering all that is interesting around you." In imagination she reconstructed her mother's visit there: "from the time you set out, we were conjecturing how far you had progressed, fearing you were detained by the rain; . . . we then in imagination saw you assembled and wished we could be there, and listen to your conversation."[43]

Richard's love of books and desire for an Aeolian harp, Robert's involvement in the cultivation of fruit trees, and Priscilla's literary flourishes and visual imagination are probably what Elizabeth Palmer Peabody meant when she spoke of "the Manning sensibility." If not exactly poets, they were not solely bookkeepers, yet it was as bookkeepers that Nathaniel Hawthorne primarily thought of them. There appears to have been a difference in their perception of and responses to the two more artistic of the Hawthorne children. They recognized Ebe's sensitivity to natural beauty and reluctantly accepted her haughty rejection of mundane chores but felt obliged to keep Nathaniel to the workaday grindstone. Robert thought of apprenticing him to a cutler and William kept him employed as a bookkeeper until they were persuaded by his teacher that he ought to attend college and prepare for a profession. The difference in these attitudes toward Ebe and Nathaniel can partially be explained by their different expectations of the two sexes, the cultivation of sensibility being a luxury allowable to a female but not to a male who had to prepare for a serious place in the world.

In addition to these gender stereotypes, the two presented themselves differently to the family. Ebe haughtily flaunted her divergence from family values, whereas Nathaniel tended to internalize it, kept it to himself, and therefore appeared more malleable. Although he eventually chose the role of artist, some part of him assented to their expectation that he would be a businessman, for he kept his writing and later much of his reading a secret from the Mannings. Although his mother and sisters knew about both, he felt that he had to protect this part of himself from Manning supervision and criticism. If his apprehension was unjust, and it may well have been, then we are led to surmise that he had early incorporated into himself what he took to be their disapproval. The Mannings seemed better able to accommodate the disparate aspects of their natures than Nathaniel did his. The split between artist and merchant expressed in a letter of 1820 to Ebe ("No man can be a Poet and a Bookkeeper at the same time") probably owes as much to his antithetical style of interpreting experience as to serious conflict between his own aspirations and Manning expectations.

Having for several years worked as a bookkeeper and letter writer for Uncle William in the stagecoach office, Nathaniel had almost ceased writing poetry. The Manning involvement with business affairs, although apparently rejected by the aspiring poet, was not entirely lost. Over and over again in Hawthorne's fiction antithetical male types are placed in opposition—the sensitive, unworldly artist such as Owen Warland or Clifford Pyncheon against the efficient, successful man of affairs like Peter Hovenden or Judge Pyncheon. This male polarity recurs as frequently as the widely observed one of light and dark women.

Very often the successful, commonsense men of the world are associated with the original Manning occupation, blacksmithing. Robert Danforth, the successful wooer of Owen Warland's beloved Annic, is a blacksmith. Peter Hovenden, her father, admires this earthy occupation: "I know what it is to work in gold, but give me the worker in iron, after all is said and done. He spends his labor upon a reality. . . . Did you ever hear of a blacksmith being such a fool as Owen Warland, yonder?" (X, 449). Lindsey, the commonsense father in "The Snow-Image," is a dealer in hardware, especially iron pots. The preoccupation of these men with iron allies them fully with Hawthorne's "Actual" in its most unredeemed form—the densest kind of matter, unalloyed with any mixture of the "Ideal." In order to associate Judge Pyncheon with unredeemed matter, Hawthorne emphasizes his "animal development," his corpulence, his greed, and his sexuality, which wore out three wives and even extends to his cousin Phoebe. This judge who "fortified his soul with iron" says proudly of himself, "I do not belong to the dreaming class of men" (II, 235).

The oppositions dramatized in Hawthorne's fiction were lodged within his own personality. He chose to be a writer, but he also took substantial pride in his few worldly successes. Although his wife was to regard him as all poet, the role he assumed with respect to her was the practical man of the world who would protect her from sordid matters that might defile her angelic nature. The delight attendant upon his election to the offices of trustee of Brook Farm and chairman of its Finance Committee shows that the bookkeeper remained alive within him. He wrote to Sophia from Brook Farm,

> Dearest love, thy husband was elected to two high offices, last night—viz., to be a Trustee of the Brook Farm estate, and Chairman of the Committee of Finance!!!! Now dost thou not blush to have formed so much lower an opinion of my business talents, than is entertained by other discerning people? From the nature of my office, I shall have the chief direction of all the money affairs of the community—the making of bargains—the supervision of receipts and expenditures &c. &c. &c. Thou didst not think of this, when thou didst pronounce me unfit to make a bargain with that petty knave of a publisher. A prophet has no honor among those of his own kindred, nor a financier in the judgment of his wife.[44]

However humorously he exaggerates his "accession to these august offices," his satisfaction is unmistakable.

The course of his career demonstrates the continuing tension between poet and bookkeeper. He wrote little or nothing during his periods of employment, and, as he records in "The Custom-House," he had to be "decapitated" as Surveyor before he could resume his writing. And when he did write, the man of affairs within him always undermined the artist, causing him first to publish anonymously or pseudonymously and later to undercut ironically both himself and many of his artist characters.

Thus it was not only his Puritan ancestors whose contempt for his profession he imagined and dreaded: "A writer of story-books! What kind of a business in life,—what mode of glorifying God, or being serviceable to mankind in his day and generation,—may that be? Why, the degenerate fellow might as well have been a fiddler!" (I, 10). He feared the same judgment much closer at hand, both from himself and from the Manning family whose values he would never escape. We might just paraphrase the concluding sentence of this paragraph from "The Custom-House" to read, "And yet, let him scorn the Mannings as he will, strong traits of their nature have intertwined themselves with his."

THREE

The Inner Circle: Hawthorne's Women

Azure, a lion's head erased, between three flower de luces.
Hawthorne family crest

From the pressure of Manning values and personalities, Nathaniel sought refuge in the inner circle of his own family. The Hawthorne women accepted him as he was and even adored him for the very traits the others wished to alter. His mother and sisters catered to his moods, whether for poetry, indolence, or "gunning" in the wilds of Raymond. Their uncritical acceptance was sorely missed during the years of separation. He longed for and idealized his mother's and Louisa's compliance and Ebe's intellectual stimulation. How different from the Mannings' prodding criticism was Ebe's judgment that Nathaniel would "never *do* anything; he is an ideal person" and Louisa's "my brother is never idle." Only in marriage to the adoring Sophia was he later able to reexperience and secure to himself such uncritical acceptance.

Although united in admiration of Nathaniel, Madame Hawthorne, Ebe, and Louisa had markedly distinct personalities. Each played a different role in his psychic economy and each contributed to his attitudes toward women. In exploring these roles and contributions we move from the mother, inmost center of the family circle, outward to the two contrasting sisters. En route we observe how metamorphoses of these primary female images link up with received literary traditions and emerge revitalized in Hawthorne's fiction. The chapter concludes with possible continuities from his first imprinted experience of femininity to his matrimonial choice.

THE MOTHER

Elizabeth Clarke Manning Hawthorne stood at the center of two concentric circles of Nathaniel's early life, the nuclear and the extended families. As the gravitational center of his entire family constellation, the connection to all other important relationships, male and female, this meek woman can be perceived in both the presences and the voids of Hawthorne's imagination.

From external evidence, this central figure was not a commanding personality, although the child's needs may have endowed her with attributes that outsiders do not perceive. Elizabeth Clarke Manning was born in 1780, the third of nine children, and received some measure of unsystematic education. Reports agree that she was beautiful, gentle, pious, and ladylike. A Salem neighbor at the time of Nathaniel's birth described her as a "beautiful woman, with remarkable eyes, full of sensibility and expression, . . . a person of singular purity of mind."[1] Her beauty later in life was praised by Elizabeth Peabody: "Widow Hawthorne always looked as if she had walked out of an old picture, with her ancient costume and a face of lovely sensibility, and great brightness."[2]

The range of her life was narrow by modern standards. At age twenty, after considerable courtship, she married her neighbor Nathaniel Hathorne in 1801 and moved across the street into the home of her husband's mother and sisters. She bore three children, the first only seven months after her marriage.[3] Her husband was absent at sea for much of their brief married life and before she had an opportunity to manage her own home he died of illness en route to Surinam. The mother of three children and a widow by age twenty-eight, she still had little experience of personal autonomy. Within three months of learning of her husband's death, she returned across the back yards connecting the Manning and Hathorne homes and retired into the bosom of her original family. Her only other recorded change of scene was a sojourn during 1816–1822 at the family homestead in Raymond, Maine.

Because early widowhood was a common fate in seafaring towns such as Salem, Elizabeth Hawthorne's refusal to remain with her husband's family and eventually inherit management of that household, or to remarry, or in some other way to establish full adult independence has led to myths of excessive dedication to her husband's memory. Had such extreme dedication existed it might easily have strengthened her ties to those who shared her loss, that is, Captain Hathorne's mother and sisters, with whom she had been living for eight years. Instead, left very little money by her deceased husband and not overly fond of his family, she chose to return to an environment more comfortable both economically and emotionally. Return to parents at a time of distress is understandable. However, a woman who had known marriage, motherhood, and eight years away from her parents might well, after an interlude of reorganizing her affairs, require privacy and independence. Had her return to the Mannings been temporary it would have occasioned little comment. But the fact that a young and strikingly beautiful woman would settle so early for daughterhood, sisterhood, widowhood, and a passive sort of motherhood points to a lack of vitality and trust in her own competence.

Elizabeth Hawthorne shared her family's liability to pulmonary disorders and headaches but lacked their compensating energy. Letters between Salem and Raymond often mention her ill health, and circumstances suggest an emotional component to these frequent illnesses. Much later Nathaniel wrote "that almost every agitating circumstance of her life had hitherto cost her a fit of sickness."[4] After the first great shock of her life she tended to insulate herself in secure and familiar circumstances. Her demeanor and "sensitive nerves" served to invite protectiveness on the part of others, especially of competent others like brother Robert.

Insulation from anxiety, agitation, and change was for her the most congenial aspect of religion. Less evangelical in religiosity than her sisters Mary and Priscilla, she expressed even in her conventional piety a characteristic insecurity. She projects this in the advice she sent brother Richard in Raymond: "Do not expose yourself, nor be over anxious about your worldly affairs, one thing only is needfull, an intrest [sic] in Jesus Christ, secure that and you will have treasures in Heaven, where neither moth nor rust can corrupt, nor thieves break through and steal!"[5]

This intrinsic insecurity was understandably reinforced by loss of her husband and brother John. Her terror that Nathaniel would become a sailor and be lost at sea extended to resisting his learning to swim, which he nevertheless managed to do. Throughout childhood he was able to strike fear into her heart and gain attention by threatening to go to sea and never return. Her fear of water was still active as late as 1823, when Nathaniel asked if he could take a steamboat home from college: "I should like to come home that way, if mother has no apprehension of the boiler's bursting."[6] Ironically, not Nathaniel but Maria Louisa was to perish by water. In 1852 the Hudson River steamboat on which she was traveling caught fire, probably from a boiler explosion. The mother's fear proved to be prophetic, although displaced.

To surmise something about her maternal style, her way of being in the world as it touched upon her children, one must make the most of sparse evidence. The style of behavior toward the Mannings that she recommended to Maria Louisa offers some hint about how she comported herself amidst her benefactors. The mother advised twelve-year-old Louisa to "make as little trouble as possible with your clothes, you must wait upon Grandmama when you are at home, and be kind and obliging to all your friends do not exert yourself too much with dancing, if you do not belong entirely to Aunt Mary you must obey her as you would a Mother."[7] Such lessons in obedience and subservience, in walking small and expecting little, tamed what small fire there was in Louisa. Although such messages did not tame Ebe's outward behavior and verbal resistance, they did, I think, affect her expectations in life, which fell far short of her possibilities.

Hawthorne's later observations on Madame Hawthorne's behavior as Una's grandmother led him to reminisce about her maternal qualities. On the subject of spoiling children she "knocked me into a cocked hat, by averring that it was impossible to spoil such children as Elizabeth and me, because she had never been able to do anything with us. This I believe to be true. There was too much gentleness in her nature for such a task." The grandmother advised Una's parents not to carry the child in their arms because she recalled that having done this with Elizabeth, she was unable to quiet her in any other way, a practice to which she "never allowed her other children to become habituated."[8]

Although need and compliant temperament led Elizabeth Hawthorne to relinquish some of her maternal presence, she was, in her quiet way, a loving mother. Her response to a gift from Nathaniel communicates this with modest eloquence: "The Coffeepot Nath'l has sent will be very usefull to me it is a very good one,—but is doubly valuable as being a present from my dear Son."[9] The scanty evidence suggests that as a mother Elizabeth Hawthorne was gentle and affectionate but not sufficiently confident of her own abilities to instill basic trust in Nathaniel. Even had she been a stronger personality, her husband's death at a particularly vulnerable period in the lives of the children would have shaken her confidence that all would be well for herself *or* her children. Such confidence is essential for the communication of what Erikson called the most fundamental of all maternal gifts, "basic trust" derived from "an almost somatic conviction that there is meaning to what they are doing."[10] Madame Hawthorne transmitted to Nathaniel her own fears and her reliance on the Mannings for guidance and resources. But the passive solution workable for a "helpless" widow of her day was less acceptable for a male child, and even then women around her were beginning to repudiate such roles.

Elizabeth Peabody's depiction of a pure-souled widow practicing an "all but Hindoo self-devotion to the manes of her husband" has been the locus of dispute ever since it was incorporated into Julian Hawthorne's biography of his parents.[11] Twentieth-century efforts to undo Hawthorne's reputation as a brooding neurotic extend to his mother. The normalizing trend encouraged by the work of Manning Hawthorne and enshrined in Randall Stewart's 1948 biography was later reversed by the psychoanalytic interpretations of Frederick Crews and Jean Normand. Recently Nina Baym has returned to the views of Hawthorne's family and great-grandson by arguing against the reclusive view of the mother.[12]

Although one must beware of judging by subjective standards of social behavior, we cannot evade this issue if we are to understand her son. Even the following brief summary of contemporaneous opinions shows disagreement about the reclusiveness of mother and son. Ebe Hawthorne and her younger cousin Rebecca B. Manning vigorously dispute the opinions of Elizabeth Peabody, Julian Hawthorne, George Parsons Lathrop, and even Sophia Peabody Hawthorne. Ebe Hawthorne and Rebecca Manning argue for the total normality of both mother and son. But impressions of the mother's reclusiveness are corroborated by Sophia Hawthorne, Horatio Bridge, and Hawthorne himself, a substantial body of testimony that Nina Baym dismisses as a plot on Hawthorne's part to derogate his mother in order to elevate Sophia to the role of his savior.[13]

The testimony of Horatio Bridge, Nathaniel's close friend from college days, may be questionable because his *Personal Recollections of Nathaniel Hawthorne* was published in 1892 after Bridge had probably read other biographies. Nevertheless, his picture of the family's isolation has the authority of long personal friendship. Bridge connects Hawthorne's personal reserve and avoidance of intimacies to his family's isolated way of life: "Hawthorne, coming, as he did from a family of exceptionally recluse habits, gained there his first practical knowledge of the world. . . . he formed few intimacies and rarely sought the friendship of others. . . . Hawthorne, previous to entering college, lived in great seclusion with his mother and two sisters at their home in Salem." Bridge also reports being "charmed with the quiet and refined manners of Mrs. Hawthorne."[14]

Sophia wrote very confiding letters to her family commenting from close observation on her husband's mother and sisters. Her emphatic descriptions of reclusive behavior during the later years of Elizabeth Hawthorne's life are untainted by outside influence, retrospective romanticizing (such as may have colored Peabody's and Bridge's views), or by any slanderous motive, for she really loved her mother-in-law. While visiting at the Herbert Street house with the infant Una, Sophia wrote to her mother:

> For the first time since my husband can remember, he dined with his mother! This is only one of the miracles which the baby is to perform. Her grandmother held her on her lap till one of us should finish dining, and then ate her own meal. . . . [Una] waked this morning like another dawn, and smiled bountifully, and was borne off to the penetralia of the house to see Madame Hawthorne and aunt Elizabeth.[15]

Prior to moving into the Mall Street house in 1847, Sophia described all three of the Hawthorne women, providing further confirmation of Elizabeth Hawthorne's reclusiveness during the later years of her life.

It will be very pleasant to have Madame Hawthorne in the house. Her suite of rooms is wholly distinct from ours, so that we shall only meet when we choose to do so. There are very few people in the world who I should like or would consent to have in the house in this way; but Madame Hawthorne is so uninterfering, of so much delicacy, that I shall never know she is near excepting when I wish it; and she has so much kindness and sense and spirit that she will be a great resource in emergencies. *Elizabeth is an invisible entity. I have seen her but once in two years*; and Louisa never intrudes. . . . It is no small satisfaction to know that Mrs. Hawthorne's remainder of life will be glorified by the presence of these children and of her own son. *I am so glad to win her out of that Castle Dismal, and from the mysterious chamber into which no mortal ever peeped*, till Una was born, and Julian,—for they alone have entered the penetralia. Into that chamber the sun never shines. Into these rooms in Mall Street it blazes without stint. [16] (italics added)

From the conflicting evidence on her reclusiveness, the following pattern emerges. While in Salem in the Herbert Street house of the Mannings, Elizabeth Hawthorne lived largely within the confines of the family. Hers was a private life but hardly solitary, since the Manning home held eleven adults and three children for several years after her return to it. Manning involvement in the Unitarian church, in a flourishing stagecoach line, and gradually in many other business activities provided her at the very least with vicarious contact with the Salem community. Her striking off with sister Mary to join the Congregational church in 1806 demonstrates a measure of communal involvement.

She was, however, somewhat swamped by her unmarried sisters and brothers, who took over a large part of her parental role even while she lived in Salem and virtually usurped it during the Raymond years. But while she was away from most of the family in Raymond, her life and contacts appear to have expanded somewhat. Here she looked after the garden and Robert's trees and distributed religious literature sent her by Mary. Although clearly still influenced by Mary and Robert from a distance, she got out of her room and into the world. There is no talk of her eating alone while in Raymond. For these reasons her children were eager for her to remain there and be "mistress of herself." Ebe and Nathaniel were in the unusual position of having to defend from the Mannings their mother's autonomy as well as their own.

Context and circumstances are important in understanding the words Hawthorne inscribed in his notebook the day before his mother died: "I love my mother; but there has been, ever since my boyhood, a sort of coldness of intercourse between us, such as is apt to come between persons of strong feelings, if they are not managed rightly" (VIII, 439). In the context of his powerful grief as he held her virtually unresponsive hand and knew that he would never be able to repair past failures of communication, that all reticences would henceforth be sealed forever, the "coldness of intercourse" can be understood as regret for all that had to remain unexpressed after the age of boyish unawareness. During adolescence Nathaniel communicated with little inhibition his yearnings for the absent mother in faraway Raymond, bringing to the surface feelings that later became difficult to "manage rightly." Most likely the later "coldness of intercourse" was on both sides a denial of unacceptable warmth.

MATERNAL DEPRIVATION: RAYMOND VERSUS SALEM

"I am here, mother, it is I, and I will go with thee to prison."
"The Gentle Boy"

Elizabeth Hawthorne did not deny herself to her son, but she allowed Uncle Robert to take him away from her and from the beloved Raymond home. The boy came to feel that he was being managed, played upon, and manipulated by the uncle who seemed so often to step between himself and his mother. In the Herbert Street days, Uncle Robert took Nathaniel out of the room he shared with his mother and sisters and into Robert's own bed. During the Raymond period the sisters were allowed for the most part to remain with their mother, whereas Nathaniel was sent back to Salem. Little wonder that he sometimes wished that he might have been a girl and pinned to his mother's apron. In Raymond was all that he loved—his mother, Sebago Lake, and the wild free life. What Ebe called "the fatality" that brought the family back to Salem despite all their resolutions and intentions was, in Nathaniel's case, Uncle Robert.

Nathaniel's emotional life was genuinely split between what he wanted for himself and what the Mannings wanted for him, between what he felt to be the legitimate authority of his mother and the inexplicably effective authority of Uncle Robert, between Salem, where fate, practical necessity, and Manning authority placed him, and Raymond, where he longed to be. Salem and Raymond, the geographical poles of young Hawthorne's life, were of imaginative significance for the future author whose work was to be organized by the principle of polarities. Salem was the old society, dominated by class distinctions and an historic past, a place where he felt the authority of grandparents, aunts, and uncles who kept him in school and tried to orient him toward a serious and productive future. Raymond was a frontier village, not fully emerged from the primeval forest, a place of hunting, fishing, and wild animals, where the boy could roam in freedom. The family referred to it as "the land of promise," and to young Hawthorne, who never actually spent more than a few months there at any one time, it loomed large in his imagination as a virtual paradise. He spoke of it always as Mark Twain spoke of the Mississippi, as a place where a boy could follow his bent undeterred by the Aunt Sallys of this world. Despite his love of reading, Nathaniel did not want to be "sivilized" by any aunts or uncles; he longed to "savagize" with Louisa in Raymond.

Late in his life, Hawthorne referred with nostalgia to the place Raymond had assumed in his imagination. To his friend Stoddard he wrote in 1853:

> When I was eight or nine years old, my mother, with her three children, took up her residence on the banks of the Sebago Lake, in Maine, where the family owned a large tract of land; and here I ran quite wild, and would, I doubt not, have willingly run wild till this time, fishing all day long, or shooting with an old fowling-piece. . . . Those were delightful days; for that part of the country was wild then, with only scattered clearings, and nine tenths of it primeval woods. But by and by my good mother began to think it was necessary for her boy to do something else; so I was sent back to Salem where a private instructor fitted me for college.[17]

James T. Fields recalls Hawthorne reminiscing in 1864 about this "happiest period of his life": "I lived in Maine," he said, "like a bird of the air, so perfect was the freedom I enjoyed. But it was there I first got my cursed habits of solitude. . . . how well I recall the summer days also, when, with my gun, I roamed at will through the woods of Maine."[18]

Uncle Richard was nearby in Raymond, having been established there since 1813 and occupying a house very close to "Manning's Folly," but Uncle Richard was married, had an adopted child, and was very much preoccupied with business affairs and his own precarious health. Although interested in his nieces and nephew, his attention was not oppressive. During her first autumn of residence in Raymond, Madame Hawthorne was ill and noticeably unhappy. Richard Manning wrote to Robert on November 10, 1816,

> She now wishes that she had gone home with Mother & Sister Mary. I thought at first that she was worried about Nath[l] as she was very lothe to part with him—I do not think that she will ever be willing (even if she should regain her health) to live on the Farm without Mother or Sister Mary is their with her, I think the Children would like to remain here, but not according to Mary's plan. Elizabeth [Ebe] in particular cannot bear to think of ever doing any kind of work, but I shall not [attempt] to influence them in any way, but let them act their plans.[19]

Knowing that Nathaniel's education was being neglected in Raymond, Robert tried sending him to a boarding school in Stroudswater, Maine. On this unsuccessful solution to the problem, Robert reported to Grandmother Manning in Salem,

> Nathaniel has been home for (3 weeks) before my arrival   in 3 Weeks more his time will be out—dolefull complaints   no mamma to take care of him. what shall I do with him when he comes. I think of sending him to Salem   Elizabeth & Maria want to see Grandma[20]

Shortly before being sent back to Salem for schooling, Nathaniel tried cajoling Uncle Robert out of the decision. He wrote him about hunting, fishing, and planting trees, implying that the women needed his help and protection, "I am sorry you intend to send me to school again. Mother says she can hardly spare me."[21]

Once back in Salem Nathaniel was assiduously observed and reported on by Aunt Mary. She reported to Robert even about the pimples on Nathaniel's face, as well as his reluctance to start school, and the fact that "he sighs for the woods of Raymond."[22] Mary's next letter reports to the boy's mother, revealing in sarcastic language her jealousy of Robert's possessiveness and lack of confidence in anyone else's ability to handle the boy.

> August 3, 1819
> Nathaniel went to school the day after I wrote my last letter to Brother Robert and since he went to school his health and spirits appear to be much better, until he went to school I do not know that a day passed without his saying "I wish I was at Raymond,["] but I do not recollect to have heard him say it since he went   Brother Samuel sleeps in the outer Chamber which you used to improve, and N. in the next one to it, and this morning he got up before six o'clock to study his lesson   *we shall be happy to see Brother R whenever it is convenient for him to come but I beg he will not hurry home on N's account, we think ourselves capable of taking care of one Boy.*[23] (italics added)

In a letter of complaint about scolding and unpleasantness in the Manning household, fifteen-year-old Nathaniel mourns the lost symbiosis of his childhood: "Oh how I wish I was again with you, with nothing to do but go agunning. But the happiest days of my life are gone. Why was I not a girl that I might have been pinned all my life to my mother's apron."[24]

A year older and ready to depart for college, he seems to have regressed even further and become more openly competitive with his uncle. He wrote to his mother:

> I shall probably see you in September, and stay 4 weeks with you. I hope you will remain in Raymond during the time I am at college, and then I can be with you 3 months out of the year. . . . It is now going on two Years since I saw you. Do not you regret the time when I was a little boy. I do almost. I [am] now as tall as Uncle Robert. . . . Do not show this to Uncle Richard.
>
> Your Affectionate Son,
> Nathaniel Hathorne[25]

Such nostalgia for childhood dependency persisting into late adolescence indicates serious problems with gender identity and too close a relationship with the mother. They show why Uncle Robert felt it to be precisely his duty to untie the lad from the maternal apron. This salutary task was to prove a thankless one. It rekindled hostility toward the intervening uncle and intensified longing for and idealization of the distant mother. At an age when other interests and objects would normally have been replacing primary ones, when the youth might have been straining forward and outward from the family for love and confirmation of identity, Nathaniel sought security in the past. This regression delayed many kinds of maturation, including development of a confident masculinity. Not too surprising, then, is his later choice of little Pearl, who was always at her mother's side, to represent his never wholly satisfied longing for symbiosis with the mother.

Mother and son missed each other intensely. The mother seemed to accept the separation fatalistically, whereas Nathaniel expressed his sense of deprivation frequently throughout the period of enforced separation. It contributed to his dislike of school, his resentment of the authority of his aunts and Uncle Robert, and most especially to his passionate desire to be "lord of himself," which he reiterated throughout the period of enforced separation.

Perhaps to encourage recovery from the boyhood foot injury, Richard Manning had given Nathaniel a gun formerly belonging to the boy's father. This weapon had been an important feature of his life in Raymond. It was part of the "savagizing" that he longed to do again with Louisa, part of the Huck Finn life he led in Raymond, and oddly enough, connected often in his letters, if only by contiguity, with Uncle Robert. To Louisa, his companion in hunting, he wrote nostalgically,

March 21, 1820

"Oh that I had the wings of a dove, that I might flee hence and be at rest." How often do I long for my gun, and wish that I could again savagize with you. But I shall never again run wild in Raymond, and I shall never be so happy as when I did.[26]

From a distance Aunt Mary was worried about Nathaniel's safety even when he was with his own mother: "I am some concerned about Nathiel [sic] useing a gun so much, do tell him to be carefull not to leave it loaded, and not to point it at any one, and do not let

Jane touch it," she wrote to Madame Hawthorne in 1818,[27] not quite trusting the mother to have even this much judgment. When Uncle Robert was visiting in Raymond, Nathaniel seemed to fear that his uncle would use his gun and be hurt by it. He wrote to Uncle Robert, now arrived at Raymond:

Salem, May 2d, 1820

Dear Uncle,

I was happy to hear you had arrived at home safe. . . . It is training day. I hope Mother is well by this time. My Gun has got a very large charge in it, and I guess it will kick. Do you intend to stay much longer? I sleep very comfortably alone. I am afraid you will scold at me if I stop here, but as one excuse I must beg leave to represent that I have from ten to fourteen lines of Latin to parse and translate.

I remain your affectionate Nephew,

Nath¹ Hathorne[28]

In sequence, his mind moves from Training Day in Salem to recollection of his unused gun in a closet up in Raymond, to the thought that Uncle Robert may be hurt by making unauthorized use of it. Having learned to fear the power of parricidal wishes, he warned his uncle against using the father's gun. Following this warning comes a query on the length of Robert's absence, and the sly words, "I sleep very comfortably alone." Clearly, Nathaniel did not like sleeping with his bachelor uncle and hoped he would stay away for a long while.

Since the Manning house was no longer crowded, one wonders just why Nathaniel had to share a bed with his uncle. He did so from the time that he was removed from his mother's chamber until he left for college. This unwanted intimacy recurs in a letter of March 13, 1821: "I dreamed the other night that I was walking by the Sebago; and when I awoke was so angry at finding it all a delusion, that I gave Uncle Robert (who sleeps with me) a most horrible kick."[29] "Kick" is what the boy was afraid his father's gun would do to Uncle Robert should he make use of it. Dreamed in disturbing proximity to Uncle Robert, this vision of escaping from him erupted into aggressive action.

He longed for the day of his majority when he could say, "I am Lord of myself." In July of 1820 he concluded a letter to his mother,

"I am 16 years old. In five years I shall belong to myself."[30] Secrecy and longing for independence permeate another letter of the same year.

Salem Oct 31st, 1820

Dear Sister,

I am very angry with you for not sending me some of your Poetry, which I consider as a great piece of Ingratitude. You will not see one line more of mine, until You return the confidence which I have placed in you. I have bought the Lord of the Isles, and intend either to send or to bring it to you. I like it as well as any of Scott's other Poems. I have read Hoggs Tales, Caleb Williams, St Leon & Mandeville. I admire Godwin's Novels, and intend to read them all. I shall read the Abbot by the Author of Waverly, as soon as I can hire it. I have read all Scott's Novels except that. I wish I had not, that I might have the pleasure of reading them again. Next to these I like Caleb Williams. I have almost given up writing Poetry. No Man can be a Poet & a Book-Keeper at the same time. I do find this place most horribly "dismal." And have taken to chewing "tobacco" with all my might, which I think raises my spirits. Say nothing of it in your letters, nor of the Lord of the Isles. . . . I do not think I shall ever go to College. I can scarcely bear the thought of living upon Uncle Robert for 4 years longer. How happy I shall feel, to be able to say "I am Lord of myself."

You may cut off this part of my letter, and show the other to Uncle Richard. Do write me some letters in Skimmed Milk. I must conclude as I am in a "monstrous Hurry."

Your Affectionate Brother,
Nath¹ Hathorne[31]

[A postscript with poetry follows.]

He did go to college in 1821 and lived largely, if not entirely, on Uncle Robert for four years longer. The following, written shortly before departure, urgently tries to arrange life according to his inner needs. Bowdoin College, only a short distance from Raymond, would bring him closer to Mother and restoration of his original family, remove him from the Mannings, and advance him toward adulthood. All very good, if only conspiratorial relatives do not persuade Mother to move south to Salem just as he moves north to Maine! He had accepted banishment to Salem so long as Mother could be kept apart from the Mannings and Uncle Robert. He is desperately afraid that as he moves back into her orbit, they will call her home to the Salem he has just left.

> Salem June 19th, 1821
>
> You can never have so much comfort here as you now enjoy. You are undisputed Mistress of your own House. Here you would have to submit to the authority of Miss Manning. If you remove to Salem, I shall have no Mother to return to during the College Vacations and the expense will be too great for me to come to Salem. If you remain where you are, think how delightfully the time will pass, with all your children round you, shut out from the world, and nothing to disturb us. It will be a second Garden of Eden. . . . Elizabeth is as anxious for you to stay as myself. . . . The reason of my saying so much on this subject is, that Mrs. Dike and Miss Manning are very earnest for you to return to Salem, and I am afraid that they will commission U.R. to persuade you to it. But, Mother, if you wish to live in peace I conjure you not to consent it [*sic*]. Grandmother I think is rather in favour of your staying.
>
> Nath¹ Hathorne
>
> Do not show this letter.³²

Sad to say, Madame Hawthorne returned permanently to Salem in 1822, after Nathaniel's first year at Bowdoin. In future he would never forget how precarious was man's hold on Eden.

Evidently his tendency to mythicize experience started early. Certain emotional concepts coalesced around the idea of Sebago Lake. Raymond becomes boyhood freedom from responsibility and authority. It is closeness with the mother. It is, to the late adolescent about to go to college, the lost Eden itself. Although he had been banished from this Eden by the educational plans of Uncle Robert, he still wanted it to remain intact, available to his imagination, and, in the practical sense, available for summer vacations from nearby Bowdoin College. Most of his letters from his return to Salem in 1816 until 1822 plead for his mother to remain in Raymond and to keep his sisters there. Even more important to him than the company of his family was the mere existence of a home away from Salem and the Mannings.

His protracted split between the ideal mother-centered home of his imagination and his actual place of residence dominated by carping relatives made "home" a problematical matter for him. Separation of the actual from the ideal, or rather conviction that the actual was always less than ideal, became a permanent mental set focused most particularly on the issue of home, which for a child is closely associated with integrity of the self.[33]

Hawthorne's concept of home had suffered from a series of losses and dissociations. From his first home on Union Street his father was mostly absent and then gone. Even this birthplace was lost to him when the family left it for the Manning house, where neither of his parents was the head or authority. Then when his mother attained a modicum of autonomy in the Raymond house, Nathaniel was removed from it. After college brought him near to Raymond, his mother returned to Salem. From this series of displacements between home and parents, home and authority, home and the self, came a lifelong sense of never being in the right place.

The sense of dislocation appeared in both his personal rootlessness (frequent moves from house to house) and in the antithetical structure of his imagination, with its constant alternations between value systems. His son Julian testifies to the perpetual rootlessness:

> He soon wearied of any particular locality. . . . Partly necessity or convenience, but partly, also, his own will, drove him from place to place; always wishing to settle down finally, but never lighting upon the fitting spot. In America he moved from place to place and longed for England. In England he travelled constantly and looked forward to France and Italy. In Paris, Rome, and Florence his affections reverted to England once more; but having returned thither, he made it but a stepping-stone to America. . . . [No sooner had he returned to Concord and enlarged his house there] than memories of England possessed him more and more.[34]

As a middle-aged man he regretted having subjected his children to such vagabondage, and named his Concord home "The Wayside" in recognition of its being more a pause on the highway of life than a permanent home.

An important fictional representation of the dissociation between home and parents appears in "The Gentle Boy," written around 1829, fairly early in the "long seclusion" in his mother's home after returning from college. At its center is Ilbrahim, a small boy passing from the care of his natural parents into that of a surrogate family. The situation is of special significance because it accounts for the loss of original parents and features the relationship between a boy and his mother.

Historically grounded in the conflict between Puritans and Quakers in the seventeenth century, the story presents mother-son figurations rather than realistic portraits. The gentle boy of this violent story is the artist as a wounded child, and his Quaker mother Catharine is a mother-figure as different from Hawthorne's own mother as is Hester Prynne. In both strong-willed fictional mothers Hawthorne created counterimages, negatives, of his own mother, endowing them with passion, self-direction, and personal magnetism. Bearing marked similarities as powerful females and single mothers, Hester and Catharine nevertheless differ significantly in the quality of their mothering, for Hester is mother to a daughter and Catharine to a son. Hester keeps her daughter near her and subordinates expression of her individual selfhood to maternal duty. Pearl and Hester are inseparable. In contrast, Catharine clearly values expression of her own ideas more highly than she values the maternal bond. Acting out her own needs, she permits separation from her son.

Little Ilbrahim knows his parents only as loss, separation, abandonment. He would willingly make his home on his father's grave or follow his mother to prison, but the mother persists in the fanatic activities that divide them. On a chill autumn evening a Puritan, Tobias Pearson, discovers the boy alone at his father's grave beneath a gallows tree. To Pearson's inquiries about where and to whom he belongs, the boy responds much like Pearl at her catechism, with an existential identification: "They call me Ilbrahim, and my home is here" (IX, 72). His mother, a Quaker fanatic, has been taken from prison and "carried into the uninhabited wilderness" (IX, 75) rather than renounce her faith. The solitary child submits to adoption by Tobias and Dorothy Pearson, whose own children have died. Somehow the prior death of the Pearson children is presented as indicative of Tobias's unfitness as a father for Ilbrahim, with the added innuendo that this adoption was less an act of benevolence than a futile move to make up the Pearsons' own losses.

Such cross-currents of complexity work against the narrative direction, which appears to be the death of a boy martyr at the hands of fanatical Puritan children. This movement is obscured by the boy's own death wishes, by the masochistic behavior of the Quakers, by the mixed motives of the Pearsons, and by the complicity of the boy's mother. The last is most pertinent for our purposes. On a brief return from the "wilderness" Catharine does not reclaim her son from the Pearsons, but in a strange encounter turns him over to them. Note how quickly, with how little interest, she accepts Dorothy Pearson as her son's foster mother and how unsettling is her confrontation with Tobias. Although perceiving Tobias's weakness and guilty hesitation, she nevertheless remits her "precious jewel" (but not her pearl of great price) to this inadequate man. Her defective maternal instincts pause only momentarily at his "hesitating air, the eyes that struggled with her own, and were vanquished; the color that went and came, and could find no resting place" (IX, 87). Unchanged by her son's embrace and declaration of love ("I am here, mother, it is I, and I will go with thee to prison" [IX, 83]), she departs, not to return until Ilbrahim's dying moment.

Despite the efforts of the delegated parents, the child suffers from "wounded love. . . . unappropriated love" and becomes depressed, passive, a willing martyr. In this state he calls for his mother in his dreams, "as if her place, which a stranger [could supply] while Ilbrahim was happy, admitted of no substitute in his extreme affliction" (I, 93). On his deathbed Ilbrahim will not be comforted by the good Dorothy but listens instead for his mother's footstep, which arrives only at the very last moment. The child dies happy, nestled on his mother's bosom.

As Frederick Crews observes, "no amount of misbehavior can make her ineligible for this reconciliation. Nothing, it seems is unforgivable in a mother; the purpose of the hero and the author is not to punish her but to restore her to her essential role."[35] Ilbrahim's saintly forgiveness may screen an underlying resentment. If Hawthorne was indeed identifying with his child hero, he must have felt some inadmissable anger at his own mother's delegation of her parental functions to others. The emotional center of his family experience, like that of "the gentle boy," was the sundering of natural parental ties and the insufficiency of substitute ones.

In violent language Catharine formulates the enduring effects she has on her son's life. Her neglect, she says, leaves him "no inheritance but woe and shame," so that for life he will "find all hearts closed against" him and all "sweet affections turned to bitterness" (IX, 84). Her Quaker heritage, which later causes Ilbrahim's death, she calls "baptism in blood," a mark she wants kept "ruddy upon his forehead" (IX, 86). Herein, then, is the content of her silent communication to Tobias Pearson, whose eyes she vanquished: from her parental guilt to his passed the masochistic message to become a Quaker and to keep the sign of alienation ruddy on his own brow and Ilbrahim's. The whole course of Ilbrahim's short life was thus determined by the red maternal sign.

REUNION

Virtually separated from his mother at the age of twelve, Hawthorne did not again live continuously in her dwelling until after his graduation from Bowdoin, when he was twenty-one. By the time he returned to his mother's home, Uncle Robert had married and moved to North Salem. The elderly grandmother died shortly after, in 1826. Aunt Mary still lived in the Manning house and Uncle Samuel came and went, but disturbing influences were substantially reduced. After long separation the geographical split was healed and Hawthorne was reunited with his original family, his mother and two sisters. Once returned, he stayed near his mother for the next twelve years.

Hawthorne's need at twenty-one was not separation from the family but reunion, restitution for the long years of maternal deprivation. Returning to Salem and Mother after college commencement, he reversed the customary direction of youthful separation. In the poignant words of his great-grandson, Manning Hawthorne, "But now, while his classmates were going eagerly forward, ready to seize opportunity and make a place for themselves in the outside world, he turned from it; and entering the seclusion of his chamber, he shut the door." [36]

Hawthorne spent most of twelve years in the "haunted chamber" of the Herbert Street house, twelve years of apprenticeship to his craft that often seemed a self-entrapment from which he felt power-less to extricate himself. He recollected both aspects of this "mora-torium" period in an autobiographical sketch he wrote for Henry Stoddard in 1853:

> It was my fortune or misfortune, just as you please, to have some slender means of supporting myself; and so, on leaving college, in 1825, instead of immediately studying a profession, I sat myself down to consider what pursuit in life I was best fit for. My mother had now returned [from Raymond], and taken up her abode in her deceased father's house, a tall, ugly, old, grayish building . . . in which I had a room. And year after year I kept on considering what I was fit for, and time and my destiny decided that I was to be the writer that I am. I had always a natural tendency (it appears to have been on the paternal side) toward seclusion; and this I now indulged to the utmost, so that for months together, I scarcely held intercourse outside of my own family; seldom going out except at twilight, or only to take the nearest way to the most convenient solitude.[37]

This mellow document supplying information for an article on the newly famous author has a plot of its own. It describes a process of normalization, taking the author from solitude relieved by occasional excursions into the world to surreptitious publication and on to full literary recognition. It states for the public record that from the solitary "owl's nest" he emerged as a literary success "pretty much like other people," not "melancholy or misanthropic" or unfitted "for the bustle of life." From the vantage point of his forty-ninth year he shapes his past experience into a narrative of destiny in which the seclusion becomes preparation ("it was the kind of discipline which my idiosyncracy demanded, and chance and my own instincts, operating together, had caused me to do what was fittest"). Having published half a dozen books, held one political office and prepared for a second, he minimizes the terror of those unproved years in the "haunted chamber," which at the time he described very differently to Sophia. In 1840, shortly after his emergence from seclusion, he wrote that in this chamber much of his youth had been wasted while he "sat a long, long time, waiting patiently for the world to know me, and sometimes wondering why it did not know me sooner, or whether it would ever know me at all—at least, till I were in my grave, and sometimes. . . . it seemed as if I were already in my grave."[38]

The period can be viewed as a professional moratorium, and indeed Julian Hawthorne perceptively described it in remarkably Eriksonian terms.* But the theme of self-entrapment and solitude expressed in the letter to Stoddard picks up motifs Hawthorne also mentioned to other friends and incorporated in his fiction, that of "stepping aside from the highway of life" and finding oneself unable to return. In a review of recent Hawthorne biographies, Alexander Welsh avers that "Wakefield," written ten years into the "long seclusion," "unquestionably reenacts that period of the writer's life," and has "nothing to do with marriage or Mrs. Wakefield, but only with the person called Wakefield and the risk he has taken." Welsh argues convincingly for the autobiographical meaning of "Wakefield," noting that the tenth anniversary of college graduation probably intensified the author's own sense of stagnation, the feeling of being "still involved in human interests, while he had lost his reciprocal influence on them" (IX, 138). He could easily have embodied that sense in a middle-aged man *called* Wakefield,[†] whose primary distinction was to have stepped aside from his own life for no apparent reason and to have unintentionally enrolled himself among the living dead with the piquant privilege of witnessing his own absence. His passion became the cultivation of "self-banishment," from which he could observe with crafty curiosity the effects of his disappearance on his wife, who infuriatingly enough does not die of grief but adapts all too readily to a placid widowhood.

"Wakefield" may well be autobiographical and in more than one way. The Hawthorne who grew up with a sense of alienation from his own home, of living in an alternate place from which he had to

---

*In "Lives of Hawthorne" (*Yale Review* 70 [Spring 1981]: 421–430), Alexander Welsh notes the Eriksonian quality of Julian's words: "There was an indolence in his nature, such as, by the mercy of Providence, is not seldom found to mark the early years of those who have some great mission to perform in the world, and who, but for this protecting laziness, would set about the work prematurely, and so bring both it and themselves to ruin." *Nathaniel Hawthorne and His Wife* (Boston and New York: Houghton Mifflin, 1884), vol. 1, p. 122. Welsh's comments on "Wakefield" occur on pages 427 and 428.

†The first line of *Moby-Dick* seems to be an allusion to Hawthorne's tendency to equivocate in just this way about the names of characters, often of those referring to himself, such as "let us call him Wakefield," or "they call me Ilbrahim." In *The Blithedale Romance* Zenobia, Fauntleroy, and Theodore are only *called* by the names assigned to them.

speculate about the effects of his removal, is reflected in the two homes of Wakefield, the primary one and that to which he banished himself. Wakefield, however, is not a wistfully exiled child, but a cruel, self-banished man who hurts a woman by walking out on her. As in the dream principle of reversal, Wakefield experiences his exile from the viewpoint of the one who abandons, not the abandoned one; he gains control of separation by becoming the "crafty" one who makes the other suffer.

Alas, his sadistic fantasy recoils. His sly observations of his wife's home reveal his own unimportance. After a brief illness (gratifying to the observer), his wife recovers and settles placidly into a contented "widowhood." The poor woman is in the unenviable position probably fantasized by many a widow, of having her readjustment to life observed by her deceased husband. The troubling memory of his crafty smile, her "doubts whether she is a widow," are the husband's legacy of spite.

Unlike Welsh, I think the story *does* have to do with a marriage, the one observed by a lost sea captain's son who had to watch his mother's adaptation to widowhood. For his father's sake he must have ached to learn how perilous it is "to make a chasm in human affections; not that they gape so long and wide—but so quickly close again!" (IX, 133). The mother who could manage without her husband very likely could make do without her son. She accepted the distance between them regretfully, but without making much effort to remedy it.

If "Wakefield" is not about a marriage, it says a good deal about widowhood, the uncanny widowhood of a woman sadistically manipulated and spied upon by her husband. The contemptuous and urbane narrator observes Wakefield observing the effects of his own absence on his wife. The story is strangely reticent about the relationship that prompted such treatment and about the personality of the wife. Her revenge is in her placidity, which communicates the man's insignificance—a cool reciprocity of injuries. With its multiple mirroring and the insistent presence of the narrator, the tale seems to be a complex dream of displacements, reversals, and condensations, with severance from an original home as its center.

Toward the end of his nearly twelve-year seclusion, Hawthorne wrote "The Threefold Destiny," a parable of a man who spent ten years wandering the exotic places of the earth in search of his remarkable destiny, only to find that it was "to till the earth around his mother's dwelling, and reap its products" (IX, 481). Ralph Cranfield, the hero, learns that his unique destiny, both personal and vocational (they are closely linked), is to derive from return to his origins—his mother, his childhood playmate, and the maternal dwelling place that had once provided unity of experience. After joyous reunion with the mother, he passes a tumultuous night "in the well-remembered chamber on the pillow where his infancy had slumbered" (IX, 477), a pillow suggestive of the maternal bosom.

Two of the three aspects of "The Threefold Destiny" he had prepared before he left. He himself had carved the word "Effode" (dig) on a tree near his mother's gate, a sign marking buried treasure for which he had searched throughout the world. And he himself had carved for his childhood playmate, Faith Egerton, a quartz heart of curious shape that was to be the sign of his fated bride. When Faith said the magical words of which he had long dreamed, "the visionary Maid . . . faded from his fancy, and in her place he saw the playmate of his childhood!" (IX, 482). The destined treasure was to be a product of the natal soil, and the destined bride was to be the playmate of his youth, much like a sister.

LOUISA AND EBE: THE DOCILE SISTER AND THE IMPERIOUS ONE

Antithetical female types, staples of Gothic romance, were filled out by Hawthorne's experience of his own two sisters. They were markedly different in personality and experience. Maria Louisa, the younger sister, has often been described as fun-loving, amiable, and ordinary. She liked dancing, parties, and pretty clothes. A capable cook and an excellent seamstress, she yet would accompany Nathaniel in his hunting and fishing in Raymond. She helped him compose his neo-Augustan *Spectator* and belonged to his secret Pin Society. Sociable and affectionate, she loved plants and animals, was very "feminine" in the nineteenth-century sense and yet always girlish in her sense of herself. With all her domesticity, she apparently never considered marrying.

In contrast to her brilliant older sister and brother, she has seemed ordinary to biographers looking for drama. Nevertheless, her homely virtues influenced Hawthorne's conception of the domestic Phoebe type, the fair woman whom the artist may marry in order to bring himself back within the bounds of society. Unlike her older sister, Maria Louisa was accepting almost to the point of passivity, and companionable without presenting intellectual challenge or competition. Her letters were mostly about her flowers and pets, dancing, and parties.[39]

Elizabeth Manning Hawthorne, or Ebe, on the other hand, was dark-haired, beautiful, imperious, opinionated, and brilliant. In Elizabeth Peabody's recollections, she seemed a "brilliant little girl" who became "a great genius . . . her bright rather shy eyes, and a rather excited frequent low laugh, looked full of wit and keenness— as if she were experienced in the world; not the least sentimental in air, but strongly intellectual."[40] She was a precocious child, and even her earliest letters show mastery of English prose. These early letters are tart, rather pert, critical of people, and impatient with even the conventions of letter writing. Even her adored brother Nathaniel is reported to have said, "The only thing I fear is Elizabeth's ridicule."[41] Ebe's haughty tone and sharp tongue emerged early. She wrote to Aunt Mary in August of 1816:

> Dear Aunt,
> I do not know what can be much more foolish than to write a long letter about nothing. This however I am required to do; much against my will I assure you. Perhaps you will call it a good exercise of my patience. It may be the same to read it. . . . Are my letters shown to Mr. Dike? If they are I shall not write any more. . . .
> I like riding about very much but if my time is at my own disposal, I shall not make one visit while in Raymond; I always disliked them but never so much as at present. People can talk about nothing tolerable but their neighbor's faults. That rouses them from the languor which otherwise overwhelms them, & then no tongue is silent. . . .
> I close my letter with an earnest request that you will ask no more letters from me, for I was never so much engaged as at present.[42]

Ebe certainly felt the family pressures to conform to their ideals of hard work and sensible living, but she resisted them far more directly than did her brother. She slept late, read long hours in her room, took walks at odd times, often after dark, and resisted all forms of housework. Richard reported in 1816 that "Elizabeth in particular cannot bear to think of ever doing any kind of Work," much as Sophia was to say in 1849, "Elizabeth is not available for every-day purposes of pot-hooks and trammels, spits and flat-irons."[43]

Despite her independent spirit, Ebe deferred to her brother and performed many self-effacing services for him. When he returned to Salem after college she fetched him books from the Salem Athenaeum, priding herself on getting the most out of this library for him. She collaborated with him anonymously when he was editor of the *American Magazine of Useful and Entertaining Knowledge*, doing research in the Salem Athenaeum and much of the writing. She also helped him with his two volumes of *Peter Parley's Universal History* that appeared in 1837. Hawthorne could not have produced the required amount of writing without Ebe's help, but he had constantly to reprove her for injecting into these necessarily bland articles her own heterodox notions. For the magazine he taught her how to paraphrase rather than quote, adding the admonition that he was "obliged to correct some of [her] naughty notions about arbitrary government."[44] Of her biographical sketch of Jefferson, he cautioned, "See that it contains nothing heterodox."[45] Ebe's imperious personality was not easily subordinated even for the purpose of collaboration.

In the years preceding Hawthorne's engagement to Sophia Peabody, Ebe was his coworker, partner, and proofreader, a closeness that she did not relinquish easily. Proud and possessive about this collaboration, she sought no recognition for her work. Years later Nathaniel wrote of her to William D. Ticknor, "She is the most sensible woman I ever knew in my life, much superior to me in general talent, and of fine cultivation; yet I suppose she would not have the ghost of a chance in literature—unless as the political editor of a newspaper, which would be queer business for a woman. . . . she has both a physical and intellectual love of books, being a born book-worm."[46]

For many years Ebe worked on a translation of Cervantes that was never published. She read widely in fiction, poetry, biography, and history, preferring to spend her scant income on books rather than clothes. She had strong and highly individual opinions about literature. Always distrustful of literary biography, especially about her brother, she expressed vigorously her view of this genre. Wishing that Julian and other members of the family "would remember their father's injunction that no life of him should be attempted," she added, "I believe all biographies are false, just in proportion as they pretend to be true, and to deal with facts. Fiction is the proper sphere for the representation of character." [47] Agreeing with Carlyle, that "the only good biography is one that ought never to have been written," [48] this sister and collaborator of an author wrote, "As to personal friends, what do they signify among literary men, who only live upon paper?" [49]

Thoroughly different from her submissive mother and sister, Ebe shared with her brother such personality traits as secretiveness and vindictiveness. Both asked correspondents not to show their letters and in later life often enjoined recipients to burn them. Both were given to highly emotional antipathies and verbal sadism. Hawthorne recorded in his English notebook that he would like to kick the posteriors of certain nude female statues [50] and that a man would be justified in murdering grossly overweight English dowagers by "taking a sharp knife and cutting away their mountainous flesh." [51] Of female authors he wrote to James T. Fields, "I wish they were forbidden to write, on pain of having their faces deeply scarified with an oyster-shell." [52] Much of Hawthorne's verbal animosity was directed toward women—"that damned mob of scribbling women," and especially toward fleshy women, "gross, gross, gross. Who would not shrink from such a mother? Who would not shrink from such a wife?" [53]

Ebe's later vindictiveness was most frequently directed toward Sophia, whom Ebe blamed for Hawthorne's death and for ruining the children. She aimed another barrage at Hawthorne biographers, especially family ones like George Parsons Lathrop: "in a newspaper . . . I observe that, in Delaware, a poor fellow has just been publicly whipped for stealing. Now I wish that George lived in Delaware, and might be tempted to steal (he is not a grain too good) and be detected, and whipped just so, before the eyes of all men." [54]

Despite their similar temperaments and interests, Ebe and Nathaniel spent little time together. In childhood they communicated by means of a rope and bucket that carried their poems and other literary efforts between his room and hers. Afraid of Ebe's outspoken opinions and her ridicule, he felt more comfortable with Louisa. By the time he returned from college, Ebe had become so withdrawn that he did not see nearly so much of her as he wished. After his marriage he saw considerably less, even when Ebe lived in the same house with him and Sophia.

Although Ebe had been sociable enough as a young girl, enjoying parties and visits to Newburyport, contemporaneous records agree that by 1825 she had become a recluse. By 1839 Hawthorne described her thus to Sophia:

> You must never expect to see my sister E. in the daytime, unless by previous appointment, or when she goes to walk. So unaccustomed am I to daylight interviews, that I never imagine her in sunshine; and I really doubt whether her faculties of life and intellect begin to be exercised till dusk—unless on extraordinary occasions. Their noon is at midnight.[55]

Sophia was to call her "an invisible entity" even when they lived in the same house.

Ebe's physical isolation was far more pronounced than Nathaniel's ever was, yet she felt no guilt about it. She was sufficient unto herself, taking pleasure in nature, cats, and books. After her mother's death in 1849, Ebe boarded permanently with the Cole family in Montserrat near the sea, only occasionally coming into Salem. She was physically but not spiritually isolated, for she took an avid interest in her brother's children and in the lives of her Manning cousins, keeping up an extensive family correspondence. These affectionate letters contain urgent invitations to cousins and nieces to visit her at Montserrat, seasonal bulletins about flowers in bloom, and frequent strong comments on political events of the day.

Whatever her eccentricities, Ebe was not troubled by self-distrust. Feeling no need to conceal her attitudes, she had little drive to express them deviously in fictional form. Considering the increasing number of women intellectuals and writers emerging in her own part of Massachusetts, many of whom she could have met through the Peabodys, she was surprisingly content with the private enjoyment of her own intellect. Her assertiveness stopped well short of publication and recognition, ambitions that she left to her brother.

87

Ebe's complex and formidable personality left its impress on the mind of young Hawthorne. Her willingness to suppress her own talents provided him an easy response to the "damned mob of scribbling women" whose success in the literary marketplace challenged his own slow rise and poor sales—women who published were "unfeminine," even immodest in risking the self-revelations he knew to be inevitable in fiction.

Ebe's possessiveness toward Nathaniel, her attempts to prevent his engagement, her lifelong avoidance of Sophia and antipathy toward her, reveal a powerful sexual motive. If Hawthorne shared her feeling, he was to reveal it only indirectly in his attitudes and in his fictional portrayals of dangerous, sexually tempting dark women forbidden to the hero by prior sexual experience, by marriage, or, in "Rappaccini's Daughter," for example, by chemical toxicity. Moreover, he was always to be both fascinated and repelled by dark, self-sufficient, strong-minded women who exuded a forbidden sexual attraction.

As biographers of their father, both Rose and Julian Hawthorne testify to Ebe's active opposition to Nathaniel's engagement and marriage. Rose depicts the Peabody sisters as clever anglers luring a trout from among the secluding ferns.[56] Julian reports many of Ebe's strategies, one of them her appropriation of flowers sent to Nathaniel by Elizabeth Peabody and delivered by Sophia. This high-handed gesture baffled the gentle Sophia, who wrote to her sister,

> I carried your packet and the flowers there on Saturday. I supposed the flowers were for him; but I received a note from Elizabeth yesterday, in which she says, "The flowers which E. sent, so sweet and tastefully arranged . . . I thought would be unworthily bestowed upon my brother, who professes to regard the love of flowers as a feminine taste. So I permitted him to look at them, but considered them as a gift to myself." Now, I am a little provoked at this, aren't you? I do not believe he does not care for flowers.

Of Ebe's appropriation of the flowers, Julian concludes, "There can be no doubt that [Ebe] took an unwarrantable and characteristic liberty. No one was more sensible than Hawthorne of the beauty and charm of flowers. . . . his sister was jealous of any attentions paid to him, and was apt to offer at least a passive resistance."[57]

Whether or not Julian is perfectly accurate in considering Ebe a Machiavellian schemer trying to prevent her brother's marriage by implying that such an event would "kill" their mother, Nathaniel delayed announcing the engagement until shortly before the wedding.[58] Fear of making such an announcement is not necessarily surprising on the part of an only son who had remained a bachelor for thirty-eight years, long enough for mother and sisters to regard him as permanently their own. Used to reliance on men, they naturally hoped to hold onto Nathaniel now that Uncle Robert had a family of his own. The unexpected loss of Nathaniel would necessarily produce fearful reactions from women of small means and dependent habits. Nor need we regard his concealment as particularly devious in view of Ebe's long history of possessiveness and his own inclination to privacy.

Madame Hawthorne was not "killed" by news of the engagement, nor did she manifest profound disturbance, but none of the "trio among the ferns" went to Boston to attend the wedding. Sophia came to love her mother-in-law, accepting her reclusive ways with great sensitivity. Between Sophia and Louisa a warm intimacy developed over the years. Louisa visited often, sewed clothes for the children, and became the recipient of many confidences from Sophia regarding the details of breast-feeding and the children's toilet-training, details worth mentioning here only because of Sophia's reputation for Victorian prudishness.

At first Sophia was awed by Ebe and wanted to love her. Before there was any sign of an engagement, Ebe once received Sophia warmly, which the latter regarded as "an unprecedented honor. . . . I all at once fell in love with her. I think her eyes are very beautiful, and I like the expression of her taper hands. . . . I think I should love her very much. I believe it is extreme sensibility which makes her a hermitess."[59]

But during the engagement and after the marriage, Hawthorne had to apologize repeatedly to Sophia for Ebe's outrageous snubs. Ebe refused to visit the newlyweds at the Old Manse and even developed an irrational hatred for Concord, their first home, considering everything about Concord, even its air, to be inferior. When they all lived together in the Mall Street house in Salem during Hawthorne's surveyorship, the "trio" had a separate entrance to their upstairs

89

apartment and Elizabeth became "an invisible entity" for months at a time to both husband and wife.

To Ebe, everything connected with Sophia and the marriage was an unmitigated disaster. She felt that her brother's writing was never as good after his marriage as before and that every family decision stemmed from a selfish plot on Sophia's part. Even Hawthorne's own intrinsic restlessness and rootlessness she blamed on Sophia and the Peabodys. Of the Hawthornes' decision to leave Lenox, Massachusetts, in 1851 to move to Newton, Ebe wrote, "I suppose it is Sophia's plan; it is so much like the Peabodys never to be settled. If Nathaniel buys a place, she will have some excuse for leaving it in a year or two." [60]

In opposition to Hawthorne's profound feeling that his wife had rescued him from a life of alienation, Ebe wrote that Sophia was a social liability to her husband, that in London society "she was a great drawback . . . but she would always stick to him" in order to enjoy the society that he alone attracted. Sophia also ruined Julian's education by putting him to school in Dresden, "because she could not bear to be separated from him. . . . It is not even Julian she cares about, but her own fancy of living where she thinks she shall be happy."

Ebe, who found all she cared to see in the vicinity of Salem, had no tolerance for people "so abject as to prefer other countries to their own." Una's Roman fever and even Hawthorne's death she blamed on Sophia's artistic interests, which kept the family too long in Europe after Hawthorne quit the Liverpool consulate. Sophia "is the only really blamable person. I shall always think that my brother might have been alive and well now if she had not kept him in Rome so long . . . it is her very want of discrimination, her inability to see anything but the shape of a building and her blindness to every thing significant." [61]

Ebe's hatred survived even Sophia's death in 1871. In 1879 Ebe wrote scornfully to her Manning cousins about people who "teach children to go the way they should not, as Sophia did, you know; yet it was not intellect that misled her, only the aping of it. . . . I might as well tell you that she is the only human being whom I really dislike; though she is dead, that makes no difference; I could have lived with her in apparent peace, but I could not have lived long; the constraint would have killed me."[62]

Ebe was possessive about her brother, tried to prevent his marriage, and felt undying contempt for his wife. In view of all this, her emotional reaction to and irate denial of Harriet Beecher Stowe's assertion that Byron committed incest with his half-sister must indicate repressed desire on Ebe's part.

> January, 1864
>
> [Mrs. Stowe] habitually mixes up fact and fiction. I dare say she does not know them apart. . . . Her Byron article is full of cant, and cant blinds the eyes like dust. . . . As to Lady Byron, she appears to be one of those people who cannot discriminate between sins, but thinks one as likely to be committed as another—or rather, who think every departure from their own particular rule of right is a sin so enormous that the person guilty of it would hesitate at nothing. . . . It is strange how persons who have very little imagination contrive to delude themselves. One would suppose that matter of fact minds would be free from idle fancies, whereas they seem to be full of them, and always of an annoying nature.[63]

Ebe's contempt for the idea of an author committing incest with his sister sprays out in all directions, even besmirching authors as a class. To the incensed Ebe, Mrs. Stowe writes sensationalist cant, authors do not know fact from fiction, and Augusta Leigh not only was incapable of incest, she was the medium of communication between Byron and his wife. Ebe accuses Lady Byron of lack of discrimination, the very sin attributed above to Sophia Hawthorne. Such overt responses in addition to Ebe's very ostentatious avoidance of him after his marriage must surely have reached her brother.

On June 27, 1848, Hawthorne recounted a dream to Sophia, who was away visiting in Newton:

> The other night, I dreamed that I was at Newton, in a room with thee, and with several other people; and thou tookst occasion to announce, that thou hadst now ceased to be my wife, and hadst taken another husband. Thou madst this intelligence known with such perfect composure and *sang froid* —not particularly addressing me, but the company generally— that it benumbed my thoughts and feelings, so that I had nothing to say.

Thou wast perfectly decided, and I had only to submit without a word. But, hereupon, thy sister Elizabeth, who was likewise present, informed the company, that, in this state of affairs, having ceased to be thy husband, I of course became her's; and turning to me, very coolly inquired whether she or I should write to inform my mother of the new arrangement! How the children were to be divided, I know not. I only know that my heart suddenly broke loose, and I began to expostulate with thee in an infinite agony, in the midst of which I awoke; but the sense of unspeakable injury and outrage hung about me for a long time—and even yet it has not quite departed. Thou shouldst not behave so, when thou comest to me in dreams.[64]

Even though Elizabeth Peabody reportedly had hoped to win Nathaniel Hawthorne for herself and was disappointed to see the election light on Sophia, the dream figure who supplants Sophia is likely to be Elizabeth Hawthorne.

There were three important Elizabeths in Hawthorne's life—his mother, sister, and sister-in-law—making it possible, even likely, that in a dream of disturbing content, the least threatening of them should be substituted for the other. Furthermore, after claiming Hawthorne as a husband, the next act of the usurper of Sophia's place is to inquire who should inform Madame Hawthorne, implying that such a shift would affect her domestic arrangements. Even the mention of Hawthorne's mother before his children leads the dream back to his primary family, as if Sophia's displacement would return Hawthorne to his childhood situation.

Julian Hawthorne's way of reporting this dream proves an illuminating act of interpretation. He combined this dream, from a letter actually written on June 27, 1848, with another letter of July 5, 1848, putting them both under the latter date, omitting a few phrases, and changing the claimant of Hawthorne's hand from "thy sister Elizabeth" to "some woman who was there present." He thus removed Elizabeth Peabody from the dream. In addition, he juxtaposed the dream to a passage from the letter of July 5 which reports that during Sophia's absence on his birthday, Ebe Hawthorne paid Nathaniel a surprise visit, evidently a rare event, during which she invited him to go walking with her. Just *before* his altered version of the dream, Julian places this paragraph from the *later* letter,

I went to town, and got home here between eleven and twelve o'clock at night. I went into the little room to put on my linen coat, and, on my return, to the sitting-room, behold! a stranger there,—whom dost thou think it might be?—it was my sister Elizabeth! I did not wish to risk frightening her away by anything like an exhibition of wonder; and so we greeted each other kindly and cordially, but with no more *empressement* than if we were in the habit of meeting. It being so late, and I so tired, we did not have much talk then; but she said she meant to go to walk this afternoon, and asked me to go with her, which I promised to do. Perhaps she will now make it her habit to come down and see us occasionally in the evening.[65]

Julian's juxtaposition brings together two events that occurred only about a week apart: Ebe's surprise visit during Sophia's absence inviting resumption of the former brother-sister walks and the dream of an Elizabeth usurping the place of Sophia. Julian appears to have sensed an incestuous awareness on the part of his father and communicates it with surprising delicacy.

Such a dream occurring during Sophia's absence indicates a charged sexual atmosphere. To the question whether Hawthorne reciprocated or even elicited incestuous feelings, we must note that the dream was his, not Ebe's. More self-conscious and cautious than Ebe, he allowed little repressed material to surface in his letters and notebooks. His fiction, however, from earliest to latest, portrays many variations of the sexually tempting but taboo dark woman. Many of these occur within a context of brother-sister incest.

Sibling incest, dark women contrasted with fair ones—these staples of Gothic romance—were amplified by Hawthorne's family experience. Literary heritage and personal experience responded to and enhanced each other. His entirely personal reaction to dark women is embarrassingly revealed in his journal depiction of the beautiful Jewess who sat opposite him at a London dinner. From this very slight *donnée* evolved a lengthy journal meditation that reveals the terror behind his many portrayals of dark, exotic, and erotically suggestive women like Hester, Zenobia, Miriam, and Beatrice Rappaccini—contact with them is dangerous. In trying to define qualities of the Jewess's beauty, her complexion and the exact texture of her hair, "a wonderful deep, raven black, black as night, black as death;

93

not raven black, for that has a shiny gloss, and her's [*sic*] had not . . . wonderful hair, Jewish hair," he finds his "pen is good for nothing."

In trying to render his powerful personal reaction, he finds Old Testament analogues like the man-slaying Judith, the adulterous Bathsheba, and finally Eve, "though one could hardly think [the Jewess] weak enough to eat the apple." This selection corresponds to the women his fictional Miriam sketched in *The Marble Faun*, women like Jael and Sisera, "acting the part of a revengeful mischief towards man." The beautiful Jewess, her Old Testament analogues, and Hawthorne's fictional dark women are all dangerous. From the real life Jewess whose beauty he found indescribable, Hawthorne recoiled physically: "I never should have thought of touching her, nor desired to touch her; for, whether owing to distinctness of race, my sense that she was a Jewess, or whatever else, I felt a sort of repugnance, simultaneously with my perception that she was an admirable creature." [66] This paradoxical personal response to dark beauty appears as a sibling metaphor in "Rappaccini's Daughter," where Beatrice treats Giovanni like a brother, a playmate from infancy, but sets up between them a stern reserve against physical contact, a barrier that he violates at his peril.

Very early in his career Hawthorne wrote a convoluted tale of brother-sister incest, "Alice Doane's Appeal," that Ebe saved from destruction. He attenuates the incest by creation of an unrecognized, long-absent twin double who acts out what Leonard Doane has succeeded in repressing, his desire for his sister Alice, and even the actuality of the incestuous act is kept ambiguous. But it is for seduction of Alice, acted or planned, that Leonard Doane kills his twin brother Walter, who is, of course, Alice's brother also. Set in the historical past, this disjointed story recalls the event recorded without names in Felt's *Annals of Salem* about Hawthorne's ancestor, Nicholas Manning, who fled into the forest to avoid being tried for incest with his sisters, Anstiss and Margaret.

In "The White Old Maid" two sisters, one lofty and proud, the other gentle and soft, meet over the corpse of a dark-haired young man: "There the two maidens stood, both beautiful, with the pale beauty of the dead between them. But she, who had first entered, was proud and stately; . . . the other, a soft and fragile thing" (IX, 371). Some unnamed act of the proud sister has caused the premature death of the young man and she exacts from gentle Edith a promise not to betray her secret, even begs her forgiveness. This Edith promises to grant if at a meeting in the distant future the proud girl can prove that she has suffered "more than death." Edith becomes "the old maid in the winding sheet," a visitor at deathbeds and funerals, whereas her proud sister makes a grand foreign marriage. On the appointed day the two meet again as old women, the proud one richly arrayed and formally attended, but now a widow. Both sisters die together in the room where the corpse had lain, their secret perishing with them. The author selects for the proud widow's armorial shield, "azure, a lion's head erased, between three flower de luces," the Hawthorne family crest.

Although this story lacks finesse, it is worthy of attention for its materials, which point backward into autobiography and forward toward a more successful artistic transformation. The opening situation, with two sisters hovering in rivalry over the corpse of a beautiful young man, is a suicidal fantasy of witnessing the grief caused by one's own death, the kind of fantasy that appears in Hawthorne's notebooks and early stories. In the two sisters, who resemble his own, he experimented with elements from which he was later to create Hester Prynne. Aspects of Louisa first appear in gentle Edith, a feared but accepted witness to the community's deaths and other rituals of passage. This role was later reworked into the "social service" side of Hester, the social outcast who belonged in the house "darkened by trouble." Like Hester's scarlet letter, Edith's white robe (from which Hilda's was doubtless later cut) evolves in the course of the story from a symbol of dread to one of holiness.

From his sister Ebe, Hawthorne's imagination drew traits for his dark women—imperious pride, beauty, and intellectual gifts, some of which emerge in the lofty sister. But such characters gather force from another source as well. The lofty sister, reentering the story as a widow whose marriage the author fails to mention, carries the signal attribute of the central figure of his own early life—widowhood. In contrast to Edith's "old maid" status, the lofty sister's offstage marriage suggests obscure sexual experience. As with Hester, Zenobia, and Miriam, carnal knowledge prior to or outside the narrative structure lends an aura of the erotic.

Hawthorne's tendency to give structural importance to the

shadowy, often ambiguous sexual experience of his dark women may well derive from the fact that he knew his mother only as a widow, a mother whose married life was completely outside his experience. Such a circumstance must have created sexual curiosity about the absence that shadowed her presence. Hawthorne's childhood situation is refracted in the adult utopian community of Blithedale, which is dominated by the parental figures of Zenobia and the stern philanthropist Hollingsworth. Zenobia is linked to two men, Hollingsworth, whom she loves but cannot win, and Westervelt, a wizardlike figure from her past who retains a mysterious power over her and the psychic medium Priscilla. Zenobia spurns Priscilla's girlish adoration and ridicules the sexual advances of the narrator, Coverdale, a timid, evasive, minor poet whom Hollingsworth tries unsuccessfully to mold into a man of his own forceful type. Coverdale speculates pruriently on Zenobia's sexuality, both present and past. The story never confirms or denies his intuition that Zenobia was one to whom "wedlock had thrown wide the gates of mystery" any more than it ever clarifies her prior relationship to Westervelt. The source of the latter's magian power over the two women is deliberately obscure, giving rise to a suggestion that Westervelt may be the father and Zenobia the mother of Priscilla. Such a speculation would raise difficulties (e.g., the respective ages of Zenobia and Priscilla), but would explain much about the behavior of the two women, especially Zenobia's rude rejection of Priscilla's public devotion to herself and her extreme response (suicide) to Priscilla's winning the love of Hollingsworth. Coverdale's prurient speculations about Zenobia are adult male versions of little Pearl's search for her father. Both seem variants of the author's early curiosity about his origins in his mother's remote sexual past.

By imagining his own begetting, young Hawthorne could try to complete the fractured parental set. If he could oust his usurping uncle from the paternal place, restore the rightful father, and complete the female role of his apparently virginal mother, he might rectify his faulty parental imagery. In such a situation, the imagination would be its own cure as well as its own guilt, a concept close to that of the primal scene, which is about where Eric J. Sundquist locates Hawthorne's sense of sin.[67] Setting Hawthorne's recurrent theme of voyeurism in a complex of related motifs, Sundquist identifies alternations such as the following: condemnation of coldhearted observation versus identification with his observers whether their object is mere prying or Faustian alchemy; the dangers of speculation versus the exhilaration of free thinking; the sinful hubris of creative activity versus the nobility of it; the fear of boundlessness versus the dread of containment; the dangers of ambition versus the dread of insignificance. Whenever Hawthorne opted for one side of the equation he simultaneously sent energy toward the other side. The likely center of all the interlinked clusters, according to Sundquist, is speculation, a transgression comprising *libido sciendi*, the lust for knowledge and the act of looking at or imagining forbidden scenes.

Provocatively, Sundquist links the sin of speculation to the sin of representation, or artistic re-presentation. Indeed, characters like Chillingworth and Coverdale speculate about sexual acts prior to and generating the narratives that embody or engender them, so that an original sinful act generates sinful speculation that in turn generates sinful representation. Almost a chain of "begats"! And if we extend Sundquist's linkage back into Hawthorne's childhood, we find a probable genesis for the thematic cluster centered on voyeurism. Speculation about his own origins in the sexuality of his parents could have led to speculation about the secrets of nature, contaminating with prurience the very act of seeking knowledge. The fact that his model for learning and knowing, even for creative activity, was actually a creative sort of scientist who hybridized plant species, tainted all such activities with guilt. Even Hawthorne's own artistic creativity was identified with the fruitfulness of a scientist whose creative acts were alternately seen as extensions of nature or as "unnatural," and therefore as either humanitarian or diabolic. From this sexualization of scientifc pursuits comes the libidinous quality of Chillingworth's psychological probings and herbalism, Aylmer's alchemical experiments in "The Birthmark", and Rappaccini's "vegetable adultery."

If Nathaniel secretly wished to oust the usurper of his father's place, he would have been guilty of ingratitude for benefits received. Moreover, because his own creativity and quest for knowledge were *like* those of the uncle, vengence would be virtually self-punishment. Maddeningly, the thread seems to run in both directions—toward recovery of the original father, which would mean a terrifying return of the dead, or toward displacement of the surrogate father, which would leave a dangerous vacuum. If one should merely do away with the interloping uncle, one would then be left in a maze of unchecked Oedipal desires. The interloper, the usurper of the father's place, is also a buffer between the boy and his mother. Just as Hamlet wished to do away with his uncle yet dreaded the vacant place his absence would create, so Hawthorne suffered from the "unappropriated" situation of his mother. He who "appropriates a lot of land that has no visible owner" (II, 3), or builds a house "over an unquiet grave," must fear the return of the *in*visible owner. Little wonder that woven through *The Scarlet Letter* and its preface are allusions to *Hamlet*, which enacts the procrastination and vacillations of a son commanded by the ghost of his deceased father to do away with his interloping uncle. Hamlet's combined sexual prurience and sexual disgust also spoke to Hawthorne's situation, as did the way Hamlet transferred attitudes toward his mother's sexuality to his relationship with Ophelia.*

For Hawthorne, the mother's seductive image merged with Ebe's incestuous aura, the two Elizabeths thus combining to create a maternal figure of dangerous sensuality. The mother was the catalytic element that made possible the fusion of all the early female images into Hester Prynne, Hawthorne's most complex literary character.

---

*The action of *Hamlet* was generated by the ghost of Hamlet's father, which charged his son to avenge his death and correct the false record. The action of *The Scarlet Letter* was initiated by the charge of Mr. Surveyor Pue, the author's "ghostly father," to do his filial duty, which is to transmit Pue's story and do justice to his memory. Like Hamlet, the Custom House narrator swears an oath of filial duty to a ghostly father. Both "sons" have difficulty stirring themselves into action. Hamlet complains that "enterprises of great pith and moment . . . lose the name of action," and the Custom House narrator bewails a lethargy that "steals the pith and availability out of whatever enterprise he may dream of undertaking." Shakespeare's cuckolded ghost cautions its avenger not to "contrive·/ Against thy mother aught. Leave her to heaven, / And to those thorns that in her bosom lodge / To prick and sting her" (I, 85–88). Similarly Chillingworth renounces vengeance against his unfaithful wife and reserves it for the man but chooses as his means psychic revenge like that the ghost selects for Gertrude. Chillingworth, thinking Hester sufficiently punished by her shame, also plans no overt violence against her lover. He tells her, "Think not that I shall interfere with Heaven's own method of retribution, or . . . that I shall contrive aught against his life" (I, 75–78). Indeed, he settles for the stinging thorns in Dimmesdale's own bosom.

The triple female figure comprehending Louisa's selfless domesticity, Ebe's pride and beauty, and the mother's single status, would eventually be transformed into Hester's solitary but proud and competent maternity. Such literary transformation of personal experience was uncannily prefigured by the Hawthorne family crest, "azure, a lion's head erased, between three flower de luces."

MATER AND MATRIMONY

An additional derivative of the natal soil was Hawthorne's matrimonial choice. Although Sophia Peabody was not the playmate of Hawthorne's youth, the two did, like his parents, grow up in close proximity in Salem. At the time he took an adult interest in Sophia, she was living on Charter Street adjoining the old cemetery where his Puritan ancestors were buried. The Sophia he then encountered had given up all expectation of marriage and acquiesced to an invalid life in the bosom of her family. He passed over her vigorous sister Elizabeth, who was equally appreciative of his gifts and person, in favor of the invalid Sophia, who first appeared before him wearing the white wrapper of her sickroom.

Elizabeth Peabody expressed surprise at the sudden attraction, or mutual recognition, of the two because the Peabody family had come to think of Sophia as a perpetual sister and daughter rather than as a nubile woman. Peabody described Sophia as one who, "having grown up with the feeling that she was never to be married, looked upon herself as practically a child."[68] Herein lay the particular quality that made marriage possible for Hawthorne. He assimilated Sophia's neurasthenic seclusion from the world to familiar Hawthorne qualities and mentally elevated her disabilities into a sign of purity uncontaminated by the world.

Sophia's undesigning and sisterly reception was the most disarming possible approach. Shortly after the meeting she wrote to Elizabeth Peabody, "I feel as if he were a born brother. I never, hardly, knew a person for whom I had such a full and at the same time perfectly quiet admiration. I do not care about seeing him often; but I delight to remember that *he is*, and that from time to time I shall have intercourse with him. I feel the most entire ease with him, as if I had always known him."[69] Sophia's unworldliness persisted so long that even well into the courtship, according to Peabody, Hawthorne spoke of her as "a flower to be worn in no man's bosom, but . . . lent from Heaven to show the possibilities of the human soul."[70]

The relationship, sheltered under such spiritual idealization and curiously enhanced by the brother-sister illusion, flowered into a rapturous union. In Sophia, Hawthorne found qualities both necessary and familiar. He had grown accustomed to and required female adoration as support for his fragile self-esteem, and his sisters, who never looked to other men, had supplied this for far too long. Sophia was fully prepared to take over this function. Moreover, her virginal, sisterly-daughterly demeanor was peculiarly compatible with his earliest impression of womanhood.

The brevity of his mother's marriage and her rapid reversion to the role of sister and daughter on her return to the parental home made her seem to him a celibate, asexual figure. This essentially virginal image, paradoxically like the "image of Divine Maternity" evoked by Hester on the scaffold, led him to locate the erotic in the "sacred image of sinless motherhood." The icon of the Virgin Mother, fusing innocence with mysterious sexuality, was the inner standard that made Sophia's maidenly reserve almost immediately familiar and desirable to him.

Having qualities continuous with his earliest needs and fantasies, Sophia served as his ideal anima figure, helping to direct these into more adult channels of sexuality and creativity. To a remarkable degree she fits Daniel Levinson's version of the anima figure as "special woman": "She shares [the Dream], believes in him as its hero, gives it her blessing, joins him on the journey and creates a 'boundary space' within which his aspirations can be imagined and his hopes nourished. . . . [She] can foster his adult aspirations while accepting his dependency, his incompleteness and his need to make her into something more than (and less than) she actually is."[71] Victorian stereotypes of the angelic woman also helped Sophia fulfill a role for which she was peculiarly fitted by experience and temperament.

Part of this stereotype was submissiveness, another cultural standard of femininity reinforced by her husband's family experience. More comfortable with docile women like his mother and Louisa, Hawthorne had always avoided female assertiveness. He chose a wife with artistic talent enough to appreciate his own gifts but the temperament of a natural acolyte. Before the marriage Sophia displayed intuitive recognition of his preferences in her sketch of his Ilbrahim, which interpreted visually what he had already expressed verbally in "The Gentle Boy." Like Hilda of *The Marble Faun*, she accepted the secondary role of interpretive copyist rather than the assertive one of original creator. Later, when Hawthorne lost his Custom House job, she made and sold decorative lamp shades to enable him to do his creative work. Although she was herself a capable writer as well as artist, she accepted during his lifetime his prohibition against publication by females. Only after his death and pressed by financial need did she publish some of her travel notes. In subordinating her own talents to his, Sophia resembled Hawthorne's gifted sister Ebe.

The marriage was beneficial for both partners. It gave Hawthorne intimate human contact and links to normal human experience. It led Sophia from chronic invalidism into sufficient health for motherhood and a fairly long, active life. Within it, both found a satisfying and enduring physical relationship that made their separations hard to endure. Sophia's frequent long visits to her parental family, sometimes for lyings-in, sometimes for reasons not so clear, indicate that even rapturous attachment to her "Apollo" did not quite eliminate her need to maintain the old sisterly-daughterly role. What evidence there is of gaps in the union (such as Sophia's retreats to Boston and Nathaniel's occasional ironies about her sentimentality) seem minor in view of their mutual devotion and esteem.

Sophia filled Nathaniel's particularly intense needs for home, an anchor, and validation as lover and artist. Like his first women, she granted priority to his wishes and whims and affirmed the importance of his work. Beyond that, she gave him what mother and sisters could not, of course, provide, which was appropriate confirmation of his manhood as a lover and a father of children.

All this Sophia performed remarkably well, especially in view of her own and her husband's unusual histories before marriage. For one who had been so long a petted invalid, she adapted with impressive speed to the roles of wife and mother. Her need for an idol and his need for adoration complemented each other beautifully, stimulating her ability to create a "home-feeling" that spoke to his deepest unfulfilled longings. He flattered and encouraged her home-building activities in the hope that she could stabilize his tendency toward alternations, oscillations, and dissatisfaction with the actualities of life.

Apparently, however, the instability of his first home was too radical to be fully overcome. His early experiences of separation of parents and authority from dwelling places and of self from parents led to continued search for the right place simply to be—the place of full presence. We know that he never stopped seeking this locus of the integrated self. If long seclusion in his mother's garret could not compensate for what the foundation stage of life failed to provide, Sophia's best efforts at homemaking would not entirely do so either.

In *The House of the Seven Gables*, Hawthorne expressed his own tension between fluidity and fixity. In Holgrave he depicted his oscillating unease and counterbalanced it with Phoebe, who sought "a house and modest garden spot of [her] own," an embodiment of Hawthorne's urgent need for stability. Such home-centered female characters, long derided by critics as tiresomely conventional, function as centripetal forces anchoring the texts as well as the vagrant artists they marry. Hawthorne recognized fully the price his artists pay for their house and garden spots (their second Edens) tended by uncomplicated homebodies, but he also felt these artists' powerful need for anchorage. Experience, however, taught him that deep childhood losses cannot be fully met even by a very good marriage. In *The Marble Faun*, written during the sad late years of his wanderings in Europe, he allows a disillusioned response to the sculptor Kenyon's anguished "O Hilda, guide me home!" Far more problematic a character than Phoebe, Hilda answers: "We are both lonely; both far from home!" (IV, 461).

Nevertheless, the successful union of such unusual people as Sophia and Nathaniel Hawthorne indicates that an adequate foundation for intimacy must have been prepared. No matter that his mother appears to have given up on her own life and to have abdicated much of her parental role. She must have been at very least a good enough mother to have generated in her son the adaptive capacity to emerge from depression and isolation, to love and satisfy a woman, to make lifelong friends, and to cope with the difficult terms of life as an artist-provider.

If never entirely happy, he proved more capable of both love and work than many who started life more auspiciously. In his chosen work he so universalized his private experiences as to speak to our common human nature more than a century after his death. He did, in fact, achieve a legacy that would have more than satisfied his "ambitious guest," the lone traveler who was willing to die if only he could leave behind a monument testifying to his having lived. In his own way, Hawthorne forged a legacy for himself out of his father's premature death. This death, which he carried within as a mutating value, served at least for a period to enhance the meaning of life and time. Although it often pushed him downward toward depression, it also pulled him forward toward achievements designed to vanquish death.

FOUR

Fathers, Uncles, and Avuncular Figures

"I came hither, and found only his grave. I knew that my father was sleeping here, and I said, this shall be my home."
"The Gentle Boy"

THE GHOSTLY LEGACY

Conscious that generations of burials had made the "earthly substance" of Salem akin to his own, Nathaniel felt keenly the paternal gap in his own continuity. His mother's body was to be placed eventually with the Manning dead, for she had ceased being a Hawthorne long before her death. But no Salem cemetery memorialized his father, whose death and burial in a remote part of the world were reported but not witnessed by the family. Nathaniel's loss of his father, in itself a severe blow although not an uncommon one, was magnified by a combination of circumstances.

Compounding his mother's diminished capacity to transmit confidence was the loss of fatherly support for growth away from the mother. At the very age when the mother-child dyad should have been opening out into a triad in which the father assumes his guiding function, that father was absent at sea. Thus even prior to the captain's death, Nathaniel was deprived of that encouragement to independence that draws a child toward autonomy. In fact, he had seen so little of his father that he had no clear image of face or voice to treasure as a stay against doubt or guilty imaginings. Nor did he have much contact with men related to his father. His one paternal uncle died in 1804, the year of Nathaniel's birth, so that of his father's immediate family he knew mainly women, a grandmother who died in 1813 and his father's sisters.

His immediate paternal legacy was further diluted by childish incomprehension of the meaning of death and the absence of any piece of Salem earth that could be viewed as his father's resting place. News of the death most likely produced changes in the mother's demeanor and behavior toward the children as she adjusted to the radical change in her own life situation. Her removal only months later to the Manning home effected further changes and severed Nathaniel from the only home he had known. Associated with the father's death, then, were many personal discontinuities working together to undermine confidence in himself and in the reliability of his world.

Perhaps on one of Captain Hathorne's rare visits to Salem, Nathaniel, accustomed to being the only male of his family, wished his father would go away and never come back. Then, when the boy was only four years old, news arrived that his father had died—would indeed never come back. The mother was thrown into disarray and panic by this news. Perhaps his powerful wishes had caused his father's death and his mother's distress.[1] He must have felt guilt over parricidal wishes unexpectedly fulfilled, anger at his father's apparent abandonment, and fear that perhaps he deserved to be abandoned.

In addition to all this, the sudden replacement of the missing father with the six Manning men must have caused additional confusion. With his father present a boy knows where to locate authority, regards it as socially authorized, and experiences it as a fixed limit to unacceptable acts and feelings, something he can push against in defining himself. In the process of finding his own identity he has a clear and socially sanctioned model of masculinity which, however much he may modify and adapt it, belongs to himself by a direct line of descent. Instead of two parents standing together in a sanctioned position of authority, Nathaniel had a confusing swarm of adults. Instead of the lost father, he acquired a multiplicity of father-figures, one of whom was to emerge with paternal authority. This was surely better than having no masculine supervision or role model, but for development of autonomy it was not the same as having a father.

Because Hawthorne was even more reticent about his father than about his mother, we find only indirect evidence for the emotional impact of this loss. What he failed to confront directly, however, emerges in journal musings on such topics as return of the dead or oppression of the living by the dead and in fiction embodying such themes. In such places, then, we find the emotional responses to his loss.

His authority confusion is vividly reflected in the doubling of adult figures in "The Wives of the Dead," a tale written in the 1820s, possibly as early as the first years of Hawthorne's return from college. It depicts two husbands and two wives, or two widows, or one wife and one widow, depending on one's reading of the ambiguously written and terminated story (it was, in fact, later published as "The Two Widows," which might be decisive if we could be sure that the author chose this title for the 1843 reprint).[2] In this highly condensed story, Mary and Margaret, two sisters sharing a home even after marriage, learn of the deaths of their husbands, two brothers, on successive days. Strikingly like Hawthorne's mother, Mary, of "mild, quiet, yet not feeble character," receives this blow with "resignation and endurance" and quickly resumes her "regular course of duties," beginning with preparation of dinner. Her countertype, Margaret, "of a lively and irritable temperament," laments passionately and refuses food. Mary's husband had been a sailor and Margaret's a landsman, a soldier in the Canadian wars.

After learning of their bereavements, the lonely sisters kept open the doors to their bedrooms, which were adjacent to a shared parlor. During the night each sister is said to be awakened separately from sleep with news that the report of her husband's death was erroneous. Each hears the knock on the parlor window from the messenger of her own good news but not the knock of the other's messenger. Each immediately wants to share her good news but, thinking the other still a widow, is too sensitive to do so. Mary, the second to receive the news, enters her sister's bedroom and hesitates to awaken the sleeper: "But her hand trembled against Margaret's neck, a tear also fell upon her cheek, and she suddenly awoke" (XI, 199). Interpretive problems result from the ambiguous pronoun reference of this final sentence of the story. If "her" and "she" refer to Mary, as seems unlikely at a first reading, she has been sleepwalking and dreaming the good news of her husband's resurrection from the deep. If the pronouns refer to Margaret, both sisters may again be wives of returning husbands, or both may have been merely dreaming their good news.

Grammatical analysis is unlikely to resolve the critical problem, but close examination of structure and details may illuminate the author's apparent syntactic carelessness, which is not characteristic. He differentiates Mary and Margaret only with respect to how they respond to news of widowhood, and events derive from this difference. Like the parable of the wise and the foolish virgins who differ in their state of preparedness for the bridegroom's arrival, this spare story is structured on the difference between the woman resisting her husband's death and the one who accepts it. Passionate Margaret, who sleeps fretfully, awakens readily for the first herald of good news and learns that her husband is among survivors of the battle. Her alertness almost seems a result of her *desire* for the news that reverses her doom: "It is difficult to be convinced of the death of one whom we have deemed another self" (XI, 194). Thinking to share her delight, she peeks into the bedroom of Mary, who sleeps so soundly that she does not hear the first knock on the window or Margaret's entrance into her room. Even when her own herald arrives later, Mary awakens very slowly.

While asleep, Mary wears a "look of motionless contentment . . . as if her heart, like a deep lake, had grown calm because its dead had sunk down so far within" (XI, 196). So newly bereaved and yet her heart is already a deep calm lake entombing her sailor husband! Indeed, the knock that awakens Mary interrupts a dream "broken in upon at the most interesting point," and when finally she responds to the summons, she finds that "by some accident" the window "had been left unhasped, and yielded easily to her hand" (XI, 197). Her herald, "a man in a sailor's dress, wet as if he had come out of the depths of the sea," appears more like a dreamed reincarnation of her drowned husband than like the friendly realistic innkeeper who brought Margaret's news.

Mary may have heard Margaret's message subliminally, incorporated it into her own dreams, fantasized a summons for herself, and then sleepwalked to the window already opened by her sister. The opened window suggests that Margaret's message occurred in "reality" as a result of her intense wish for it and that Mary's was only a dream. Furthermore, when Mary in turn enters Margaret's room to impart her good news, she finds that the door left open the evening before is now closed. She finds Margaret, whom she hesitates to awaken, in a sleep very different from her own placid slumbers. Margaret is restive, her body feverish, her cheek rosy, her expression joyous, her drapery "displaced," all suggestive of an erotic dream. This description added to the minute details of the unlocked window and the closed bedroom door suggest that passionate Margaret has "really" learned that her married life is to be resumed and now wants privacy. Now that she is again to be a wife she will not leave her bedroom door open in sisterly fashion. Margaret's shutting of the door directs attention to the fact that wifehood and sisterhood in this story are alternative ways of being and that Margaret clearly prefers the former whereas placid Mary can accept either status with equanimity.

Reversals of each other, the paired sisters, one so like Hawthorne's mother, the other so like Hester Prynne (or perhaps even Ebe Hawthorne) are differentiated specifically with respect to the intensity of their temperaments, the power of their passions and wishes. One seems destined to be a widow content with a sisterly relationship and the other to be a wife. Conceivably, the tear that Mary drops is for herself, because *her* herald from the sea is only a dream and she herself only a sleepwalker. If so, her acceptance of her husband's death serves only to ratify it. Perhaps Hawthorne allowed the syntactically ambiguous "she" to stand for his hesitation in judging his own mother's deficiencies and his own ambivalence about return of the dead. The sailor presumed dead, according to Mary's new report, saved himself on a spar, "when [his ship] the Blessing turned bottom upwards" (XI, 198). These ironic words to a widow whose dead had already sunk deep into the lake of her contented heart were written by a son who wished for but feared his father's return.

Had Hawthorne wished to write only of a woman's good fortune in discovering that her husband was alive, he need not have diminished realism by doubling the wives, the husbands, the deaths, and the apparent resurrections. If, as I speculate above, Margaret's husband lives and Mary's does not, the continuing marriage of Margaret and the landsman could represent the child's fantasies about his mother's close relationship to her landsman brother Robert, which to a child could easily have looked like a marriage. Given the delicate autobiographical nature of the materials, the story's doublings and ambiguous syntax suggest a process of transformation similar to that of dreams, with their reversals, doublings, condensations, and complexes of meaning.

Although his father did not perish by drowning, Hawthorne had reason to associate sea voyages with death. Entries in his notebook of 1838 suggest that in childhood he may have thought of his father as still lying at the bottom of a lake and susceptible to resurrection: "All the dead that had ever been drowned in a certain lake—to arise," followed by "the history of a small lake, from the first, till it was drained" (VIII, 179). Such thoughts link the entombment of the dead in the calm lake of Mary's heart to the "icy sepulchre" of "Alice Doane's Appeal."

This early tale begins abruptly with the discovery of an unburied body on the edge of a lake, where a murderer had attempted to submerge it: "There had been a slight fall of snow during the night, and as if nature were shocked at the deed, and strove to hide it with her frozen tears, a little drifted heap had partly buried the body, and lay deepest over the pale dead face" (XI, 269–270). The story is an account of a fratricide that is in effect a partial suicide, elimination of the unacceptable, incestuous part of the self. It also carries intimations of parricide, or guilt over an imagined parricide such as a young child might feel after the mysterious death of a father. The framing narrative is set on Gallows Hill, a significant spot in Hawthorne's paternal history, where witches were executed and "without a coffin or a prayer, were buried" (XI, 267). The narrator regrets that the boys who light bonfires on this "haunted height" every fifth of November do not pay funeral honors to these improperly buried dead.

The narrator later moves back to the cause of the murder, the severing of the close relationship between Leonard Doane and his sister Alice by the arrival of Walter Brome, Leonard's long-absent twin brother. Oddly unaware that Leonard's identical twin brother is also her own brother, Alice falls in love with him. Walter boasts of having seduced Alice, thus provoking Leonard to murder him. We see Walter's unburied corpse twice in the story, a sight so shocking that nature herself attempts to cover it with snow. Gazing on the face of his victim, which is the same as his own, Leonard has a vision of his murdered father.

But it seemed to me that the irrevocable years since childhood had rolled back, and a scene that had long been confused and broken in my memory, arrayed itself with all its first distinctness. Methought I stood a weeping infant by my father's hearth; by the cold and blood-stained hearth where he lay dead. . . . As I gazed, a cold wind whistled by, and waved my father's hair. Immediately I stood again in the lonesome road, no more a sinless child, but a man of blood. . . . But the delusion was not wholly gone; that face still wore a likeness of my father; and because my soul shrank from the fixed glare of the eyes, I bore the body to the lake, and would have buried it there. But before his icy sepulchre was hewn, I heard the voices of two travellers and fled. (XI, 273)

Hawthorne tried to distance the urgent, extremely personal dream fantasies of this inner tale by inserting it into an ironic frame. The frame dramatizes an artist's attempt to shape his own fantasies into material designed to affect an audience, but the basic material is, as Hyatt Waggoner says, "too transparent and too close to the forbidden." [3]

A corpse that lies unburied for eighteen years dominates "Roger Malvin's Burial" and haunts the younger man who failed to bury it until it is lightly covered by leaves from a withered tree, as Walter Brome's was covered by falling snow. Throughout his marriage Reuben Bourne was conscious "that an unburied corpse was calling to him out of the wilderness" (X, 349). The story's title reflects the importance in Hawthorne's mind of proper funeral obsequies, which serve not only to honor the dead but to appease them in hopes they will not haunt the living.

Having failed to experience this terminal ritual for his father, Hawthorne was unable to incorporate the full reality of his death or accept a substitute father. Around 1838 he wrote: "Stories to be told of a certain person's appearance in public, of his having been seen in various situations, and of his making visits in private circles; but finally, on looking for this person, to come upon his old grave and mossy tombstone" (VIII, 170). Like Reuben Bourne he spent his life haunted by the dead. Long after his father's death and two years after that of Uncle Robert he wrote in his journal: "To represent the influence which Dead Men have among living affairs;—for instance, a Dead Man controls the disposition of wealth; a Dead Man sits on the judgment-seat, and the living judges do but repeat his decisions;

Dead Men's opinions in all things control the living truth . . . everywhere and in all matters, Dead Men tyrannize over us" (VIII, 252).

Sometimes in private musings Hawthorne imagined the dead as immortal observers of the living: "Solomon dies during the building of the Temple, but his body remains leaning on a staff and overlooking the workmen, as if it were alive" (VIII, 227). Even his contradictory attitudes toward the past involve something of his feelings about his dead father. On the one hand the past is tradition, rest, peace, security; on the other it is a suffocating oppression. Residence in ancestral England stimulated both views, but relics of the past in the British Museum made him wish that "all the material relics of so many ages had disappeared with the generations that produced them. The present is burthened too much with the past. . . . I do not see how future ages are to stagger onward under all this dead weight, with the additions that will be continually made to it."[4]

Employing the same image of staggering under the dead weight of the past but heightening its implications, Holgrave exclaims in *The House of the Seven Gables*,

> Shall we never, never get rid of this Past! . . . It lies upon the Present like a giant's dead body! In fact, the case is just as if a young giant were compelled to waste all his strength in carrying about the corpse of the old giant, his grandfather, who died a long while ago, and only needs to be decently buried. Just think a moment; and it will startle you to see what slaves we are to bygone times—to Death, if we give the matter the right word! (II, 182–183)

In the tragic agon the young living giant is less potent than the dead old one, at least so long as the corpse is unburied. Calling the old giant a grandfather instead of a father typifies Hawthorne's processes of condensation and displacement. Directing attention to the painful area but disguising it, he conflates departed paternal figures so that the persistent dead who watch over and dominate the living include his father, grandfather, and four of his five Manning uncles, all dead by the time he wrote *The House of the Seven Gables*. Late in life, when residence in England had stirred up ancestral longings, he was still looking for his Uncle John Manning, who never returned from the War of 1812:

If it is not known how and when a man dies, it seems to make a ghost of him for many years thereafter. . . . I had an uncle John, who went a voyage to sea, about the beginning of the war of 1812, and has never returned to this hour. But as long as his mother lived (as much as twenty years afterwards) she never gave up the hope of his return. . . . Thus, so far as her belief was concerned, he still walked the earth. And even to this day, I never see his name (which is no very uncommon one) without thinking that this may be the lost uncle.[5]

The lost uncle had become emotionally identified with the lost father,[6] a more manageable variant of the same fear that the dead whose departure was not witnessed or confirmed may return, or may be watching and judging the living. A persisting need for a terminal ritual may have motivated his decision while a busy consul in Liverpool to attend the funeral of one Captain Auld, a mariner who died alone in this foreign port. Unable to put the "perturbed spirit" of his father to rest, Hawthorne wrote about the unquiet dead with varying degrees of obliquity over the years. The father-figure had come to be freighted with obligations beyond any owing to a natural parent and resentments beyond any rational justification—the products of displaced, unresolved, and therefore unburied Oedipal hostility.

UNCLE ROBERT AND AVUNCULAR FIGURES

"And because you have been a father to me, should I therefore leave you to perish and to lie unburied in the wilderness?"
"Roger Malvin's Burial"

Considering the emphasis on filial piety and proper funeral obsequies, it is remarkable that when Robert Manning died in 1842, Hawthorne found trivial excuses for not traveling the short distance from Concord to Salem to attend the funeral. He wrote to Louisa,

Concord, October 12th, 1842
My dear Sister,
I have just received your letter, containing the sad intelligence of Uncle Robert's death. If there were a little more time, I would certainly be present at the funeral, although I should be compelled to return hither tomorrow night; but I could not arrive in Boston this evening, till between nine and ten oclock, and could scarcely be with you before the appointed

hour. I cannot, at present, leave Concord for any long space; because my domestic affairs, orchard, potatoes &c have to be attended to this week; and, I have also a guest (Mr. Farley) who has been invited to stay several days—not to mention a literary matter, which must be completed within a specified time. . . .

Say everything that ought to be said on my behalf, to Mrs. Manning. Something must be done for the children. This also we must talk about, when we meet. Believe me (not the less because I seldom say it) your very loving brother,

Nath. Hawthorne[7]

It would be simple enough to explain Hawthorne's abstention by saying that he was unwilling to disturb his routine for an uncle he had never really liked or that by staying home he avoided having to pretend a grief he did not feel. And this may be all there was to it. However, the failure visually to confirm Uncle Robert's demise leaves this death very much like those of the father and Uncle John. In turn, Robert's death doubtless carried with it reminders of the cumulative childhood losses that the boy could not have understood, much less effectively mourned. The uncle who had stood *in loco parentis* thus could join previously missing father figures whose vague departures from this world might be unconsciously regarded as not quite final.

Well before Robert Manning's death, the way had been prepared for such a fusion of the father and father-surrogate. The image of a symbolic father sitting unburied at the base of a pre-inscribed granite marker dominates the life of a man from youth until middle age in "Roger Malvin's Burial," one of a cluster of tales written in the 1820s that focus on initiation of young men into guilt by older ones.[8] The blighting of Reuben Bourne's spirit, marriage, and work—that is, the substance of his adult life—by conflicting attitudes toward a father-figure conveys the enduring power of this kind of surrogate relationship.

Near a granite rock compared to a gravestone, Reuben Bourne, an injured young soldier, and Roger Malvin, his fatally wounded companion and father of his fiancée, find themselves too weak to return together to their village. The old soldier invokes his nearly paternal authority to argue down Reuben's moral scruples against leaving a dying man and to persuade him to depart that he may marry

Malvin's daughter Dorcas, who would otherwise be bereaved of both father and lover. Reuben promises to return, either to bring aid to Malvin or to bury his bones.

Half-conscious motives complicate the already conflicting values of reason and honor. In the older man's benevolent argument are probably embedded some self-interested thoughts about his daughter's welfare, and in Reuben's acceptance is a reasonable loyalty to the unfulfilled life within himself. In obedience to Malvin's seductive logic the conflicted young man departs. His inability to admit to Dorcas after returning home that he has left her dying father makes it difficult for him to fulfill the vow to return and bury Malvin's bones. Receiving unmerited praise for his supposed fidelity, he marries Dorcas and inherits Malvin's flourishing farm. The thought of the unburied dead calling to him from the wilderness blights his marriage and his fortunes to such a degree that after eighteen years of failure he must strike out into the wilderness to make a new start. While stalking deer in the forest Reuben is unconsciously led back to the site of Malvin's death, where, firing at a movement in the underbrush, he accidentally shoots his son Cyrus.

Disturbingly for readers and critics, the story concludes with Reuben's liberation from years of self-enclosed bitterness by this "sacrifice" of his son on the altar of his own guilt. The filicide, sometimes interpreted as a symbolic suicide, makes a morally unacceptable act of atonement in that it deprives Cyrus of life, Dorcas of her son, and Roger Malvin of posterity. As Frederick Crews asserts in "The Logic of Compulsion," Hawthorne's treatment of the actual slaying as Reuben's expiation for an imaginary murder points toward a psychological interpretation.[9] But what psychological theory can account for Reuben's relief on learning that he has shot his son?

Reuben Bourne behaves toward his fiancée's father not only with filial respect but also with filial hostility. As the story is structured, Malvin's benevolence in seducing Reuben into leaving him to die alone paradoxically blights the remainder of Reuben's life. Insofar as Malvin's wiles give Reuben the gift of continued life, they generate a sense of obligation; insofar as they cause him to violate his sense of honor and experience guilt, they occasion resentment. Such incompatible feelings toward this second father paralyze Reuben emotionally, so that his future actions become self-canceling and self-punitive.

His first self-punitive action, procrastination about burying Malvin's remains, generates the haunting image of the unburied father-figure. Because guilt connected with this image transforms the sanguine youth into a morbid and depressed man, and because this lapse could so easily have been remedied, we must conclude that Reuben unconsciously chooses this form of self-torture. He continues through life in a series of self-canceling actions. He marries Dorcas but cannot love her, inherits Malvin's farm but neglects it, fathers a son but slays him. If we ask *why* Reuben could not accept from Roger Malvin the gift of continued life, we are led back to the original source of Reuben's life, the biological father for whóm Malvin is a surrogate.

Of Reuben's actual father, the author says nothing, but the story opens and closes with a massive granite rock "not unlike a gigantic gravestone, upon which the veins seem to form an inscription in forgotten characters" (X, 338). Because Roger Malvin (whose initials are the same as those of Robert Manning) dies at an already inscribed funerary monument, his death seems to revive some "prehistoric" event, possibly the death of Reuben's own father, which may have involved an earlier legacy of irrational guilt. The unburied figure at the waiting tombstone looms so large in Reuben's psyche that it dominates his adult life and compels him to return to it at the specific time that Cyrus is on the threshold of manhood, no sooner and no later.

A deep Oedipal confusion results from the fact that Reuben has married the daughter of his surrogate father. The marriage is experienced as incestuous and the issue of it seems tainted by this flaw. Seeking punishment for this assumed guilt that may have reactivated earlier Oedipal feelings, Reuben yields to flimsy excuses for not keeping his vow to return and bury Malvin's bones. By procrastinating he retains the accusing image of Malvin watching over and censuring the most intimate acts of his life, magnifying his guilt until it comes to include the murder of his father-in-law. The destruction of Cyrus, which cuts off Roger Malvin from his only line of posterity, could scarcely expiate any sin, real or imaginary, but it could serve the psychological functions of self-punishment and the surrender of the fruits of a primal sin.

The dimly inscribed and waiting tombstone, Reuben tells Dorcas, is the gravestone of her father and her son; it is also the grave of

Reuben's own symbolic father and his own son, and the grave of all their posterity. In shooting Cyrus, Reuben not only kills what was best in himself, he terminates the cycle of fathers and sons before it can be repeated by Cyrus's succession to manhood. If the "accidental" gunshot enacts a ritual of ending all parricidal rituals by killing a son, it expiates one curse deeply rooted in human psychic experience by another that would end all human experience. The only credible relief at the conclusion of the story consists in the sudden termination of emotional paralysis by explosive, unmeditated action. For this discharge of blocked emotion the price will be the interment of posterity in the sepulcher of the ancestors.*

Underlying this entire inquiry is the difference to a proud and sensitive young boy between a father and a father-surrogate. The surrogate in Nathaniel's case was surely no ogre; very likely the same man would have affected him quite differently as a father. But as an interloper in the vacated paternal position, Robert Manning assumed psychic magnification sufficient to have influenced Hawthorne's imagination as well as his personality.

The relationship was a two-way interaction. A man of Robert Manning's responsible temperament was likely to behave more prudently, less intuitively, toward a sister's son than toward one of his own, especially in reaction to the nephew's impractical temperament. Responsibility for ensuring the manliness and economic viability of just such an indolent, artistic boy doubtless elicited Manning's most authoritarian tendencies. He might well have been more flexible had the boy been different or his own. Conversely, the boy, perceiving duty and responsibility instead of paternal love, and resenting the intrusion, resisted Uncle Robert in such a way as to stimulate even more authoritarian behavior. And implicated in all this was Nathaniel's burden of obligation for benefits that a father gives freely.

---

*In Lovewell's fight at Pigwacket, the historical basis for this story, Massachusetts men fought near Fryeburg, Maine, not far from Raymond. The emotionally determined discharge of Reuben's musket suggests young Nathaniel's dream in Salem of blissfully "walking by the Sebago" in Maine only to awaken and find himself kicking Uncle Robert. It was at this time that he worried about his gun accidentally discharging and injuring the uncle who kept him in Salem and away from Raymond.

The result was an emotional knot that grew tighter with all attempts to loosen it.

When Hawthorne wrote about guardians, he expressed a conflict between importunate and not overly reasonable resentment and a desire to do justice to a genuine benefactor. The following, from "Passages from a Relinquished Work," shows more overtly than the polished tales the difficult process of assessment, of efforts to adjust complex feelings and square them with reality. The passage occurs when the itinerant narrator recalls conflicts with his guardian over the choice of a literary vocation:

> Though Parson Thumpcushion had an upright heart, and some called it a warm one, he was invariably stern and severe, on principle, I sup-pose, to me. With late justice, though early enough, even now, to be tinc-tured with generosity, I acknowledge him to have been a good and wise man after his own fashion. If his management failed as to myself, it suc-ceeded with his three sons. . . . We could neither change the nature that God gave me nor adapt his own inflexible mind to my peculiar character. Perhaps it was my chief misfortune that I had neither father nor mother alive; for parents have an instinctive sagacity in regard to the welfare of their children, and the child feels a confidence both in the wisdom and affection of his parents which he cannot transfer to any delegate of their duties, however conscientious. An orphan's fate is hard, be he rich or poor. As for Parson Thumpcushion, whenever I see the old gentleman in my dreams he looks kindly and sorrowfully at me, holding out his hand, as if each had something to forgive. (X, 406)

This condensed and balanced assessment, so different from the el-derly author's long and agonizing ones about Doctor Grimshawe, can serve as navigational guide in steering between the realities of Robert Manning and the mythic role he played in Hawthorne's in-ner life. The brief early portrait of Parson Thumpcushion, written before Hawthorne had expended a lifetime of psychic energy resist-ing domination by the internalized avuncular figure, seems both sane and sad. Both guardian and ward might have loved each other but for the fixed circumstances of their relationship. The complex interaction inevitably left traces both favorable and otherwise on Hawthorne's personality, affecting his self-image, sense of vocation, and attitudes toward authority.

Although Uncle Robert clearly intended to "make a man" of Nathaniel by separating him from his mother and by encouraging practical rather than literary endeavors, his powerful, decisive personality fostered instead self-distrust, dependency, and passivity. Of this cluster of traits, Hawthorne seemed most consciously aware of dependency, which throughout life he alternately sought and then resisted as shameful. Some innate tendency toward passivity seems to have been magnified by this dependency and by the enforced intimacy of sharing a bed with Uncle Robert over many years. The nephew's remarkable good looks and the uncle's prolonged bachelorhood lead inevitably to suspicions that despite the boy's expressed dislike of sleeping with his uncle, an erotic attachment developed between them. The relationship was almost certainly tinged with enough eros to encourage a passively feminine identification in Nathaniel, but one need not posit an actual "homosexual assault," as does biographer James R. Mellow.[10] The characters of Robert Manning and Nathaniel Hawthorne make the notion of an overt homosexual assault seem unlikely and unnecessary.

The evidence of Uncle Robert's probity and self-discipline make such a breach of trust improbable. His continued air of authority in dealing with Nathaniel would have been grossest hypocrisy after such a lapse and would likely have provoked rebellion far more immediate and direct than the subtle, surreptitious kind he generated. Given Nathaniel's sensitivity to nuances of behavior and his imaginative ability to extrapolate from slightest hints (an ability intensified by his earlier attempts to construe his family constellation), homosexuality need only have hovered in the atmosphere between them to have provoked guilty desires, dreams, and fantasies. The mere suggestion of homosexuality planted in such an active imagination would turn the "unpardonable sin" onto the imaginer, where it seems to have been located. Hawthorne's self-punitive tendency as well as his urge to be fair to a decent and well-meaning guardian (as expressed above in the passage on Parson Thumpcushion) make it more likely that the sin was in the fantasy of the nephew rather than in overt acts of the uncle. Hawthorne would not have been so covert, so self-canceling, in expressions of his anger had his uncle been guilty of homosexual "assault." Direct assault would probably have left Hawthorne more retributive, less conflicted, perhaps less seriously affected, than a subtle aura of seduction of which the source, whether self or other, was uncertain.

Assurance is not possible in such a matter, and there are additional possibilities that cannot be excluded definitively, such as a continuing reciprocal homosexual relationship, one or more overt acts provoked by the nephew rather than the uncle, and so forth. The hypothesis of an atmosphere ambiguously charged with homoerotic potential is not only more conservative than one of overt action but more consonant with the continuing course of the relationship and the ways it unfolded in Hawthorne's life. While speculating on the personal and literary sequelae of this relationship in which the real uncle became transformed into an avuncular figure, an internalized imago, we might find guidance in Erikson's schema of the stages of human development.

Having identified so far certain flaws in parental presence that marred Hawthorne's passage through Erikson's first stage of Basic Trust, we find a shaky foundation for the second, Autonomy versus Shame and Doubt. Once the child "standing on its own feet" has perceived how small it is in comparison to adults, it is especially subject to a sense of shame. The developmental task of the second stage is self-mastery or autonomy through maturation of sphincter control. If the child develops favorably and masters control of the contrary functions of "holding on and letting go," it can develop enough autonomy to overcome the feeling of shame. It is at this stage in Nathaniel's development that Uncle Robert began assuming the paternal functions that ideally should lead to Autonomy, which in turn is the foundation for the next stage, Initiative versus Guilt.

Without being rigidly schematic, we can discern personality traits distinctively Hawthornian in Shame and Doubt, the "defaults" of the second stage as Erikson defines them.

> Shame supposes that one is completely exposed and conscious of being looked at: in one word, self-conscious. One is visible and not ready to be visible; which is why we dream of shame as a situation in which we are stared at in a condition of incomplete dress, in night attire, "with one's pants down." But this, I think, is essentially rage turned against the self. He who is ashamed would like to force the world not to look at him, not to notice his exposure. He would like to destroy the eyes of the world. Instead he must wish for his own invisibility. . . .

Doubt is the brother of shame. Where shame is dependent on the consciousness of being upright and exposed, doubt . . . has much to do with a consciousness of having a front and a back—and especially a "behind." For this reverse area of the body, with its aggressive and libidinal focus in the sphincters and in the buttocks, cannot be seen by the child, and yet it can be magically dominated and effectively invaded by those who would attack one's power of autonomy. . . . This basic sense of doubt in whatever one has left behind forms a substratum for later and more verbal forms of compulsive doubting; this finds its adult expression in paranoiac fears concerning hidden persecutors and secret persecutions from behind and from within the behind.[11]

This sense of an exposed rear, an unguarded second self subject to unexpected attacks is, according to Erikson's theory, the origin of the divided self, of self-consciousness. In etymological progression from Erikson's "doubt" we might add doubleness and duplicity, both well-recognized Hawthornian traits. If "doubleness" and self-doubt do indeed stem from vulnerability about what is going on behind one's back, that is from the side visible to others but not to the self, any degree of homoerotic sensitization derived from Nathaniel's years of supervision by and sleeping with Uncle Robert could have evolved into a complex of permanent personality traits, even of that "duplicity" identified by D. H. Lawrence in *Studies in Classic American Literature*.

That the bedroom intimacy had psychic importance is evidenced by journal entries alluding to it over many years. During the important transition period of 1837–1838 Hawthorne recorded among a particularly reflective group of entries:

In the Duke of Buckingham's comedy—"The Chances"—Don Frederick says of Don John, (two noble Spanish gentlemen), "One bed contains us ever,"

immediately followed by:

A person, while awake and in the business of life, to think highly of another and place perfect confidence in him; but to be troubled with dreams, in which this seeming friend appears to act the part of a most deadly enemy. Finally it is discovered that the dream-character is the true one. The explanation would be—the soul's instinctive perception. (VIII, 181)

The last indicates to me that it was the "soul's instinctive perception" rather than an overt act that prompted young Nathaniel many years earlier to kick his uncle on awaking next to him in bed.

The adult Hawthorne retained strong feelings about men sleeping together. On an early visit to a Shaker community with Uncle Samuel, he was so impressed with their way of life that he considered joining them. But on a later visit with Herman Melville and Julian in 1851 he experienced a rush of disgust when he discovered their overly intimate sleeping arrangements:

> And then their utter and systematic lack of privacy; their close junction of man with man, and supervision of one man over another—it is hateful and disgusting to think of; and the sooner the sect is extinct the better—a consummation which, I am happy to hear, is thought to be not a great many years distant. (VIII, 465)

By this time a family man who had no thought of joining the Shakers, he surely overreacts in his vindictive desire for their extinction. The conjunction of ideas—"the junction of man with man" to violation of privacy and the "supervision of one man over another" directs us to the kind of problem generated by the avuncular relationship. The problem extends beyond sexual identity (no small matter) to more generalized relationships between self and others. The feeling of having been watched even in sleep, like that of being spied on behind one's back, could make almost desperate the need for privacy, for protecting one's self from the gaze of others. The result would be slyness, secretiveness, fear of intimacy, dread of exposure.

In Hawthorne's private notebooks as in his scenes of public shaming, the act of watching is perceived as aggressive, a penetration of the private sphere of the one who is seen. The notebooks record numerous permutations of this theme, one of the milder being, "The strange sensation of a person who feels himself an object of deep interest, and close observation, and various construction of all his actions by another person" (VII, 183). But for the connection of secret sexuality to public exhibition of shame we do best to consider the most famous example, the first scaffold scene of *The Scarlet Letter*, which, we recall, has as antecedent the exposure of ancestral Manning women to prolonged public shaming for the sin of incest.

Hawthorne sets his scene to maximize the agony of shaming. Displayed on a scaffold in broad daylight, Hester stands before public gaze for hours wearing the badge of shame, holding her sin-born child, and then is subjected to public inquisition into most intimate matters. The Puritan custom of public exposure of sexual sinners allows Hawthorne to introduce Hester with shame rather than guilt or penitence, a strategy that aligns our sympathy with her and against the Puritans. Shame, more primitive than guilt, and less a product of society and the superego, is more readily mobilized for empathic purposes. Says the narrator, "There can be no outrage, methinks, against our common nature . . . no outrage more flagrant than to forbid the culprit to hide his face for shame; as it was the essence of this punishment to do" (I, 55). Hester cannot hide her face from the stares of the hostile crowd; rather, from among these stares she identifies the coldest, most unloving of them all—that of her husband.

On this same scaffold Dimmesdale, privileged to enjoy subtler sublimations of his sexuality than is Hester, both dreads and desires to expose his own offenses. For him, too, the merciless probing of a single totally interested but coldhearted observer is more agonizing than the gaze of impersonal multitudes. Having lived under the same roof with Chillingworth, having been watched covertly (behind his back, as it were), so intently as to have become the principal object of the physician's highly sexualized scrutiny, and having himself come to practice self-flagellation as penance, Dimmesdale has more than mere adultery to expiate. By the conclusion of the novel he has far surpassed that first and simpler sin which earlier he had duplicitously exhorted Hester to reveal "if it be for [her] soul's good." Now a master of transformations, he attempts ambiguous self-exposure in the subtext or scarcely audible undertone of his final public address, the Election Sermon. Because this submerged meaning is audible only to Hester, who knows it already, he restates his insufficiently publicized message more openly by exposing his bare bosom, which again can be read only by those who already understand. He makes his final and also misinterpreted statement by embracing Pearl only moments before death enables him to hide his face forever. One motive for all this dubious public exposure is to escape the torturing scrutiny of Chillingworth. Paradoxically, even ambiguous or duplicitous publication of shame distributes it and helps dilute its corrosive sting, its "agenbyte of inwit."

Hester's shame, frontally visible in her pregnant belly and then in the letter on her bosom, is published before the world. Dimmesdale's, in contrast, is private, but continuously observed by the hostile eyes of the older man with whom he lives, generally thought to be his benefactor. This covert supervision of one man by another is a fictive transformation of Hawthorne's own dread of coldhearted judgment, of which we have already seen considerable evidence. Preferring inconspicuous mediocrity to being judged, he found even praise uncomfortable. Being judged made him doubt the very powers that he was protecting from the eyes of others.

The self-distrust for which his college friend Horatio Bridge so often castigated Hawthorne led to the ambivalent action of publishing his stories but without his own name attached. In the late 1830s, however, he made two moves indicative of a major emotional transition away from his "long seclusion." In 1837 he allowed Horatio Bridge to woo him into publishing *Twice-told Tales* under his own name, and in 1838 he became engaged to Sophia. Thus in close succession he committed himself to public acknowledgment of his own works and to the shared intimacy of marriage. "Publication," or going public, is exposure of oneself to public gaze, which may make one an object of unloving and uncontrollable scrutiny. Hawthorne countered this self-exposure by falling in love, which is to find an "other" whose gaze is not alien or hostile, but rather a loving mirror of one's best self. Indirectly, journals of this period indicate anxiety about this transition but also an interesting variant of the self-observer split. It had become internalized:

A perception, for a moment, of one's eventual and moral self, as if it were another person,—the observant faculty being separated, and looking intently at the qualities of the character. There is a surprise when this happens,—this getting out of one's self,—and then the observer sees how queer a fellow he is. (VIII, 178)

After departure from his mother's home to work in the Boston Custom House, Hawthorne did little writing beyond amorous letters to his betrothed. Now he had a new kind of exposure to fear—that personal intimacies would creep into his fiction and be displayed before the eyes of the world. He wrote in his journal: "Some most secret thing, valued and honored between lovers, to be hung up in a public place, and made the subject of remark by the city—remarks, sneers, laughter" (VIII, 185). He came to fear this because he had long been an observer of the intimacies of others, presumably as a way of controlling anxiety about being the object of speculation. By becoming the observing subject, he could reverse the subject-object relationship and put himself in the position of power. Increasingly he identified with those aloof spectators whom his fiction so often castigates, the "spiritualized Paul Pry" or the Coverdale watching unseen from a treetop observation post. Zenobia recognizes the aggression contained in Coverdale's spying by calling it "eye-shot."

The self-doubts, the uncertainty, the sense that even his best gifts were not entirely admirable did little to enhance Hawthorne's confidence in his own masculinity. In this area, too, he was split, and in ways recognizable to his contemporaries. Lowell, Longfellow, Alcott, Emerson, and Margaret Fuller all observed a doubleness of sensibility to which Julian Hawthorne also testified. These observers reported traits of coyness, passivity, and an intuitiveness regarded as feminine but mingled with genuine manliness. They reported the double sensibility without sneers, but rather as indicative of a fuller nature than uniformity would produce.[12]

This passive side of Hawthorne's nature sometimes amounted to what Edward Wagenknecht calls "a gift for being served."[13] Correspondence with publishers Ticknor and Fields shows Hawthorne demanding and receiving various time-consuming services from these busy men, from serious matters of financial investment and real estate selection to menial acts such as delivering parcels, directing mail, paying bills, purchasing wine and cigars, and even selecting a wrist watch for Sophia. These and similar services performed by Horatio Bridge and Franklin Pierce suggest that in adult life Hawthorne found substitutes for the oft-resented benefactions of his Manning uncle. His greater closeness with practical men like Bridge

and Pierce than with literary men like Emerson, Melville, or Longfellow suggests that despite his desire for independence, his long relationship with Robert Manning created a need for reliance on practical men along with a comparative distrust of literary ones.

Hawthorne's requirement for an ideal friend combined qualities
inherent in his problematic uncle—sternness and sensibility. In ex-
plaining to Sophia why John O'Sullivan, an amiable friend over
many years "never stirred [him] to any depth," he revealed what he
needed for deep friendship: "I should wish my friend of friends to be
a sterner and grimmer man than [O'Sullivan]. . . . the truest manly
delicacy is to be found in those stern, grim natures." [14] His own ability to combine delicacy and severity and his longing for continued
contact with men so constituted indicates that Uncle Robert's puritanical traits were partially elicited by a deep need emanating from
a boy afraid of his own feminine potential. The need for a rock to
rely on was so deep in both Melville and Hawthorne that neither
could be the completely satisfying "friend of friends" for the other.

Hawthorne transferred the avuncular relationship into his closest
male friendships. Even in the last year of his life he tended to inter-
pret the generosity of friends in this light. He wrote to James T.
Fields on October 18, 1863: "Julian told me that he borrowed $10 of
you. Please to record it against me, and don't let the little scamp
have any more. An Uncle (and your kindness places you in the position) is a very dangerous member of the family." [15]

Fields's familial behavior only earned him extra doses of Hawthorne's sadistic vindictiveness. Hawthorne wrote to Ticknor on
April 11, 1856: "Fields writes me that, in case of a war between
America and England, he is going to fight for the latter. I hope he
will live to be tarred and feathered, and that I may live to pour the
first ladleful of tar on the top of his head, and to clap the first handful
of feathers on the same spot. He is a traitor, and his English friends
know it." [16]

When Franklin Pierce became president of the United States he
had the power to bestow large gifts. Although Hawthorne had said
he wanted no reward for writing Pierce's campaign biography, both
he and Bridge waited like expectant sons to see whom the president
would favor. Hawthorne received the Liverpool consulate and tried
to console Bridge for his failure to receive an appointment. He wrote

in 1854: "Do not mistrust him; and when we three come to sit down together, as old men, let there be no ugly recollections to disturb our harmony. You say that it is easy for me to feel thus towards him, since he has done his very best in my behalf; but the truth is (alas for poor human nature!) *I should probably have loved him better if I had never received any favors from him*" (italics added).[17] Hawthorne repeated to Bridge his displeasure at having accepted Pierce's benefaction in December of the same year; "I envy you, for not having received any favors from him."[18] Letters to Bridge and others show Hawthorne becoming critical of Franklin Pierce only *after* receiving the consular appointment.

Throughout his tenure as consul Hawthorne was restless and dissatisfied, continually planning and threatening to resign. After he did resign, however, the friendship resumed its original loyalty, even tenderness. At the funeral of Pierce's wife, the ex-president, overwhelmed with grief at the graveside, reached over to draw up the collar of Hawthorne's coat to protect him from the December cold.[19] Hawthorne's loyalty to Pierce was such that he persisted against all advice in dedicating *Our Old Home* to the former president, who had become discredited throughout abolitionist New England for his pro-Union stand. It was in the company of this man that Hawthorne died.

Late in March of 1864 William D. Ticknor accompanied a debilitated Hawthorne on a trip south to benefit the latter's health. They met with bad weather, which they waited out in New York City, with Ticknor keeping close watch on Hawthorne's frail condition and looking for signs of improvement. When they reached Philadelphia, Ticknor developed a cold and died suddenly on April 10, leaving an appalled Hawthorne to make arrangements. Afterward Hawthorne staggered home to Sophia, barely able to walk from the train station.

Visibly ill and deeply shaken by witnessing this wayside death of his friend, he set off with Franklin Pierce only a few weeks later on a New England tour with an ostensibly similar purpose, traveling to regain health. Knowing his end was near and having had a shocking preview of death in a wayside hotel, he yet left home and Sophia to die peacefully in the company of this fatherly friend.

The depth and complexity of Hawthorne's filial feelings are revealed by his lengthy involvement with the story of Samuel Johnson's penance in the Uttoxeter marketplace. Repeatedly over a period of twenty-five years he told this story of the great man's compulsion to stand at his deceased father's bookstall at noon before the public gaze. Hawthorne seemed haunted by this image of the aged man of letters choosing public shame in the marketplace to expiate imagined guilt for contributing to his father's death. He recorded this public penance in his notebook in 1838, told it in *Biographical Stories for Children* (published 1842), and recounted his own pilgrimage to Litchfield and Uttoxeter in *Our Old Home*, his last completed work, published in 1863. In the version for children, he concluded the story of Samuel Johnson's fifty-year penance for a small act of filial impiety with,

> My dear children, if you have grieved—I will not say, your parents, but, if you have grieved—the heart of any human being, who has a claim upon your love, then think of Samuel Johnson's penance! Will it not be better to redeem the error now, than to endure the agony of remorse for fifty years? (VI, 248)

Like Samuel Johnson's fifty-year penance, the dashes above have a very wide embrace; within them are a repetition and a slight corrective pause that bridge the gap between the general human condition and Hawthorne's own, the gap between fathers and uncles. Hawthorne's equally long period of guilt, confusing a sense of implication in his father's early disappearance and unwitnessed burial with an inability to feel unmixed gratitude for his uncle's benefactions, was not subject to either expiation or resolution. Like Reuben Bourne, he suffered from an obscure sense that the guilt he felt toward his father-surrogate was reciprocal—each had failed the other. If Hawthorne dreamed of his guardian, it must have been as his Story Teller did, a figure who "looks kindly and sorrowfully at me, holding out his hand as if each had something to forgive" (X, 406–407).

By refusing to read Parson Thumpcushion's letter, the Story Teller kept open the possibility that his guardian finally had softened "his authority with the gentleness of love, as a father might, and even [admitted that] my errors had an apology in his own mistaken discipline." Burning the Parson's letter unread, like failing to attend Robert Manning's funeral, allowed imagination to supply what the soul required. Both real and fictive storytellers could cherish a hope that their guardians' final messages were words of "paternal wisdom, and love, and reconciliation, which [they] could not have resisted, had [they] but risked the trial" (X, 421).

THE DISPLACED CENTER

If we try to unravel the literary influences of Robert Manning from the personal, we find them closely interwoven, virtually continuous. Hawthorne's experience of paternal authority in a psychically unmanageable form which he had no acceptable way to challenge, led him to deal with it obliquely in his fiction—frequently in the triangular pattern of a young man, a sexually tempting young woman, and an older man who has a blighting effect on the younger one. Whichever aspect of Robert Manning the older man displays, the scientist or the successful man of affairs, he is always somehow related to the desirable woman. Often this older man works through the woman, using her as an agent or temptress through whom he gains access to the soul of the youth, to pry into his secret life or to tempt him into sin. In this process, the relationship between the two men comes to displace the sexual one as the center of the story.

The triangular pattern utilizing woman as the link between men appears in its purest form in *The Scarlet Letter*, but it recurs throughout Hawthorne's fiction. We are all aware that the scientist-sorcerer Chillingworth preys on the soul of young Dimmesdale in such a way that their relationship becomes the central one of the book. Only through the silent cooperation of the woman does this hideous intimacy become possible. A similar dynamic occurs in "Roger Malvin's Burial," where Dorcas forms the link creating a father-son relationship between Reuben and Roger Malvin. In "Rappaccini's Daughter" Beatrice is the lure that puts Giovanni under the power of her scientist father. Annie Hovenden's relationship to "the artist of the beautiful" is of less structural or emotional importance than is the artist's tie to her father. Similarly, the monk in *The Marble Faun* who lures Donatello into crime with the silent acquiescence of Miriam, has had an earlier, unspecified relationship with this exotic woman. The monk haunts Miriam, but his major function in the book is to corrupt Donatello, a purpose for which Miriam is an unwitting agent.

Critical attention to *The Blithedale Romance* has only recently begun to shift from Coverdale's prurient lust for Zenobia and his claim to love Priscilla and toward his most meaningful relationship, which is with Hollingsworth. In "The Crisis," the central chapter of the book (number fifteen out of a total of twenty-nine) Hollingsworth brushes aside as unimportant his involvement with the two women and makes a tremendous effort to woo Coverdale. Hollingsworth argues that joining his cause will give the wavering poet a purpose in life, so that he shall "never again feel the languor and vague wretchedness of an indolent or half-occupied man . . . there shall be strength, courage, . . . everything that a manly and generous nature should desire!" (III, 133). With tears in his eyes Hollingsworth holds out his hands and murmurs, "there is not the man in this wide world, whom I can love as I could you. Do not forsake me!" (III, 133). When asked how Zenobia and Priscilla fit into this scheme, Hollingsworth responds fiercely, "Why do you bring in the names of these women? . . . What have they to do with the proposal which I make you? . . . Will you devote yourself . . . to this great end, and be my friend of friends forever?" (III, 135).

Coverdale is fully responsive to Hollingsworth's magnetism ("I loved Hollingsworth, as has already been enough expressed") and even recognizes its sexual dimension ("There was a tenderness in his voice, eyes, mouth, in his gesture, and in every indescribable manifestation, which few men could resist, and no woman" [III, 28]). Nevertheless, Coverdale does resist this magnetism and remain in his own timid orbit. Of this refusal he says, "I never said the word . . . that cost me a thousandth part so hard an effort as did that one syllable. The heart-pang was not merely figurative, but an absolute torture of the breast. . . . It struck him, too, like a bullet. . . . One other appeal to my friendship . . . would completely have subdued me" (III, 135–136). Following this crisis (the rift between the two men) Coverdale takes leave of Blithedale, finding that "everything was suddenly faded."

Hollingsworth's seductive offer and Coverdale's pained refusal to accept his domination make this central chapter the emotional crisis of the book. Even if, as many critics believe, the Melville-Hawthorne relationship is a source of this intense male seduction and refusal, Hawthorne's earlier experience with his uncle may stand behind both. Ingrained resistance to seductive behavior by a dominating male may well explain Hawthorne's reserve before Melville's advances.[20] The power relationship between the men in *Blithedale* is that of a firmly defined older man to a wavering, uncommitted younger one even though their ages are not very different. Hollingsworth offers to make a man out of Coverdale if only the poet will identify with him. To designate Melville as the model for Hollingsworth is to ignore the fact that Melville was half a generation younger and at that time professionally less defined than Hawthorne. In fact, Melville wished to identify with the admired author of *Mosses from an Old Manse* and *The Scarlet Letter*, not the other way around.

Vis-à-vis the former blacksmith, a man to whom iron metaphors cling like magnetized particles, Coverdale is seen and sees himself as trivial, the polar opposite to Hollingsworth's inflexible purpose. Hollingsworth expressed the contrast: "I have always been in earnest, . . . I have hammered thought out of iron, after heating the iron in my heart! . . . Miles Coverdale is not in earnest, either as a poet or a laborer" (III, 68). Associated by his former occupation, blacksmithing, to the Mannings, and by metaphors of iron to fictional "iron men," like Peter Hovenden, Robert Danforth, Mr. Lindsey, and Judge Pyncheon, Hollingsworth (unlike Melville) is the quintessential anti-artist. Hollingsworth is the most successful of the lot in undermining the artist's self-esteem, for in this book distrust of the artistic enterprise is incorporated into the narrative itself, which is told in the very voice of the emasculated artist. The middle-aged Coverdale who tells the story many years after the events still tends to "exaggerate his own defects" and portrays himself as still petty, indolent, and essentially impotent.

Paradoxically, Hollingsworth's philanthropy is a perversion of his initial benevolence, a virtue misdirected by egotism into a destructive vice. Says Coverdale of such reformers, "And the higher and purer the original object, and the more unselfishly it may have been taken up, the slighter is the probability that they can be led to recognize the process, by which godlike benevolence has been debased into all-devouring egotism" (III, 71). Hollingsworth even tries to win Coverdale by assuming toward him a nurturant role, which leads to suspicion that Hollingsworth had used his kindness as a means of enthrallment when he tenderly nursed the younger man through an illness. Subjected to this destructive benevolence, the artist's mind tends to diabolize the benefactor, to cast him as a satanic seducer. In the iron features of the philanthropist the rest of mankind sees "only benignity and love," but the artist subjected to them at close quarters exaggerates the dichotomy. Apologizing for his exaggeration, Coverdale explains it as the only way to express his conflicting feelings: "In my recollection of his dark and impressive countenance, the features grew more sternly prominent than the reality, duskier in their depth and shadow, and more lurid in their light; the frown, that had merely flitted across his brow, seemed to have contorted it with an adamantine wrinkle. On meeting him again, I was often filled with remorse, when his deep eyes beamed kindly upon me, as with the glow of a household fire" (III, 71) This conflicted relationship resembles that of the Story Teller to Parson Thumpcushion—a guardian-ward relationship rather than that of an established older writer to an aspiring younger one like Melville.

Hawthorne's penchant for botanical imagery and his attitudes toward scientific experimentation owe much to the horticultural-scientific interests of Robert Manning. These attitudes were transmuted into fictional plots featuring obsessed scientists who use their high talents to pervert the innocence of nature. At the end of the catalogue of fruit trees offered for sale in 1843 from the Robert Manning estate is an item that probably amused the author of "Rappaccini's Daughter": "A large variety of Apples, budded on Paradise Stocks, for dwarfs." Hawthorne's tale of an "Eden of poisonous flowers" was written in 1844, two years after Robert Manning's death. The gardener-scientist Rappaccini is only one of many Hawthorne scientists who attempt to improve upon nature, utilizing their subtle knowledge of natural processes only to create something unnatural.

Horticultural improvements fall into the ambiguous area between nature and artifice. Whether hybridization of species, for example, is an extension of the natural or a lapse into the artificial is an insoluble question. One may, with Shakespeare's Perdita, shun "piedness" because crossbreeding seems adulterous and because the art of making hybrids "shares with great creating nature." On the other hand, one may take the larger view of Polixenes, that "Nature is made better by no mean, but Nature makes that mean" (*The Winter's Tale*, IV, iv). The conflict is as old as the Faust myth and equally unresolvable.

Hawthorne's stories of scientists vibrate to both views, but the plot resolutions always confirm Perdita's position that altering nature vies with the Creator and is therefore sinful. Alchemists like Rappaccini and Aylmer, as artists in living material but tamperers with the divine order, are both the highest and the lowest of mankind. Hawthorne's opposition to scientific endeavor, part of the Wordsworthian heritage, was intensified by his exposure to Robert Manning's pomological experiments. The attitude early expressed in "Rappaccini's Daughter" is like that expressed many years later in Hawthorne's notebooks. Of English attempts to grow peaches, pears, and figs in a cold climate by espaliering them to internally heated brick walls, he wrote, "It seems as if there must be something unreal and unsatisfactory in fruit that owes its existence to such artificial methods; it is at best, no more than half natural."[21]

Indeed, the narrator describes Rappaccini's experiments in language of sexual revulsion, for the experiments pervert "the most simple and innocent of human toils," gardening, into a species of adultery. By the light of Giovanni's inflamed imagination, the results "would have shocked a delicate instinct by an appearance of artificialness indicating that there had been such commixture, and, as it were, adultery of various vegetable species, that the production was no longer of God's making, but the monstrous offspring of man's depraved fancy" (X, 110).

The "depraved fancy" moves from vegetable adultery to innuendos of incest. The language of perverse sexuality and the repeated use of sibling metaphors suggest that the barrier between Giovanni and Beatrice is indeed this family taboo. Giovanni converses with Beatrice "like a brother," and whenever he appears she flies "to his side with confidence as unreserved as if they had been playmates from early infancy—as if they were such playmates still." Frederick Crews insinuates that the situation is Oedipal but does not explore the autobiographical connections. He says that "Rappaccini serves as a check upon frankness, an escape valve for dangerous auto-biographical meaning." Rappaccini with all his exaggerated and imaginatively intensified resemblances to Hawthorne's pomologist uncle is less an escape valve than the autobiographical link validating Crews's statement that "the hero's vacillations and fantasies are so urgently those of the author."[22]

MATTER VERSUS SPIRIT

The avuncular relationship was subject to many transformations, splits, and recombinations. Important among these is the polarization of spirit and matter, or artistry versus materialism. In a cluster of works treated here not chronologically but in an ascending sequence of intensity, the business or "man of affairs" aspect of Uncle Robert helps to define by opposition the spiritual nature of the artist. Although "The Snow-Image" is not greatly admired, it exemplifies the psychological center of this complex—the misguided, art-destroying or perhaps art-challenging nature of the man of worldly affairs even, or especially, when his intentions are entirely benevolent. Even from the early years when Hawthorne produced a newspaper, *The Spectator*, with his sister Louisa, he tended to treat the subject of benevolence with irony. In later work he frequently attributed benevolence to father-figures whose effects are unintentionally destructive. Note, for example, the following story idea listed in his notebook:

> A benevolent person going about the world, and endeavoring to do good to every body; in pursuance of which object, for instance, he gives a pair of spectacles to a blind man—and does all such ill-suited things. Beautiful pictures & statues to one intellectually blind. (VIII, 285)

In addition to an overemotional and outraged view of benevolence erupting into "The Snow-Image," an interesting minor detail connects it to the avuncular relationship—the use of Robert Manning's favorite tree outside the Lindsey house. This particular fruit appears in inconspicuous ways in story after story, always associated with a materialistic father-figure who blights the life or aspirations of a young person. "The Snow-Image" contains so inconspicuous a use of the pear tree that one must be alert to Hawthorne's special use of this word even to notice it. Among other trees, the pear grows outside the house of Mr. Lindsey, a commonsense, "matter-of-fact man, a dealer in hardware," who is off at his practical business affairs while his two children are creating a snow image so realistic that it dances and flits about the snowy garden. The poetic mother and the imaginative children immediately believe in the possibility of a living work of art, the ringlets of which are made from the lightest kind of snow found "on the lower branches of the pear tree." The artistic members of the family simply enjoy the beauty of the snow girl. But at the father's approach the snow birds fly off and the snow girl backs away. Thinking her to be an underdressed neighbor child, Mr. Lindsey insists on bringing her into the house and placing her next to the stove. Of course, the snow image melts into a puddle as a result of this practical man and his unimaginative benevolence. I would not make this much of so trivial and sentimental a story, which pits materialism against artistic faith, if at the conclusion Hawthorne had not erupted into furious moralizing against the father and people of his kind.

> One of its lessons, for instance, might be, that it behooves men, and especially men of benevolence, to consider well what they are about, and, before acting on their philanthropic purposes, to be quite sure that they comprehend the nature and all the relations of the business in hand. . . .
> But, after all, there is no teaching anything to wise men of good Mr. Lindsey's stamp. They know everything,—oh, to be sure!—everything that has been, and everything that is, and everything that, by any future possibility, can be. And, should some phenomenon of nature or Providence transcend their system, they will not recognize it, even if it come to pass under their very noses. (XI, 25)

By the time the snow image melts, Mr. Lindsey's commonsense materialism and misguided benevolence have been so thoroughly established through repetition that the rancor of this emotional tirade is gratuitous. Reiterating the word "benevolent," used at least three times previously in describing the father, Hawthorne loses authorial control and wreaks on the uncomprehending provider of material comforts a highly personal resentment.

In "The Artist of the Beautiful" the conflict moves from that of mindlessly benevolent father against artistic children to the displaced family triangle that we have so often noted in Hawthorne's work. Here the prudent, skeptical materialism of Annie Hovenden's father diminishes the self-respect of his undersized, unworldly apprentice, thus intensifying the dynamics of Hawthorne's characteristic male relationship. To the detriment of his story, he so polarizes the antithesis that Owen Warland becomes a ludicrous child-man and Peter Hovenden a devil of malevolent skepticism, each intensifying the extremism of the other.

In couching such an unrelenting allegory of matter and spirit in the terms of his father-surrogate relationship, Hawthorne risks much artistically, but his purpose may have been more therapeutic than artistic. At the time of writing, in 1844, he was facing the impracticality of his literary vocation as the economic support for his growing family. In this year of Una's birth he was living cheaply at the Old Manse but earning little and, though dedicating himself to writing, not producing much in quantity or quality. His lack of literary success and the realities of his family situation may have reawakened the disapproving voice of his guardian chiding him for not taking up more manly and remunerative work. Although happy in his family situation he may even have felt the absence of a familiar goad since the death of Uncle Robert two years earlier. Lacking any overt opposition from Uncle Robert and languishing instead in Sophia's enthusiastic encouragement, he may have written this strange story in order to reawaken the counterforce that had previously helped define him as an artist and piqued him into productivity. In this story he marshalls his arguments against the internalized avuncular figure in order to rouse himself into renewed creative activity.

Paradoxically, Peter Hovenden's materialistic influence helps to shape Owen Warland's artistic career by repeatedly challenging his creative spirit: "There was nothing so antipodal to his nature as this man's cold, unimaginative sagacity, by contact with which everything was converted into a dream, except the densest matter of the physical world. Owen . . . prayed fervently to be delivered from him. . . . Owen never met this man without a shrinking of the heart. Of all the world, he was the most terrible, by reason of a keen understanding, which saw so distinctly what it did see, and disbelieved so uncompromisingly in what it could not see" (X, 456 and 463). Hovenden's unimaginative utilitarianism and Robert Danforth's virile strength diminish Owen's personal life but by their very opposition serve to refine, or to Platonize, his conception of art. Peter Hovenden is Annie's father and Robert Danforth becomes her husband. Annie serves as Owen's muse, but her father is more important in shaping his career.

Hawthorne was trying to work out serious personal and vocational problems in this story. His reduction of Owen's physical self to elfin dimensions is a bizarre way of expressing the insubstantiality he felt vis-à-vis men of action. Against little Owen are two such men, a skeptical older one who denigrates the impracticality of his endeavors and a brawny younger one who is Hovenden's ideal of young manhood—a blacksmith, a worker in iron, a laborer among realities, and therefore worthy of wife and family. Each intrusion of the Hovendens into Owen's private world causes a destruction of his work following which Owen declines morally and physically, first into drunkenness, then into infantile obesity, and finally into spiritual lethargy. When not functioning artistically, the story implies, the artist is even grosser, more material, than the reality-oriented men he scorns. If he cannot be more than such men, he becomes less. Owen regresses into a deep sloth that eventually proves to be not a death but a sleep of the spirit, a prerequisite to his spiritualization of matter, his one great burst of achievement. Owen's butterfly, like Hawthorne's story, is an allegory of self- and artistic reintegration. Like a real butterfly, Owen emerges from a wormlike condition after a period of dormancy to enjoy a brief moment of flight that justifies all the preparation. In putting Owen through phases of creativity and decline, periods of energetic invention, then successive destructions of his work followed by intervals of lethargy, Hawthorne was examining his own oscillations. Combating doubts about himself and his work, he used the story to revive the drama of psychic antitheses that had so long stimulated his artistic energies.

Owen works to spiritualize the clockwork mechanism, a measure of time that in youth he scorned in favor of eternal values. But the artist trying to transcend time is yet in his own person subject to time as measured out by his inner clock and the rhythms of his creative ebb and flow. The forty-year-old author who had not yet validated his artistic vocation with a substantial book was surely invested in the long disquisition on time, death, and the artist that follows immediately on Owen's recovery of his talents: "He was incited to toil the more diligently, by an anxiety lest death should surprise him in the midst of his labors. This anxiety, perhaps, is common to all men who set their hearts upon anything so high, . . . that life becomes of importance only as conditional to its accomplishment. So long as we love life for itself, we seldom dread losing it. When we desire life for the attainment of an object, we recognize the frailty of its texture" (X, 466–467). Owen Warland, the superior watchmaker, tries to transcend time much as his creator tried to idealize the actualities of daily life, but neither could do so without first incorporating the message of time. Spurred by chronological urgencies to deeper integration of this message, both had first to conquer the time-consuming sin of spiritual sloth, which today is more often called depression.

More pointedly, both transcended their own deficiencies by incorporating and inwardly transforming their materialistic opposites. In his deepest stage of regression and just before his final reawakening, Owen had lost his "faith in the invisible" and come to trust only "what his hand could touch" (X, 466), and in these terms he presents his mechanical marvel to Annie, now Mrs. Robert Danforth, "You shall know, and see, and touch, and possess, the secret" (X, 469). Before presenting his life's work to Annie and her "iron men" Owen has come to terms with their incomprehension and prepared himself for the philistine reception that his work indeed receives: "He knew that the world, *and Annie as the representative of the world*, whatever praise might be bestowed, could never say the fitting word, nor feel the fitting sentiment which should be the perfect recompense of an artist. . . . Not at this latest moment, was he to learn that the reward of all high performance must be sought within itself or sought in vain" (X, 472–473; italics added). But even in this exalted state Owen is not above feeling a "secret scorn" for the incomprehension behind Annie's wondering admiration, a scorn so subtle that only an artist would discern it. Annie's role as uncomprehending muse (itself a product of the artist's enhancing imagination) is a lesser stimulus to the creative process than is her father's belittling provocation. Like the author putting his book before the public, Owen has prepared himself in advance for the world's response and, in anticipation, largely risen above it. Having recognized the Doubting Thomas within himself, he can forgive it in others. Realizing that in the process of producing the work he has become a different person from the one who conceived it, he discovers that the butterfly now has a different meaning for him. He can do without the perceptible representation of his ideal, for his real achievement is in what he has become, and this his public and perhaps even his muse, cannot fully appreciate. In this odd little story we can see the forty-year-old Hawthorne reviving his old antagonist in order to rally himself for a renewed assault on the citadel of fame and rehearsing various prospective scripts for the outcome. Should he fail to achieve fame he could always dismiss it as "the last infirmity of noble minds."

THE HOUSE OF MANY GABLES

In *The Scarlet Letter* Hawthorne achieved a substantial success durable enough to be mauled by a century of critics without either collapsing or yielding up all its secrets. Less ephemeral than Owen Warland's butterfly, it nevertheless shares the position of a culminating achievement, the center of Hawthorne's reputation. He intended the next novel to be a sunny antidote to the gloom and sorrow of the first. He deliberately interlarded *The House of the Seven Gables* with episodes of comic relief, but despite these intentions it emerged the most death- and ancestor-ridden of his completed romances.

Seven Gables is also the most home- and family-centered of these works, not only utilizing familial materials but multiplying each of the key elements. It features a toweringly oppressive paternal figure who epitomizes an ancestral line of just such figures. Judge Jaffrey Pyncheon has not just a single quavering artist as victim of his domination but two artists, three if we include the narrator who forgets his carefully cultivated urbanity when dealing with this formidable "kindred enemy."

The paternal figure who oppresses so many characters and so strongly affects his creator gathers energy not only from Hawthorne's political confrontation with Charles W. Upham but also from aspects of his maternal and paternal lineage as well. There are indeed likenesses between Pyncheon and Upham, who was responsible for Hawthorne's "decapitation" as Surveyor of the port of Salem, and when this was recognized, Hawthorne did not demur. "Like Judge Pyncheon, Upham had served one term in each branch of the state legislature, was (in Hawthorne's view) a hypocrite, and had a forebear who was a Loyalist during the American Revolution." [23]

The Judge's political connections may tie him to Hawthorne's recent political enemy, and his witch-persecuting predecessors who incurred the curse of Matthew Maule certainly link him to Hawthorne's Puritan forefathers, but other traits also connect him to the Mannings. Jaffrey Pyncheon's obsession with obtaining the deeds to eastern lands in Maine, as well as his commercial speculations and horticultural pursuits suggest the Mannings in general and Uncle Robert in particular. The portrayal of Judge Pyncheon is a calculated mixture of ancestral Hathorne and contemporary Manning, of cruelty, greed, and hypocritical benevolence, including even an attenuated sensibility. In his horticulture and his hankering for the quite unnecessary eastern lands Pyncheon even displays a touch of pastoralism, a longing for a home elsewhere that somewhat extenuates his greed. His frequently mentioned sensuality differs from anything Hawthorne wrote about his "steeple crowned" Puritan ancestors.

The chapter called "The Scowl and the Smile" distinguishes the Judge's public image of smiling benevolence from the oppressive, blighting effect he has on his relatives. The smiling public man is depicted in a remarkably long, breathless sentence of heavy irony. Even the punctuation serves an ironic purpose:

The purity of his judicial character, while on the bench; the faithfulness of his public service in subsequent capacities; . . . his remarkable zeal as president of a Bible society; *his unimpeachable integrity as treasurer of a Widow's and Orphan's fund; his benefits to horticulture, by producing two much-esteemed varieties of the pear,* and to agriculture, through the agency of the famous Pyncheon bull; the cleanliness of his moral deportment, for a great many years past; the severity with which he had frowned upon, and finally cast off, an expensive and dissipated son, delaying forgiveness un-til within the final quarter of an hour of the young man's life; his prayers at morning and eventide, and graces at mealtime; his efforts in further-ance of the temperance-cause; his confining himself, since the last attack of the gout, to five diurnal glasses of old Sherry wine; the snowy white-ness of his linen, the polish of his boots, the handsomeness of his gold-headed cane. . . . the smile of broad benevolence wherewith he made it a point to gladden the whole world;—what room could possibly be found for darker traits, in a portrait made up of lineaments like these! (II, 230–231; italics added)

All of the above, in addition to much that has been omitted, is one long sentence, syntactically so overwhelming that it virtually oblite-rates the sly allusion to Uncle Robert in the Judge's pear-hybridizing activities.

Phoebe found herself "quite overpowered by the sultry, dog-day heat, as it were, of benevolence, which this excellent man diffused out of his great heart into the surrounding atmosphere;—very much like a serpent, which, as a preliminary to fascination, is said to fill the air with his peculiar odor" (II, 119). She is unwilling to yield him a cousinly kiss because "the man, the sex, somehow or other, was entirely too prominent in the Judge's demonstrations of that sort" (II, 118). The Judge's smile of benevolence is offset by the scowl made visible by Holgrave's "prophetic picture," a daguerreotype that penetrates the public image and reveals the Judge's true familial character.

As the representative of the Actual, this man of iron is the ulti-mate anti-artist whose pride is in never mistaking a dream for a real-ity. Against his inflexible will Hawthorne pits different kinds of art-ists, and the distinctions among them indicate developments in his thinking on this subject. Given the fact that Clifford had a lifetime of painful experience with Judge Pyncheon and Holgrave had only an ancestral grudge, it is odd that both artists felt oppressed by him in very similar ways. Holgrave reacts as personally to the Judge as does Clifford but often has to disguise his animus as political theory. After spouting on for several pages about the past as a "giant's dead body" lying upon the present, the power of the dead over the living, the control of the dead over all aspects of life, Holgrave finally fo-cuses so violently on Jaffrey, the living incarnation of all the past mischief, that Phoebe questions his sanity.

Although Holgrave is young and flexible and has had an amazing variety of life experiences for his twenty-two years, he talks like one immobilized by the past, which is closer to Clifford's situation. Indeed, when Clifford breaks out in a brief resurgence of vitality and energy he espouses Holgrave's progressivist views on houses and inheritances. As different as they at first appear, the aged aesthete and the practical Yankee stem from a common source. As artistic men at different ends of the age spectrum, they represent phases of response to that "kindred enemy" or "Evil Destiny," the corpulent embodiment of authoritarian oppression.

The bursting of one of Clifford's soap bubbles on Jaffrey's nose epitomizes the Judge's effect on an artist who grew up in his presence. Fragile art and massive materialism collide much as they do in "The Snow-Image" and "The Artist of the Beautiful":

> "Aha, Cousin Clifford!" cried Judge Pyncheon. "What! Still blowing soap-bubbles!"
> The tone seemed as if meant to be kind and soothing, but yet had a bitterness of sarcasm in it. As for Clifford, an absolute palsy of fear came over him. Apart from any definite cause of dread, . . . he felt that native and original horror of the excellent Judge, which is proper to a weak, delicate, and apprehensive character, in the presence of massive strength. Strength is incomprehensible by weakness, and therefore the more terrible. There is no greater bugbear than a strong-willed relative, in the circle of his own connections. (II, 172)

The fragile aesthete Clifford is an aged Owen Warland cheated of his creative opportunity by the Judge's perfidy. Having spent thirty years imprisoned, he emerges too late to recover the use of his talents. In fact, the stifling of these gifts has left him self-centered and sensual. He develops a voracious appetite for food and a somewhat leering voyeurism with respect to Phoebe's developing womanhood. His excessive carnal appetites recall Owen Warland's during periods of regression and, like Owen's, mirror the sensual qualities of his opponent.

Clifford's true release from imprisonment comes only after the death of Jaffrey, when he boards a train with Hepzibah, plunges into a throng of humanity, and enjoys a brief recrudescence of emotional and intellectual vitality. In a sudden flare of eloquence he announces the advent of the future, of change, of freedom from past tyrannies, in words much grander than Holgrave's and always tied to the image of the dead man sitting upright in the house of seven gables. Feeling rejuvenated, the exuberant Clifford pronounces the message of time:

> No longer ago than this morning, I was old. I remember looking in the glass, and wondering at my own gray hair, and the wrinkles, . . . and the prodigious trampling of crow's feet about my temples! It was too soon! I could not bear it! Age had no right to come! I had not lived! . . . [Now] I feel in the very hey-day of my youth, with the world and my best days before me! (II, 262)

But Clifford is carried away by exuberance, as the many exclamation points suggest. The two gray "owls" return tired to their nest, their situation materially and emotionally improved, but with no great future before them. Clifford's day is past and he has only decadent aestheticism to show for his lost talents.

Holgrave, as descendant of the Maules, derives his talents and his motivation from ancestral sources. As a hypnotist and seer he turns the inherited Maule gift into an instrument of revenge so powerful that he fears its exercise. His chosen medium of photography seems to be a recapturing of the aggressive aspect of vision. By photographing Jaffrey unawares, Holgrave can penetrate his hypocritical mask and thereby his private sphere. Holgrave's photography, then, is the enhancement of his ancestral Maule gift of "seeing" and by seeing, controlling events. Success in his sworn mission is too frightening for Holgrave. The extinction of the male Pyncheon line in the deaths of Jaffrey and his son is so like the fulfillment of a parricidal wish that Holgrave virtually renounces his prophetic powers in fear of their efficacy. His decision to marry Phoebe, made impulsively in the presence of his defunct enemy, and his entire swing over to conservatism seem a retreat before visionary powers that are simply too dangerous.

Until the death of Jaffrey he had been in no haste "to betake himself within the precincts of common life." Hawthorne makes it quite clear that Holgrave had probably intended to let his romantic inclinations "die in their undeveloped germs" (II, 305). With his ancestral enemy dead, however, he leaps impulsively into the most conventional of marriages. His failure of nerve, like Clifford's brief recrudescence, is a direct response to Jaffrey's death.

The narrator's response to the open-eyed corpse is no less remark-able. He positively gloats over the seated body of the older man, taunting it with the passage of time, the fly that buzzes on its nose, the unreaped honors that the Judge had hoped to enjoy but never will, the unfinished business on his schedule, which slyly includes, "To give orders for some fruit-trees of a rare variety, to be deliver-able at his country-seat, in the ensuing autumn. Yes; buy them, by all means; and may the peaches be luscious in your mouth, Judge Pyncheon!" (II, 272). The vindictive chapter spoken entirely in the author's voice concludes,

> And, all these great purposes accomplished, will he walk the streets again, with that dog-day smile of elaborate benevolence, sultry enough to tempt flies to come and buzz in it? . . . Will he bear about with him—no odious grin of feigned benignity, insolent in its pretence, and loathsome in its falsehood—but the tender sadness of a contrite heart? . . . Rise up, Judge Pyncheon! . . . Rise up before it is too late. . . . Canst thou not brush the fly away? Art thou too sluggish? Thou man, that hadst so many busy projects, yesterday! Art thou too weak, that wast so powerful? (II, 282–283)

Sadistically entitled "*Governor* Pyncheon," this chapter empha-sizes the Judge's unfulfilled ambitions just approaching fruition at the time of his death. Could the narrator make room for compassion, he might pity a man who dies suddenly with his schedule filled with anticipated events—social, gustatory, commercial, and political. But no, he gloats over the figure seated with open eyes (so like Reuben Bourne's dreaded image of Roger Malvin), punctuating his glee with reference to the ticking clock in Judge Pyncheon's motionless hand, the "never-ceasing throb of Time's pulse," which continues after its owner's has stopped.* With demonic pleasure the narrator exults in being able to look at the powerless Judge whose open eyes can no longer judge him. The hated face disintegrates with the loss of sight, and the meaning of death now penetrates even the exulting survivor: "There is no face! An infinite, inscrutable blackness has annihilated

---

*This chapter bears uncanny resemblance to Emily Dickinson's "A Clock stopped / Not the Mantel's" which also contrasts the continuance of measurable time after the stopping of the inner metronome and concludes with "Decades of Arrogance be-tween / The Dial life / and Him."

sight! Where is our universe? All crumbled away from us; and we, adrift in chaos, may hearken to the gusts of homeless wind, that go sighing and murmuring about, in quest of what was once a world!" (II, 276–277). The "we" shows a moment of human identification before the taunting resumes.

When the tension becomes unbearable, the shop bell rings, breaking the spell as does the knocking at the gate in *Macbeth*, and "we breathe more freely, emerging from Judge Pyncheon's presence into the street before the seven gables" (II, 283), releasing both narrator and reader from the weighty presence of the seated corpse. All nature reflects this release in the sunshine and verdure of the next chapter. Of all the "vegetable productions" that rejoice in the death of the Judge, none seems so alive as the Pyncheon elm, which now is "in perfect verdure, except a single branch . . . [which] had been transmuted to brightest gold. It was like the golden branch, that gained Aeneas and the Sibyl admittance into Hades" (II, 285). This prophetic branch, autumnal in spring and reminiscent of Reuben's withered branch in "Roger Malvin's Burial," hangs over the doorway inviting passers-by to enter and learn the secrets of the house.

Part of the resurgence of natural and communal life following Jaffrey's death is the reappearance of the Italian organ-grinder, whose mechanical minstrelsy seems a counterpart to Holgrave's photography. This vagabond musician appears in intuitive response to the death of the anti-artist within the house.

> It really seemed as if the touch of genuine, though slight and almost playful emotion, communicated a juicier sweetness to the dry, mechanical process of his minstrelsy. These wanderers are readily responsive to any natural kindness—be it no more than a smile, or a word, itself not understood, but only a warmth in it—which befalls them on the roadside of life. They remember these things, because they are the little enchantments which, for the instant—for the space that reflects a landscape in a soap-bubble—build up a home about them. (II, 293)

This mechanical "grinding out of jigs and waltzes" before the collapse of the Pyncheon world is the final insult art tosses at Jaffrey's "solid unrealities." The insolent notes of the vagabond musician glancingly allude to the author's abandoned fantasy of becoming a roving storyteller and presage the union of Maule and Pyncheon, which restores social order by taming Holgrave. Had Holgrave not been so dangerously successful at wizardry as to witness the fall of the house of Pyncheon and to catch Phoebe in his "web of sorcery" (that is, if he had not absorbed some Pyncheon traits in combating them), such an itinerant artist might have been more at home in the still virgin "eastern lands" in Waldo County, Maine, than in Jaffrey's own country seat. Holgrave's acceptance of property and limits instead of "lighting out for the territory" prepares us for the fact that when Hawthorne is ready to leave ancestral Massachusetts, he will head not for the Maine frontier but for still more ancestral Europe.

FIVE

Doctor Grimshawe and Other Secrets[1]

Such whenas *Archimago* them did view,
He weened well to worke some uncouth wile,
Eftsoones untwisting his deceiptfull clew,
He gan to weave a web of wicked guile.

The Faerie Queene, II, 8

[Doctor Grimshawe] must have the air, in the Romance, of a
sort of magician, without being called so; and even after his
death, his influence must still be felt. Hold on to this. A dark,
subtle manager, for the love of managing, like a spider sitting in
the center of his web, which stretches far to east and west.

Doctor Grimshawe's Secret

ARCHIMAGO'S WEB

Until the very end of his life, perhaps especially at the end of it,
Hawthorne struggled with unresolved feelings about his guardian.
Of all his works, *Doctor Grimshawe's Secret* contains the most autobiographical material and is the most preoccupied with father-
substitutes. Feeding into this unfinished work are materials drawn
from the author's own life experiences—his emotional return to the
land of his fathers, his early reading in Spenser, and residual feelings
about his own childhood. All four of the late romances deal with
personal preoccupations of the sick and aged author. To a greater or
lesser degree, these works focus on a central set of symbols and situations that Hawthorne seemed unable to discard even when he was

unsure of their meaning and value. Among these are the scientist whose demon or familiar is an enormous spider, an American claimant to an ancestral English estate, and the legend of the Bloody Footstep.

Doctor Grimshawe's Secret is really a fuller version of *The Ancestral Footstep*, abandoned when Hawthorne decided to write *The Marble Faun* after his visit to Rome. The major difference between the two English romances is that *The Ancestral Footstep* begins in England, with the American claimant to an ancestral English estate wandering on the grounds of the family mansion, whereas *Grimshawe* starts with the orphaned hero's childhood in America. The American opening provides two important elements absent in the earlier version—the figure of the spider-cultivating guardian, Doctor Grimshawe, and a transatlantic basis for satirical American-English contrasts that were part of Hawthorne's original intention.

Both grew out of Hawthorne's experiences in England. As American consul to Liverpool, he met many deluded Americans who thought they had claims on English estates and titles, even one who thought he was related to Queen Victoria. Although Hawthorne had no such delusion, he was greatly moved by the thought of having returned to the home of his ancestors and even played with the notion that he was a reincarnation of the first emigrant to America, now returned to join the broken thread of family history. He recorded this idea in his notebook of October 9, 1854,

My ancestor left England in 1635. I return in 1853. I sometimes feel as if I myself had been absent these two hundred and eighteen years—leaving England just emerging from the feudal system, and finding it on the verge of Republicanism. It brings the two far separated points of time very closely together, to view the matter thus.[2]

Asking James T. Fields to inquire of an antiquarian from just what part of England the first Hathorne had emigrated, he wrote: "Of all things, I should like to find a gravestone in one of these churchyards, with my own name upon it, although for myself, I should wish to be buried in America."[3] The phrasing indicates that thoughts of his own death accelerated his lifelong search for origins, a combination that surfaces in *Doctor Grimshawe's Secret*. For both the hero of this book and its author, the approach to death and to ancestral origins leads back to a reexamination of the meaning of childhood experiences.

As this chapter will show, there is a good deal of disguised autobiography in the Salem childhood of Ned Etherege, brought up by a bachelor foster-father who educated him conscientiously but unlovingly. Hawthorne wrote the childhood section twice, reworking and expanding what was to have been a mere preliminary to the English part of the romance, and in the process he reexamined the determining power of childhood relationships. As the protagonist comes to realize the extent to which his whole life was dominated by his foster-father, the book loses its satirical purpose and becomes a psychological study of the process of enthrallment. Doctor Grimshawe's pseudoscientific obsession with spiders evolves into the symbol of the enmeshing web of ever larger extent, while the Doctor himself becomes the epitome of all Hawthorne's wizard figures who control the destinies of his characters and often the plots of his tales. Some of Doctor Grimshawe's fictive predecessors are the wizard who stage-manages the plot of "Alice Doane's Appeal," the sorcerer Chillingworth who manipulates the soul of Arthur Dimmesdale, and Doctor Portsoaken, who directs the Faustian endeavors of Septimius Felton.

The device of the controlling wizard may appear to be derived from Hawthorne's interest in the Salem witch trials or from Gothic romances, but its most direct source is probably Hawthorne's early reading of and lifelong interest in Spenser's *Faerie Queene*. In this work Archimago, or the ruling magician, is the protean source of delusion whose powers are unlimited by time and space. In Book II Spenser calls the arch enchanter's guile a web, the leading metaphor of *Doctor Grimshawe's Secret*. In fact all the central symbols as well as aspects of characters in this uncontrolled romance can be found in Book II of *The Faerie Queene*—the magician's web, the casket of golden treasure, an orphaned child born after his father's disappearance bearing on his hands blood that cannot be washed away, the vine-covered entrance to the Bower of Bliss, and descent into the underworld. Although Ned Etherege is not an allegorical figure, he is, like Sir Guyon, engaged in a quest involving sequential experiences leading to the climactic one of entering a tempting and forbidden place. Like Sir Guyon, Ned Etherege is guided in his English experiences by a kindly old man, the Palmer, later called Pearson and the Pensioner.

One may well wonder why use of an allegorical model should have produced so unmanageable a book that the author constantly struggles to locate his theme, to define his symbols, and to portray characters who finally escape all coherent formulation. Certainly Hawthorne does not use Spenser as James Joyce uses Homer. Employing the pattern of quest romance, Hawthorne depicts a failed search for an unmentionable goal, setting up expectations of circular fulfillment that he cannot realize, utilizing symbols like a casket full of golden hair that he cannot connect to his plot, and creating characters who refuse to maintain the needed archetypal and dialectical clarity. The quest of Sir Guyon underlies *Grimshawe* but does not help Hawthorne master his materials.

Like *Septimius Felton*, *Doctor Grimshawe's Secret* was left uncompleted at Hawthorne's death; both were abandoned in a fragmentary state that mingles narrative portions with the author's working notes. *Septimius*, which was edited by Una Hawthorne with the help of Robert Browning, contains a few bracketed passages that show how the author intended to amplify or change certain parts. In editing *Grimshawe* Julian Hawthorne also retained some of the author's working notes, smoothed out the names of the characters (Grimshawe is variously named Etherege, Ormskirk, Archdale, Gibbiter, and Norman Hanscough), and selected one of the two versions of Ned Etherege's childhood. In addition to bestowing on the manuscript the title *Doctor Grimshawe's Secret*, Julian made a great many other changes that render the text far more orderly than it was. In 1954 Edward Davidson published a reconstruction of the original manuscript with all its variants, errors, recapitulations, and lengthy working notes.[4] In 1977 Davidson, along with Claude M. Simpson and L. Neal Smith, issued a revised edition as part of volume XII of the Centenary Edition.[5] The reconstructed manuscript alternates narrative with the author's brooding meditations on his fictional problems, revealing Hawthorne struggling to order his material, a process that earlier was not difficult for him. Material that he considered the very backbone of *Doctor Grimshawe's Secret*, such as that on the secret prisoner, remains in the notes and scarcely enters the narrative at all.

With its interrupted narrative, lengthy authorial meditations, and prevailing dream-state, the reconstructed manuscript of *Grimshawe* is a text overrun with interpretation, the author constantly commenting on the process of writing it, searching for meaning among fictionalized shards of his own childhood experiences, trying sometimes to evolve meaning and sometimes to evade it. It contains a collection of characters whose motivations are as puzzling to the author as they are to his hero. With the exception of Elsie they are a fixed constellation of older men who dominate the hero's consciousness successively yet in a sense simultaneously. These men are extremely important in defining the meaning of his life. Their influence vacillates continually between beneficent and destructive, with all but one of these older men bifurcating at some point in the story into good and evil before finally collapsing into hopeless ambiguity. Even though trying hard to assess the precise value to the protagonist of each of these older men, Hawthorne was unable to decide on their character or motivation. The interest and the problem of *Doctor Grimshawe's Secret* lie in the fact that the quest is the same for both hero and author.

The protagonist, Ned Etherege, is at a point of stasis in his life. He has behind him achievements of a political nature and ahead of him a choice between an American diplomatic future and an English title. Before he can choose he must find out who he is, what his roots are, what values he places on his American and his English origins. In other words, he seeks his future in his past. This is where the second or English section of the romance opens—at a point of stasis or stocktaking during which Etherege must clarify to what extent he is determined by his orphaned childhood, whether he is a free American with no past at his back—or whether he is bound by blood ties to a static but restful English title. Is he free, or is he determined by his childhood relation to Doctor Grimshawe, whose long arm seems to reach beyond death and across the ocean?

In this book, as in *The House of the Seven Gables*, there are forces pulling in contrary directions. The protagonists keep exclaiming, "Onward, onward," but are palpably urged backward, toward the past. The urge toward the past, felt in the very blood, is a pull toward identification with the dead fathers, toward peace, rest, home, whereas the onward urge is treated as the manly, normal, optimistic American thrust into the unknown and unmastered future. In *Grimshawe* the author repeatedly reminds himself, "Try back, try back again," whereas his protagonist repeatedly tries to counteract the backward tug with Holgrave's words, "Onward, onward." Thus in both late English romances, the two countries, England and America, take on symbolic values, and the frequent debates between the heroes and representative Englishmen about the respective merits of the two countries involve the author's inner debate between two forces within himself. The two countries represent past and future, parent and child, restful return and onward striving, giving in to a predetermined destiny and manfully forging one's own. It is not surprising, then, that the debate is so often taken up in *Grimshawe* and so often ends in a draw, one statement canceling out another.

The two forces coexist in genuine tension. "America" is the conscious drive to be free, not only politically but psychically. The orphaned Ned Etherege acts out the dangerous dominance of the past, while his creator, though emotionally bound to him, effectively bars him from consummating this return. The author plans two routes of return to the past and then closes them off. Violating the romance pattern on which the book was to be based, he forbids the marriage to Elsie and invalidates Ned's claims to nobility. The almshouse foundling is not, after all, a nobleman in disguise; he does not marry the heroine; either he dies or remains on the road. Despite heroic attempts at circular closure, Hawthorne is unable to complete the pattern of quest romance.

What started out as a satirical international novel ridiculing Americans trying to claim hereditary English estates becomes a psychological study truly remarkable for its time. In it a man on the balancing point between past and future enters a time interval during which his mind relinquishes rational control and moves dreamily backwards, forwards, and sideways, making connections among various aspects of his life. Wandering blissfully around the part of England to which he was brought up to believe he is the claimant, he is shot by what he thinks is a stray bullet. This injury, which turns out to be intentional, frees him from all purposeful activity for a long period of recuperation during which his mind wanders uncontrolled. For the duration of the romance, Etherege's actions and thoughts remain dreamlike, directed by his psychological needs rather than by conscious purposes. He experiences strange recognitions and affinities generating a compulsion to reenter the family mansion at any cost, to reclaim the estate to which he believes he was born, to relinquish his American striving and rootlessness, and to find rest in English peace and ancestral soil.

Having been brought up on the edge of an American graveyard by a demented scientist, he finds England to be what it was to Hawthorne himself, "our old home." Etherege seeks in England both his origins and a peace like unto death. The grave dominates both his childhood and his English experiences. Etherege insists on entering the ancestral mansion despite frequent passionate warnings that to do so is to risk death. Although the forward action of the book points toward losing himself in the past, toward annihilation by the master of the estate whom he more and more wishes to displace, the effective force is the backward one of reevaluating his personal past with his father-surrogate, Doctor Grimshawe. As he moves deeper and deeper into the dream-state he finds that his personal past is the determinant of whatever future he has. Despite his patriotic declarations that he is a free, unfettered American, his life has been controlled by the spider-loving Doctor. The young man is, in fact, enmeshed in his guardian's enormous web.

CHILDHOOD ON THE EDGE OF A CEMETERY

Of the two versions of Ned Etherege's childhood with the grim Doctor, Julian used the second in his edition of the book. In both versions the Doctor's character and the nature of his relationship to the two foundling children evolve gradually. In general, the first draft, entitled "Etherege" in the Centenary Edition, depicts a kindly but eccentric doctor whose motives are on the whole benevolent, who responds amiably to the inquiries of the visiting Englishman seeking an ancient grave, and who wishes only to educate Ned as conscientiously as possible. In the second draft, the Doctor becomes coarse, animalistic, hostile to the visiting stranger, and interested in

Ned primarily as an instrument of revenge against the English hold-ers of the estate and title. Grimshawe's relation to Ned and Elsie shifts constantly; sometimes he loves the girl and not the boy, some-times the boy and not the girl, and most often he loves neither. Al-ways he is seen as the educator of the boy, although with varying intentions and attitudes.

The Doctor is both benefactor and destroyer, a combination mad-dening to character and author, both of whom struggle to define the precise nature of that benevolent despotism. Ned's Salem childhood with Doctor Grimshawe shares certain parallels with that of Haw-thorne, but never exact ones. The most important difference is that Ned and Elsie are orphans, Ned having been salvaged from an Eng-lish almshouse. The origins of his foster sister Elsie are kept vague because the author was saving her for a later marriage with Ned, although ultimately he changed his mind. The absence of a mother serves to intensify the decisive role of Grimshawe in Ned's inner life as well as the boy's urgent need for contact with his origins. Most of all it allows for a more poignant expression of maternal deprivation, as in the following:

> Then growing up without a mother, to cultivate his tenderness with kisses and the inestimable, inevitable love of love breaking out on all little occasions, without reference to merit or demerit, unfailing whether or no . . . mother's generous interpretation of all that was doubtful in him . . . mother's deep intuitive insight, which should see the permanent good be-neath all the appearance of temporary evil. (XII, 429)

Death dominates the childhood of Ned and Elsie. Their cobweb-filled home is on the edge of Salem's Charter Street cemetery and they play among the remains of the first English settlers. The very dust of the house is described as the decomposed substance of Eng-land, so that the first of many English-American correspondences is set up at the beginning of both drafts of the book. Death permeates the air that the children breathe. It is the sign under which this book is written, recapitulating a life dominated by the awful emblem— the grim reaper, the grim shaver, Doctor Grimshawe—death. The father-surrogate leads Ned to seek the true father, who is dead, and in his mind may even be death itself.

Nevertheless, Ned feels that his death-dominated childhood had beneficial effects upon him, that "the mild, gracious, genial, though sad paternity of the old Doctor . . . had fostered everything deep, sweet, and high in him, and rooted out, so far as it could, all evil weeds" (XII, 119). In this draft, the childhood period is treated less extensively and less negatively than in the second. It seems that only after Hawthorne had brought the narrative to conclusion, though not to completion, he felt called upon to reexamine the childhood in the light of what he discovered in the process of writing. In this later version of the American childhood, Doctor Grimshawe becomes brutish, drunken, coarse, and cruel enough to use the boy as an instrument of vengeance. In both drafts, however, the relation of Grimshawe to Ned is one of bachelor father-surrogate whose principal activity is to educate, and to provide education for, the orphaned boy. In both drafts, the Doctor is a benefactor to a child who would otherwise have been destitute and uneducated, and in both drafts the boy feels that whatever the negative aspects of his rearing, the Doctor helped him to become a sensitive, proud, imaginative person. The boy Ned, like the boy Nathaniel, was handsome and aristocratic in person, apt in learning, imaginative, and given to literary pursuits.

Even in the sunnier first draft, however, ambivalence creeps into the depiction of the Doctor as educator; we see that he teaches the boy dutifully and conscientiously, but without real paternal love. We see also a rivalry with Elsie for the Doctor's love and the pride with which the boy hides this feeling. We sense also in the following passage that the boy believes himself to have a soft effeminate nature, which his educator wisely intends to toughen.

[The boy], as we have already hinted, was not apparently a favorite with his guardian; not that Dr. Etherege [sic] did not act towards him with even paternal care and consideration; with even more, indeed, than towards the girl. But there was a character of carefulness and study, a lack of spontaneity in this. There were no kindly impulses; all was a well-planned, wise, and kind order of education, independent of feeling, and such as a tutor, if a man of conscience and sagacity, might have instituted for the education of a boy. . . . The boy had pride, too, as well as sensibility and affection; and he seemed to make no effort to win the demonstrations of tenderness that flowed spontaneously towards Elsie. . . . Doubtless, this

154

coldness, as respected him, in the temper of his patron, was of no real disadvantage to the boy. It gave him, perhaps, an energy which the softness and impressibility of his nature needed. (XII, 95–96)

Much of Hawthorne's feeling about his childhood is reflected in this passage and in the modifications of it that he made further on in the book. Here we see a reflection of Uncle Robert's probably salutary efforts to toughen up an overly soft boy. We catch, too, a reflection of the differing attitudes that Uncle Robert manifested toward his nieces and his nephew. Although he felt that the nephew was of more importance to the family, being at that time the only male descendant, he felt more comfortable with and affectionate toward his nieces, especially Maria Louisa.

In the second draft Hawthorne repeats this image of conscientious, untender education but very quickly cancels it out.

One effect of his zealous and analytic instruction of the boy was very perceptible. Heretofore, though enduring him, and occasionally making a plaything of him, it may be doubted whether the grim Doctor had really any strong affection for the child; it rather seemed a self-imposed task, which, with his strong will, he forced himself to undertake, and carry sedulously forward. All that he had done—his rescuing the bright child from poverty, and nameless degradation, ignorance, sordid life, hopeless of better fortune, and opening to him the whole realm of mighty possibilities, in an American life—did not imply any love for the little individual whom he thus benefitted. It had some other motive. (XII, 377)

The seclusion from society in which the children are brought up creates in Ned a paradoxical sense of himself very like Hawthorne's own.

It had made him think ridiculously high of his own gifts, powers, attainments, and at the same time doubt whether they could pass with those of others; it made him despise all flesh, as if he were of a superior race, and yet have an idle and weak fear of coming in contact with them, from a dread of his incompetency to cope with them; so he at once depreciated and exalted, to an absurd degree, both himself and others. (XII, 426)

At this point in the second draft comes an interchange between the Doctor and Ned that in no way furthers the purposes of the narrative, but instead voices Hawthorne's inner debate about the true feelings of his own benefactor toward him. The Doctor confronts Ned suddenly with misgivings about the boy's manliness. This confrontation and its amorous reconciliation break through the surface of the narrative in an embarrassing manner. It causes the grim Doctor to conclude that Ned has been brought up in too much isolation from his kind and to take him off to an academy or boarding school.

"Ned," said the Doctor to him one day, in his gruffest tone, "you are not turning out to be the boy I looked for, and meant to make you. I have given you sturdy English instruction . . . I looked to see the rudiments of a man in you, by this time; and you begin to mope and pule, as if your babyhood were coming back to you. You seem to think more than a boy of your years should; and yet it is not manly thought, nor ever will be so. What do you mean, boy, by making all my care of you come to nothing, in this way?"

"I do my best, Doctor Grim," said Ned, with sullen dignity. "What you teach me, I learn. What more can I do?"

"I'll tell you what, my fine fellow. . . . You disappoint me, and I'll not bear it. I want you to be a man. . . . If I had foreboded such a fellow as you turn out to be, I never would have taken you from the place where . . . I found you—the almshouse!" . . .

"There is nonsense that ought to be whipt out of you, Sir," added the Doctor, incensed at the boy's aspect.

"You have said enough, Sir," said the boy. "Would to God you had left me where you found me! . . . It was not my fault that you took me from the almshouse. But it will be my fault if I ever eat another bit of your bread, or stay under your roof an hour longer." (XII, 426–427)

Perhaps all this is inspired by the Doctor's earlier discovery that his introspective ward wrote poetry, with which the Doctor was accustomed to light his pipe, but the confrontation leads to a scene of passionate reconciliation, a renewal of love, which is of great moment to this orphan hungry for tenderness: "Doctor Grim, in his way, had the same kind of enjoyment of this passionate crisis; so that though the next day, they all three looked at one another a little ashamed, yet it had some remote analogy to that delicious embarrassment of two lovers at their first meeting after they know all" (XII, 428). The analogy is odd and rather embarrassing.

Had the presentation of the boy's youthful relation to his bachelor-benefactor been merely a preparation for the events later to occur in England, there would have been no need for such complicated assessment and reassessment of the Doctor's emotional vagaries with respect to the children. Were the book a purely conventional romance we would need only be told of the Doctor's education of the alms-house boy to noble accomplishments and a sense of noble destiny. The vacillation about the degree and kind of the Doctor's paternal feelings, between true and adoptive paternity, between harshness and passionate love, advance no narrative goals. They are instead a quest for understanding on the part of an author still tortured by ambivalent feelings toward a long-dead father-surrogate who was indeed his benefactor, but whose benefactions left a residue of life-long resentment.

Of course the varied portraits of Doctor Grimshawe are not literal portraits of Uncle Robert, who certainly was not cruel, drunken, rude, nor vengeful. The book depicts childhood feelings rather than actualities, the benevolent tyrant as experienced by the child's emotions and thus become monstrous. Parallels between the actual and the literary father-surrogates abound. We may start with the obvious fact that Dr. Grimshawe is a scientist of a bizarre sort. Even the early description of his scientific activity in the first draft reveals parallels with the pomologist uncle; not only did Grimshawe fill his house with domestic spiders and cobwebs, "he even sent to some torrid region or other to obtain a spider such as heretofore had only been seen, dead and dry, in the collection of naturalists" (XII, 93–94). He wished to benefit society by making a life-saving extract of cobwebs and had specimens sent him from all over the world.

The spider's web is the Doctor's emblem throughout the many drafts and studies of the book, but it takes the author a long time to grasp the significance. The man and his symbol are firmly connected, as firmly as is anything in this variable work, but the meaning of the symbol is only gradually revealed to both protagonist and author. At first it is only a semi-ludicrous pseudoscientific obsession, but gradually the great spider acquires demonic significance as the Doctor's familiar. Even in the first draft, before the Doctor is viewed as vile and vengeful, Hawthorne is groping toward significance in the conjunction of man, spider, and web. Let us follow some part of this process in sequence as it occurs in the working notes.

It shall seem as if the great spider's web were a charm, by means of which the Doctor is enthralling his enemies. (XII, 128)

The Doctor must have a great agency in these doings, both of the Pensioner and Etherege, making tissues of cobwebs out of men's life-threads; he must have the air, in the Romance, of a sort of magician, without being called so; and even after his death, his influence must still be felt. Hold on to this. A dark subtle manager, for the love of managing, like a spider sitting in the centre of his web, which stretches far to east and west. (XII, 224)

The great spider shall be an emblem of the Doctor himself; it shall be his craft and wickedness coming into this shape outside him. (XII, 226)

This old Doctor's spider's web must of course have a signification; it signifies a plot in which his art has involved the story and every individual actor; he has caught them all, like so many flies. (XII, 287)

Even by the last of these statements, Hawthorne has not yet really evolved the plot in which the Doctor has enthralled his enemies. In the first draft narrative, the Doctor has only unintentionally and without clear purpose given Ned an intimation of his descent from a noble English family, whereas in the later authorial meditations and in the narrative of the second draft, Grimshawe is consciously and intentionally misleading the boy by training him to depose the present holder of the estate. The element of enthrallment occurs in the authorial meditations in draft one and not yet in the narrative, where Doctor Grimshawe is still a benefactor. In this draft Grimshawe has not yet enslaved the man whom he saved from hanging to act as foreign agent to fulfill the Doctor's purposes in England. The web is the Doctor's sign, but it has not yet a material counterpart in the form of characterization and plot. That does not come until Hawthorne rewrites the childhood episode in the light of the conclusion in which Etherege turns out after all not to be the missing heir. In the second version of Ned's childhood, he is deluded all his life and it is the wicked benefactor who created the delusion.

But the wickedness of the benefactor does not dawn completely on either character or author until Ned's conscious control is weakened by his injury. In the dream-state of the final section of the English part of the book, Etherege fully realizes his enthrallment by his childhood guardian. In an intervening period of relative sanity spent in the home of the Warden, the only unambiguously generous man in the novel, Ned returns to thinking of the Doctor as his kindly benefactor. In this lucid interval between residence with yet two more ambivalent father-figures, Ned reveals to the Warden that he came under the Doctor's care at the age of four, the very age at which Nathaniel Hawthorne lost his father and moved with his family into the Manning home.

Another reflection in *Grimshawe* of Hawthorne's early family constellation is the ghostly influence of a missing sailor-relative, who appears to have been linked in Hawthorne's mind to his sailor-father. The homes of both Etherege and Hawthorne were overcast by a missing brother of the father-surrogate. John Manning never returned from the War of 1812, his death was never reported, and throughout the years there came rumors of his appearance here and there. Grandmother Manning never accepted the idea of his death and always awaited his return. So, too, the Doctor had a missing brother who is gothicized in the first draft into the Expected One, for whom a room is always kept in readiness:

> But it was said that the Doctor always kept a chamber in the house ready for the occupancy of the brother when he returned; a fire burning, a meal, some say, prepared, a pair of slippers and a night cap by the bed. . . . And this was said to have been the custom of the family from time immemorial. . . . a fire in winter, in the chamber, a fresh arrangement every morning through the year, a plate always at the board, for some shadowy guest, who had never yet appeared. (XII, 112–113)

Ned begins to wonder whether his family is strange in its dedication to the memory of the Expected One and queries the Doctor whether others have such customs:

> In every house, is there a chamber for some guest that never comes; at every table, a plate for a person who never sits down to eat a mouthful? "I know not how that may be, my boy," said the Doctor. "But in most hearts, there is an empty chamber, waiting for a guest." (XII, 115)

The legend of the Expected One, doubled by different versions on either side of the Atlantic, suggests that Hawthorne was in some sense expecting or fearing his father's return, a ghostly sense stimulated by residence in the ancestral country.

Grimshawe contains other parallels with Hawthorne's own experience, some of them quite minor. The housekeeper, Crusty Hannah, starts out as a portrayal of Hannah Lord, both a relative and a servant to Miriam Lord Manning, Nathaniel's grandmother. Hannah evolves, however, into something bizarre in the second draft, "a mixture of Indian and Negro, & as some say, Monkey" (XII, 344). Like other characters drawn from life, she bifurcates during the course of composition, but in this case, to no discernible purpose.

In addition, there are several minor bits of self-reference in *Grimshawe*. For example, Ned passes his time in the Warden's house reading county history and genealogy. One work "seemed particularly full . . . and contained many incidents that would have worked well into historical romance" (XII, 150). The Warden's view of this book seems an unmistakable comment on Hawthorne's own practice as a historical romancer:

> "My old friend Gibben, the learned author of this work (he has been dead this score of years, so he will not mind my saying it) had a little too much the habit of seeking his authorities in the cottage-chimney corners. I mean that an old woman's [tales] were just about as acceptable to him as a recorded fact; and to say the truth, they are really apt to have ten times the life in them." (XII, 150)

Like Hawthorne, Gibben had a preference for the preternatural rather than the natural explanation of legendary events: "there was an odious rumour that what was called the Bloody Footstep was nothing miraculous, after all, but most probably a natural reddish stain in the stone door-step; but against this heresy the excellent Dr. Gibben set his face most sturdily" (XII, 151). Hawthorne's notebooks record the skeptical and rational view of the Bloody Footstep that Dr. Gibben rejects, but his four late romances utilize the preternatural version.

THE PASSIONATE PILGRIM

The English section, part of the first draft, introduces the adult Etherege without transition, walking about the very part of England that he was led to think of as his ancestral estate. Once arrived there he lives successively in the homes of three older men, the Pensioner, the Warden, and the master of Brathwaite, each of whom leads him a step closer to his goal. Of these three older men, only the Warden is treated consistently; the characterizations of the Pensioner and the Italianate master of Brathwaite, like those of most father-surrogates in Hawthorne's fiction, bifurcate into good and evil.

Ned's first view of England is a vision of paradise, but in the course of a few pages it turns out to be a dangerous domain, containing not a serpent, but hunters pursuing human game. A jealous master who does not welcome the return of a possible usurper to his rights presides over this family estate. The English section of *Grimshawe* opens very much like the beginning of *The Ancestral Footstep*, revealing something important about the quests of both Americans, Etherege and Middleton, for their places of origin. The first paragraph of *The Ancestral Footstep* concludes thus:

> In all his life, including its earliest and happiest days, he had never known such a spring and zest as now filled his veins, and gave lightsomeness to his limbs; this spirit gave to the beautiful country which he trod a still richer beauty than it had ever borne, and he sought his ancient home in it as if he had found his way into Paradise and were there endeavoring to trace out the signs of Eve's bridal bower, the birthplace of the human race and all its glorious possibilities of happiness and high performance. (XII, 3)

In both books the ancient home is felt to be a paradise because it is the long-lost origin, the birthplace not so much of the human race as of the orphaned wanderer, a place to which he longs to return. The gateway to the paradise of the human race is guarded by cherubim and a flaming sword that none may reenter. The ancestral home in these two romances is guarded by a jealous master who is ready to destroy any usurper who seeks to displace him. This original home symbolizes the orphan's mother, his own birthplace. Guarding it is the jealous father of tradition. The Bloody Footstep points away from the threshold of the mansion, not toward it. The proper direction for the son of the house is away from the mother; reentry is forbidden and dangerous. As Hawthorne says just before Etherege is shot while blissfully wandering near the mansion, "there is a foreboding, a sense within us, that the traveller is not going the right way" (XII, 131).

THE PALMER-PENSIONER

Ned awakens from this gunshot injury in an ancient hospital donated to the care of impoverished aged family descendants by the founder of the Brathwaite family as atonement for his sins. Still delirious, Ned regains consciousness in an antique chamber in the presence of the venerable Palmer dressed in the style of three hundred years before. He awakens, in other words, into the past and in the kindly company of a figure of the past who is all paternal solicitude. At this point in their acquaintance, the wise old figure suggests the ideal father to attend a wounded orphan in a state of enforced passivity. He talks in a "grave, impressive voice of authority, not unmixed with a paternal sort of kindness" (XII, 134), gives the patient soothing potions, bids him rest, and seems to be present even in his sleep and dreams. The Pensioner is benign, "thoughtful, speculative, commanding" although a beneficiary of the hospital's charity. In some versions of the narrative this old Palmer, as he is sometimes called, is the same person as the Alcott-like tutor who back in America had taught Ned in the Doctor's house. In a late authorial recapitulation of the plot "Etherege vaguely recognizes the holy presence that has never quite died out of his memory" (XII, 232).

For Etherege the approach to death and the slow recovery in an almshouse tended by a kindly pensioner are like a rebirth into his own past. For a while the Pensioner is a kindly father and the hospital a sheltering mother.

> "Be weak, and be the stronger for it," said the old man, with a grave smile. "It is not in the pride of our strength that we are best or stronger. To be made anew, the man must be again a little child, and consent to be enwrapt quietly in the arms of Providence, as a child in its mother's arms."
>
> "I never knew a mother's care," replied the traveller, in a low, regretful tone. . . . "Since my boyhood, I have lived among hard men—a life of struggle and hard rivalry. It is good to find myself here in the long past, and in a sheltered harbor." (XII, 455)

In numerous authorial meditations Hawthorne tries desperately to objectify in plot and characterization what he so strongly feels in the image of the Palmer-Pensioner. The man is saintly but somehow suspect, benevolent but somehow infuriating; sometimes he is said to be preserving the title for Ned but, in the end, is himself the holder of the title. Hawthorne strives to formulate what becomes over the course of the meditations an impossibly mixed personality. Every time he posits a saintly character, it bifurcates into something dubious or deadly.

A study of the characterization of the old Pensioner shows just how complex is the question of literary models. As a palmer he resembles the aged guide who accompanied Spenser's Sir Guyon through his temptations. In the working notes, Hawthorne mentions both Emerson and Alcott as models, and Alcott was most probably the model for the Pensioner in his earlier incarnation as the excessively mild tutor in Ned's childhood. Edward Davidson makes a very convincing case for the use of George Bradford as model for the old Pensioner by setting side by side very similar descriptions of the Pensioner and Bradford, the latter taken from the *English Notebooks*, showing Hawthorne's exasperation at the minute conscientiousness and excessive scrupulosity of both.

> Mr. Bradford has the blood of martyrs in him, through two channels; and I doubt not there is the substance in himself to make a martyr of;— and yet he is a wonderfully small pattern of a man. He has a minute conscientiousness which is continually stumbling over insignificant matters; and trifles of all kinds seem to be matters of great moment with him. There is a lack of strong will, that makes his conduct, when not determined by principle, miserably weak and wavering. . . . He is always uneasy what to do next; always regretting the last thing he did.[6]

This passage certainly corresponds remarkably well with the saintly religious character of the Pensioner and with the scene in which Etherege suddenly becomes wildly inflamed at the old man's overscrupulosity in gardening. If saintliness and excess of conscience were the entirety of the characterization, Davidson would have made his case—Bradford, along with a touch of Emerson and Alcott, would be the model. But Davidson does not account for either the feeling associated with the Pensioner or the complex, infuriating, self-canceling process by which Hawthorne was trying to depict a presence that he felt but could not objectify.

The notebook portrait of Bradford is complex but cool, objective, and discerning, with no signs of struggle. In contrast, Etherege's reaction to very similar personality traits in the Pensioner is homicidal fury followed by his characteristic attitude of appreciation for the old man's benevolence. This complexity delays and obfuscates the action, seemingly more an eruption of irrelevant feeling than a functioning part of the story. The very *benevolence* of the Pensioner, disturbing to both Etherege and author, points behind Bradford to a source of genuine emotional confusion.

Hawthorne sought by an agonizing process to convey a presence that he felt psychically but could not formulate. We have already seen that at the opening of the English section, the Palmer or Pensioner is a wise, kindly, benign figure. Ambiguity creeps in almost immediately and is full-blown in a long authorial meditation that recapitulates the whole story once more.

> [Etherege] is taken up by the old pensioner, as before, who must be drawn with traits of a deep, sad tenderness, which makes a profound impression on Etherege. It shall be shown, however, that he is an object of vague suspicion and dislike among his associates in the Hospital, and even the Warden shall not have escaped this influence. It spreads, in some degree over Etherege, in spite of his gratitude to the old man. (XII, 205–206)

> What shall be his distinguishing trait;—merely, a conscience, and the inveterate habit of acting on it. . . . Perhaps the moral may be, that there is nothing so disorganizing—so certain to overthrow everything earthly, if it can only have its own way, as conscience. . . . Let the weakness of too much conscience be fairly brought out;—the indecision, the incapacity, of action that must result from it; the inability for anything but suffering. (XII, 207)

At this point Hawthorne determines that this petty, feeble yet strong, sublime, meek martyr of an old man should be the true heir of the Brathwaite family. Suddenly he resumes the narrative with Etherege watching the old man gardening, an activity associated with someone far older to Hawthorne's acquaintance than George Bradford. The overscrupulosity of conscience attributed to Bradford and quoted above is now applied to the old Pensioner as gardener, an absurd but potent combination.

[Etherege] could not help being struck by the scrupulous care with which he attended to the plants; it seemed to him that there was a sense of justice—of desiring to do exactly what was right in the matter, not favoring one plant more than another, and doing all he could for each. . . . Then he was so minute; and often, when he was on the point of leaving one thing to take up another, some small neglect that he saw or fancied, called him back again, to spend other minutes on the same task. He was so full of scruples. It struck Etherege that this was conscience, morbid, sick, a despot in trifles, looking so closely into life that it permitted nothing to be done. . . . Here was a lily that had been neglected, while he paid too much attention to a rose; he had set his foot on a violet. (XII, 208–209)

Etherege then expostulates with the old man, telling him that the ability to act is more important than minute matters of conscience, becomes abashed at the gardener's humble demeanor, and finds himself unable to continue. Suddenly, and for no reason that either the character or the author can give, Etherege now breaks out into a homicidal rage against his gentle benefactor.

But he was surprised to find how he had to struggle against a certain repulsion within himself to the old man. He seemed so nonsensical, interfering with everybody's right in the world; so mischievous, standing there and shutting out the possibility of action. It seemed well to trample him down; to put him out of the way—no matter how—somehow. It gave him, he thought, an inkling of the way in which this poor old man had made himself odious to his kind, by opposing himself, inevitably to what was bad in men, chiding it by his very presence, accepting nothing false. You must either love him utterly, or hate him utterly; for he would not let you alone. Etherege, being a susceptible man, felt this influence in the strongest way; for it was as if there was a battle within him, one . . . party pulling, wrenching him towards this old man, another wrenching him away; so that, by the agony of the contest, he felt disposed to end it by taking flight, and never seeing the strange individual again. He could well enough conceive how a brutal nature . . . might find it so intolerable that it must needs get rid of him by violence—by taking his blood if necessary.

All these feelings were but transitory, however; they swept across him like a wind, and then he looked again at the old man and saw only his simplicity, his unworldliness. . . . And then Etherege went away, in a state of disturbance for which he could not account to himself. (XII, 211–212)

This is clearly something more than a failed satire on Transcendentalists, as Davidson supposes.[7] Emerson, Alcott, and Bradford may well be involved here as models, but the wild extrapolation from painstakingly slow progress in gardening to "interfering with everybody's right in the world" is motivated by some emotion more primitive than satire. The battle within Etherege and the murderous rage seem unmistakably to be inspired by a father-figure with whom the character and the author have not yet come to terms.

Only a few pages after the inexplicable outburst of homicidal fury, Etherege returns to his original view of the Pensioner: "I shall find it impossible to call up this scene, any of the scenes hereafter, without the venerable figure of this, whom I may truly call my benefactor, among them. I fancy him among them from their foundation—young then, but keeping just the equal step with their age and decay—and still doing good and hospitable deeds to those who need them" (XII, 217). Not only is the Pensioner again a good and kindly figure, he is again a paternal figure seeming to belong to the entire lifespan of the speaker. Like Grimshawe, he is described in Ned's more rational moments as benevolent, a quality linking him to the chain of well-meaning but disturbing father-figures that we have been tracing. Out of many possible passages that show ambivalent feelings toward the Pensioner, I select one that follows hard upon the words just quoted above. The lines come from a long authorial meditation in which Hawthorne tries yet again to define the character of this troubling figure.

His whole life shall have been petty in its means, noble, sublime in its spirit. . . . A certain property shall attend him wherever he goes; a bloody footstep. Pshaw! He shall have the fatality of causing death, bloodshed, wherever he goes; *and this shall symbolize the strife which benevolence inevitably provokes, because it disturbs everything around it.* . . . Some secret mischief he must inevitably do, immense, of bloody consequences, yet consistent with his mild and beautiful nature. (XII, 220; italics added)

The almost unbearable ambivalence abates for a brief interlude during which Etherege stays at the home of a truly kind and comfortable Englishman, the Warden of the hospital. Here the American indulges in tourism, recovers strength and lucidity, and prepares himself for his final trial, the assault on the ancestral home. No longer in a dream-state, Etherege discourses with the Warden on his origins, confesses his hitherto unformulated desire to claim his birthright, and manages to speak positively of the Doctor's benefactions. Etherege says, "I have no ancestry; at the very first step, my origin is lost in impenetrable obscurity. I only know that but for the aid of a kind friend—on whose benevolence I seem to have had no claim whatever—my life would probably have been poor, mean, unenlightened" (XII, 149). This is similar to the rational, daylight view of the man who educated Hawthorne; it is the view of Robert Manning's benefactions taken by Ebe Hawthorne and other members of the family as well as by most Hawthorne biographers. The diabolic view of Doctor Grimshawe appears to Ned only when, in a dreamlike state, his mind wanders out of conscious control. Ambivalence toward Grimshawe and the Pensioner appears in authorial meditations and in Etherege's mental reflections, but Etherege never *speaks* of either benefactor in other than favorable terms.

A BOX WITHIN BOXES

From the respite of the Warden's hospitality, Etherege moves into the final phase of the quest for which his entire life has prepared him. The special meaning of the ancestral home to this orphan was already present in the early, childhood phase of the book when Ned revealed that England and the house were part of his unconscious mind. At this point in the first draft of the book the Doctor had not yet planted delusions in the boy's head about the old home. The Bloody Footstep is like a dangerous repressed idea that surfaces only when brought forth by association.

> To tell you the truth, Uncle, and Elsie, either my nurse or my mother told me the story, when I was a baby, or else I dreamt it; but there is in my mind a thought about this Bloody Footstep, that is imprinted somewhere in England, and which no rain will wipe away. When it happened, or where it is, I don't know; but I never think of England without seeing that in my mind's eye; and it seems as if all England was nothing else but

the ground sufficient for this great Bloody Footstep to be imprinted in! (XII, 108)

These shadowy intimations, not the Doctor's diabolical plot, motivate Ned's passionate determination to enter the house at all risks despite warnings from both Elsie and the Pensioner. Even death, should that be the price of entry, is not too much to pay for a reunion with the source of his being. The most urgent elements of his identity require this material connection to his origins, the maternal and the paternal, now fused into one unfulfilled yearning.

All my dreams, all my wishes hitherto, have looked forward to precisely the juncture that seems now to be approaching. My dreaming childhood dreamt of this. If you know anything of me, you know how I sprang out of mystery, akin to none, a thing concocted out of the elements, without visible agency—how, all through my boyhood, I was alone; how I grew up without a root, yet continually longing for one—longing to be connected with somebody—and never feeling myself so. Yet there was ever a looking forward to this turn on which I now find myself. If my next step were death, yet while the path seemed to lead onward to a certainty of establishing me in connection with my race, I would yet take it. I have tried to keep down this yearning, to stifle it, annihilate it, with making a position for myself, with being my own past, but I cannot overcome this natural horror of being a creature floating in the air, attached to nothing; nor this feeling that there is no reality in the life and fortunes, good or bad, of a being so unconnected. There is not even a grave, not a heap of dry bones, not a pinch of dust, with which I can claim connection, unless I find it here. (XII, 257–258)

To his disappointment, Ned does not see the footstep when he arrives at the public front door of the family mansion. Only by taking a circuitous route that leads past the place where he had been shot does he find the private family entrance, "a very pleasant entrance it was, beneath a porch, of antique form, and ivy-clad, hospitable and inviting" (XII, 282). This porched private entrance is strikingly similar to the second gate opening into Spenser's Bower of Bliss, an association that reinforces the sexual symbolism of the private entrance:

Till that he came unto another gate;
No gate, but like one, being goodly dight
With boughes and braunches, which did broad dilate
Their clasping armes, in wanton wreathings intricate.

So fashioned a Porch with rare device,
Archt over head with an embracing vine,
Whose bounches hanging downe, seemed to entice
All passers by, to tast their lushious wine.

(Faerie Queene, II, 12:53, 54)

At the family entrance Ned finds on the white marble the emblem that haunted his mind from its earliest days.

For it was the mark of a footstep, very decidedly made out, in red, like blood—the Bloody Footstep—the mark of a foot, which seemed to have been slightly impressed into the rock, as if it had been a soft substance, at the same time sliding a little, and gushing with blood. The glistening moisture, . . . made it appear as if it were just freshly stamped there; . . . It was well that there was no spectator there; for the American would have blushed to have it known how much this old traditionary wonder had affected his imagination. But, indeed, it was as old as any bugbear of his mind—as any of those bugbears and private terrors which grow up with people, and make the dreams and nightmares of childhood, and the fever-images of mature years. . . .
The foot was issuing from, not entering into the house. Whoever had impressed it, or on whatever occasion, he had gone forth, and doubtless to return no more. *Etherege was impelled to place his own foot in the track . . . and he felt a strange, vague, yet strong surmise of some agony, some terror and horror, that had passed here,* and would not fade out of the spot. While he was in these musings . . . he saw Lord Brathwaite looking at him through the glass of the porch, with fixed, curious eyes, and a smile on his face. (XII, 282–283; italics added)

Even the purest mind could not avoid the implications of forbidden sexual approach. The inviting, porched, ivy-clad private entrance stained by the blood of a long-past agonizing event surely suggests maternal genitalia. Into the mark of a foot "issuing from, not entering into the house," Etherege is compelled to place his own foot, glad to think that he is unseen in this furtive act. But in fact he is being watched all the time—coolly and sardonically—by the

master of the house. The interchange between master and interloper, though urbane in language, contains a veiled threat. Etherege
feigns a skeptical attitude, claiming to believe that the stain is only a
natural discoloration in the stone. "'Do you [think] so, indeed?' re-
joined his lordship. 'It may be; but in that case, if not the record of
an actual deed . . . we may consider it as prophetic;—as foreboding,
from the time when the stone was squared and smoothed, and laid at
this threshold, that a fatal footstep was really to be impressed here'"
(XII, 283).

Subsequent events show that to the master Etherege's furtive step
is a fatal misstep, a trespass punishable by death. The Italianate,
Popish master, a Gothic villain and the very image of the evil punitive father, having failed to kill Etherege on his first trespass, has
lured him into his web for the final kill. The master's house, too,
contains a giant spider of the same species as Doctor Grimshawe's
pet one. Insofar as the house and its bloody threshold represent the
longed-for mother, its proprietor is the castrating father, ever alert to
the invasion of his domain by the son who wishes to displace him.

The determination to enter the house represents an incest wish,
personal to Etherege but mythic as well:

> Was he himself—in another guise, as Lord Brathwaite had been saying—
> that long expected one? Was his the echoing tread that had been heard so
> long through the ages—so far through the wide world—approaching the
> blood-stained threshold?
>   With such thoughts, or dreams (for they were hardly sincerely enter-
> tained enough to be called thoughts) Etherege spent the day; a strange,
> delicious day, in spite of the sombre shadows that enveloped it. He fan-
> cied himself strangely wonted, already to the house; as if his every part
> and peculiarity had at once fitted into its nooks, and corners, and cran-
> nies. (XII, 285)

Undeterred by his lordship's threat, Etherege passes a strange, delicious day indulging in such sexually suggestive fantasies. Although
Hawthorne finally does not allow him to displace the master, Etherege has stolen some secret satisfaction in placing his foot in the
Bloody Footstep and finding that "his every part and peculiarity had
at once fitted into [the house's] nooks and corners and crannies."

This much of the private bugbear of his mind is allowed to attain the fulfillment of circular completion.

Etherege's incest wishes extend even to his adopted sister Elsie, to whom he proposes marriage, apparently as an alternative to entering the house. From both alternatives the sister recoils with extreme revulsion, urging him to leave her, the house, and England. Says Ned:

> "Away with this strangeness that lurks between us. Let us meet as those who began life together, and whose life-strings, being so early twisted in unison, cannot now be torn apart."
>
> "You are not wise . . . to break the restraint which we have tacitly imposed upon ourselves. Do not let us speak further on this subject. . . . It is best that we should meet as strangers, and so part."
>
> "No, no," cried Etherege. . . . "Circumstances have shown that Providence has designed a relation in my fate to yours. Elsie, are you as lonely as I am?"
>
> "No," she replied, "I have bonds, ties, a life, a duty! I must live that life and do that duty! You have, likewise, both. Do yours, live your own life, like me."
>
> "Know you, Elsie," he said, "whither that life is now tending?"
>
> "Whither?" . . .
>
> "To yonder hall!" said he.
>
> She started up, in wild excitement, and clasped her hands about his arm.
>
> "No, no," she almost shrieked. "Go not thither! There is blood upon the threshold! Go not thither! Return, return, to the haunts where we erst knew each other. A dreadful fatality awaits you here."
>
> "Come with me then," said he, "and I yield my purpose."
>
> "It cannot be," said Elsie.
>
> "Then, I, too, tell you it cannot be," returned Etherege.
>
> (XII, 260–261)

Entering the ancestral mansion and marrying this adoptive sister seem equally horrifying to Elsie and both are clearly linked in the feelings of Etherege. Elsie responds with all the horror that a proposal of incest might evoke, and even the author, who has carefully specified that they are not siblings, draws back from such a union.

Looking up after this intense interchange, Etherege finds that Lord Brathwaite has been observing them unseen, just as he had when Etherege placed his foot into the Bloody Footstep. At one point Hawthorne even considers creating a rivalry between Etherege and Brathwaite by having Brathwaite fall in love with Elsie. Although the girl has little function in the narrative, she figures frequently in the author's meditations, where she is connected in turn with Grimshawe, the Pensioner (as a daughter), and finally with Brathwaite. She thus follows more fully than any other of Hawthorne's female characters in the pattern of a dangerously tempting young woman related to a destructive or punitive older man. In this case, Hawthorne has too many older men and cannot integrate this familiar pattern into his plot.

One puzzling motif runs through the book—the coffer that in the final denouement turns out to be full of golden hair. Nothing in the narrative explains its significance, nor has it any visible relation to the action. Only in one of the authorial meditations does the coffer acquire meaning. "It awakens an unhallowed ambition, and madness of lust for something that ought not to be—cannot be possessed. It speaks of a great beauty to be won; and she is found in the old coffer" (XII, 287). The coffer full of golden hair appears to be a transformation of the caskets of gold in the deepest subterranean chamber of the Cave of Mammon, the final temptation of greed to temperate Sir Guyon. The transmutation of a beautiful woman who ought not to be possessed into golden hair, thus conflating two of Sir Guyon's temptations, the sexual and the material (both forbidden, but only the sexual truly tempting to Etherege), perhaps tells something of the process by which Hawthorne transformed the Spenserian quest. The golden hair is the lifeless residue of the multiplied temptation.

The tresses are found in a coffer in the chamber of the man imprisoned for seducing the Doctor's sister, a chamber deep in the subterranean bowels of the house. It is the inmost secret of the mansion and perhaps of the book—a box within boxes, to be opened only on the final pages. It is much like the central ebony cabinet of *The Ancestral Footstep*, a miniature replica of the ancestral house containing in its secret innermost compartment only a pinch of dust. Both coffers open only to keys mysteriously possessed by the young Americans. The house and the box at its center that opens only to a key held by the long missing son of the house surely symbolize an incest wish.

THE KISS OF DEATH

Hawthorne also had difficulties with the characterization of Lord Brathwaite, the fourth older man with whom Etherege dwells in the course of the romance. The incumbent of the disputed estate is frankly a villain, stagey and overdrawn, but even so, more suitable to a romance because of the relative clarity of his presentation, than are Grimshawe and the Pensioner. The four or so pages in which Hawthorne tries to locate the right character for this villain are desperate and hilarious; he even mocks his own methods as his imagination searches far and wide for the crime that corresponds to the villainy. The list is so long and thorough that it omits few offenses except incest. A brief sampling should give some indication of Hawthorne's difficulties in characterization.

> The Lord of Brathwaite Hall shall be a wretched, dissipated, dishonorable fellow. . . . He shall (perhaps) be in love with Elsie. Up to his death, he must feel as if this American had come to thwart him and ruin him in everything, and shall hate him accordingly, and think he is doing well to kill him if possible . . . a fiend, a man sold to the devil, a magician, a poison-breather, a Thug, a pirate, a pickpocket. . . . If I could only hit right here, he would be the centre of interest. . . . Nothing mean must he be, but as wicked as you please. . . . A monkey? A Faulkenstein? A man of straw? . . . Wicked as he must be, there shall still be relations between him and the pauper Saint. . . . What? What? What? A worshipper of the Sun? A cannibal? A ghoul? a vampire? . . . He has something to do with the old Doctor's spider-theory. . . . He has been poisoned by a Bologna sausage. . . . He shall need a young life every five years . . . and he shall have fixed upon Elsie. . . . At any rate, he must have dreadful designs on Elsie—dreadful, dreadful, dreadful. (XII, 264–265)

On and on goes the author with growing desperation and abandon. Hawthorne's desire to connect this evil figure to the Doctor and the Pensioner indicates that in a sense all three men are one man, various projections of Etherege's mind, various visions of the controlling figure who stands between the orphan and his real father.

The first two father-surrogates start out benevolent and then turn diabolical and oppressive. The last one starts out pure villain and bifurcates at the last moment into the ultimate ambiguity, a kindly killer. But this split occurs only in Etherege's mind after he has come under the influence of the house, when conscious control no longer checks or modifies his wandering perceptions. "The mansion itself was like dark-colored experience, the reality; the point of view where things were seen in their true lights; the true world, all outside of which was delusion, had here—dreamlike as it sometimes seemed—the absolute truth" (XII, 209). Under the influence of this inverting experience, Etherege comes to fear that the place is taking hold of him—"the tendrils of the ivy seemed to hold him"—and that he will never be able to resume his active life among men. As he finds himself coming more and more under the control of Brathwaite and the house, feeling that he will decay there, he discovers just how much he has been under the stealthy observation and control of Doctor Grimshawe.

> He looked back through the vanished years to the time which he had spent with the old Doctor, and he felt unaccountably as if the mysterious old man were yet ruling him, as he did in his boyhood; as if his inscrutable inevitable eye were upon him in all his movements; nay, as if he had guided every step that he took in coming hither, and were stalking mistily before him, leading him onward. . . . So here, in this darkened room, he waited for what should come to pass. . . . the witchcraft of the place was really to be recognized, the old witchcraft, too, of the Doctor, which he had escaped by the quick ebullition of youthful spirit, long ago while the Doctor lived; but which had [been] stored up till now, like an influenza that remains latent for years, and then breaks out in active disease. (XII, 296)

This remarkable analysis of the cause and process of mental collapse does not prove to be therapeutic. Etherege finds himself becoming a prisoner, a feeling that later materializes as the prisoner in the subterranean chamber. But now, wandering among the dark passages of the house and frightened by his circumstances, he sees only visions of control:

> A great disturbance there was in his being, the causes of which he could not trace. It had an influence on his dreams, through which the Doctor

seemed to pass continually, and when he awoke, it was often with the sensation that he had just before been holding conversation with the old man, and that the latter—with that gesture of power that he remembered so well—had been impressing some command upon him. . . . It seemed as if he was under a spell; he could neither go away nor rest—nothing but dream troubled dreams. He had ghostly fears, as if someone were near him whom he could not make out; stealing behind him, and starting away when he was impelled to turn round. (XII, 297–298)

These visions of the past are a prelude to Etherege's growing suspicions that the master of the house intends to poison him, but in a loving, seductive manner. What follows is said to be merely the "dreamy suppositions of Etherege, in the idleness and languor of this old mansion, letting his mind run at will, and following it into dim caves whither it tended" (XII, 301). Sensing danger from the master of the house, Etherege yet

did not think that Mr. Brathwaite had the slightest hostility towards him. It might make the thing more horrible, perhaps; but it has been often seen, in those who poison for the sake of interest, without feelings of personal malevolence, that they do it as kindly as the nature of the thing will permit; they, possibly, may even have a certain degree of affection for their victims, enough to induce them to make the last hours of life sweet and pleasant, to wind up the fever of life with a double supply of enjoyable throbs, to sweeten and delicately flavor the cup of death that they offer to the lips of him whose life is inconsistent with some stated necessity of their own. (XII, 299–300)

Despite his suspicions, the warnings of his friends, and the threats of the master, Etherege makes known to his host the possibility that he will displace him and accepts two glasses of a strange wine that the host himself does not drink. The wine at least will bring matters to a conclusion, prevent his taking up his active life again, and unite his fate to that of the house. Death is one form of the peace that he has been seeking in England and Etherege acts as if he deserves it. Indeed, death by the master's hand seems like an erotic consummation toward which he is drawn.

The wine brings on the culmination of that truth-revealing dream-state toward which everything has been tending.

It had, he thought, a singular effect upon his faculties, quickening and making them active, and causing him to feel as if he were on the point of penetrating rare mysteries, such as men's thoughts are always hovering round, and always returning from. Some strange, vast, sombre, mysterious truth, which he seemed to have searched for long, appeared to be on the point of being revealed to him . . . an opening of doors, a drawing away of veils, a lifting of heavy, magnificent curtains, whose dark folds hung before a spectacle of awe;—it was like the verge of the grave. (XII, 307)

THE SECRET PRISONER

This second descent into the valley of death brings Ned's mind back to his earliest unremembered childhood. In a dim, confining chamber deep in the bowels of the house, a room unknown to all but initiates, he returns unwillingly to life. As in his prior return from a brush with death, he awakens in the presence of an aged man in the garb of centuries before. This time it is the prisoner who, after surviving in the secret chamber deep in the house from youth until old age, dies as soon as he is identified by the awakening Etherege. Who he is and why he was imprisoned are not revealed until after the close of the narrative in a long authorial meditation that reviews the entire action of the romance. It begins, "Try back again."

In the interest of economy I shall extract those passages in which Hawthorne evolves his conception of the prisoner—a character, let me add, wholly extraneous to the action and serving no apparent purpose other than to embody Etherege's newly surfaced awareness of the Doctor's lifelong remote control over his soul. The Doctor employs as his agent in subduing the prisoner "an imperfectly hanged person" whom he had saved from the scaffold and then made into a moral slave. The agent in turn enslaves the prisoner either by drugs or by "some continual operation on his mind" that causes the prisoner to isolate himself from society. The captive depicted below is both self-imprisoned and the prisoner of the Doctor. Hawthorne's backing and filling on this point indicate that he was portraying psychic rather than physical enslavement and was still unresolved how to assign responsibility for such a situation.

[The agent] does not imprison his foe, but induces him to imprison himself. Lack-a-day! Let it be with his own consent, that he inhabits the secret chamber of the old mansion, and sometimes prowls about the neighborhood. Vastly probable. . . . Try back! What had this gentleman done? He had seduced the young wife of this man? I don't like that. Or his daughter or sister? not much better, though the sister a little. . . . What is the crime? Each son murders his father at a certain age; or does each father try to accomplish the impossibility of murdering his successor? [This striking pre-Freudian Oedipal statement and its inversion may shed some light on the shooting of Cyrus in "Roger Malvin's Burial."] This is not the right tack. . . . He secludes himself, from a morbid impulse, and finds himself caught, and can never get back again into society; so that he has given up all the opportunities of life by that one act. The Doctor promotes it in the first instance, and makes it next to impossible for him to return into the world in the next. . . . There must be a motive, in the first place, strong enough to keep him secluded a week; then, let him get out if he can. The fact should show that a strange repulsion—as well as a strong attraction—exists among human beings. . . . It is a very common thing— this fact of a man's being caught and made prisoner by himself. . . . Now what can be the motive; he has fallen in love with and tried to seduce, the Doctor's young sister; possibly he has seduced her, and she has died. . . . There must be one [chapter], in which this self-imprisoned man must be described—still young, cherishing purposes of coming out into the world, but deferring it till another day. . . .

Again, at an after period, . . . the prisoner must be introduced, now some years older; the effect of these imprisoned years must be developed; his growing horror of the world, yet sometimes a passionate yearning to get back into it. . . . Show him with the marks of coming age, and his faculties, growing torpid through disuse. . . .

His mind, I think, should at all times be full of the Doctor—haunted by some impression of him. . . . [The prisoner is to be sensitive, poetic, imaginative.] A lack of animal spirits, of active energy. He has books and writing materials. . . .

This runs through the Romance like the vertebrae of the back-bone. There should be a reference to it in everything, grave or gay. (XII, 324–331)

Of this confusing meditation, we can say one thing that is certain—the prisoner does not run through the romance like a backbone. He is hardly there at all in the narrative as written, although he may indeed be the backbone of the personal romance rising up from the depths. The confusion of pronouns and antecedents that may have disturbed the reader is only partly a result of excision. Primarily, it is Hawthorne's own confusion of one man with another as principals and agents, enslavers and victims merge. His vacillation about just who enslaved the prisoner runs throughout the passage. We see him move from the idea of purely Gothic revenge on the seducer of the Doctor's sister, to more and more subtle forms of enslavement—from drops of poison to something far more maddening, inducing the prisoner to enslave himself, and then back again, over and over again. The punishment by the older man is somehow justified by this seduction of a sister, which is mentioned far more frequently than the excerpt indicates. Throughout the passage we see this pattern—seclusion of a young man in a secret chamber by an older man whose sister was seduced or ruined by the younger man, then an attenuation of the punitive action of the older man, so that punishment becomes internalized into self-imprisonment, then again an angry rejection of self-blame and a reassertion of the older man's punitive and destructive influence.

And far more frequently than our excerpt shows, the crime of the younger man is generalized away from seduction of the Doctor's sister to the possibility that the Doctor or his agent enslaved the prisoner by an all-inclusive permissiveness. By pandering to "all the desires of his heart," the agent causes evil desires to become deeds. The author cannot specify these evil desires, but as the young man in the chamber comes more and more to resemble Hawthorne's descriptions of his own solitude, both in the "haunted chamber" and later, the autobiographical implication is that the self-immured prisoner is suffering profound guilt for "evil" desires for his father-surrogate's sister, that is, Hawthorne's own mother. His personal confusion is such that he is not certain just who is punishing whom for what; the prisoner's own conscience has become indistinguishable from the Doctor's punitive ire.

Hawthorne reiterates frequently his intention that Etherege must at the end confront this prisoner. This confrontation, which does in fact occur within the narrative, although the nature of the prisoner is given only in the working notes, seems to be a confrontation of the active aspect of Hawthorne's personality with the withdrawn part. It occurs only after Etherege has reached back into his own past deeply enough to realize his enthrallment by the Doctor. At the time of this meeting, just before the conclusion of the narrative, Etherege is near death from poisoned wine administered by Lord Brathwaite, and the prisoner dies. Ned Etherege approaches death twice within the short span of this romance and witnesses the death of the prisoner, an aspect of himself and of the author. It is not clear whether or not Ned dies at the conclusion, but he is found at the end with the dead prisoner "at the bottom of a winding descent, that seemed deep and remote, and far within" (XII, 321–322) in the presence of the coffer full of golden hair, the symbol of something that should never be possessed. He has carried his quest as far as it could be carried.

When the narrative proper has ended and the nine-page authorial meditation is concluded, the narrative voice suddenly shifts to the first person in a brief passage depicting the prisoner at an earlier time. He is discovered in a narrow, oppressive, unlighted antique chamber in which all the emblems of the romance are resumed. Here, in a chamber likened to Spenser's Cave of Despair and furnished with instruments of suicide, are the prisoner, his keeper, the ancient coffer, and a plenitude of cobwebs. This hallucinatory section begins:

> There is—or there was, now many years ago, and a few years also, it was still extant—a chamber, which when I think of it, seems to me like entering a deep recess of my own consciousness, a deep cave of my nature; so much have I thought of it and its inmate, through a considerable period of my life. (XII, 235–236)

This "haunted chamber" deep in the bowels of the ancestral mansion was indeed a chamber of the author's own consciousness, so much so that in the final words of the manuscript, he suddenly drops the posture of objectivity and lapses into the first person. In this chamber of his consciousness the narrator discovers the secret prisoner as a young man contemplating suicide. The final paragraph of the first draft describes the mental state of this subterranean prisoner, but seems also to describe the condition of Etherege after he has come to a realization of his enthrallment, and perhaps also that of the creator of both these victims of wizard control:

> By and by, by what impulse or cause it is impossible to say, he started upon his feet in a sudden frenzy of rage and despair. It seemed as if a

179

consciousness of some strange, wild, miserable fate that had befallen him had come upon him all at once; how that he was a prisoner to a devilish influence, to some wizard might, that bound him hand and foot with spider's web. So he stamped, so he half-shrieked, yet stopped himself in the midst so that his cry was stifled and smothered. Then he snatched up the poisoned dagger and looked at it; the noose and put it about his neck; evil instrument of death, but laid it down again. (XII, 341–342)

By having both Etherege and the prisoner bound in a "wizard-woven web" Hawthorne reveals the final metaphoric value of the spider's web. The cobweb is a soft and silken trap seductive enough to paralyze the human victim's will. Thinking he can always burst such fragile bonds, he reposes in them forever. In 1837, as Hawthorne was just beginning to emerge from his twelve years of seclusion, he wrote to Longfellow of his own sense of self-imprisonment in language less feverish than his depiction of the prisoner, but still reminiscent of it.

> You would have been much nearer the truth if you had pictured me as dwelling in an owl's nest; for mine is about as dismal, and like the owl I seldom venture abroad till after dusk. By some witchcraft or other . . . I have been carried apart from the main current of life, and find it impossible to get back again. Since we last met . . . I have secluded myself from society; and yet I never meant any such thing, nor dreamed what sort of life I was going to lead. I have made a captive of myself, and put me into a dungeon, and now I cannot find the key to let myself out,—and if the door were open, I should be almost afraid to let myself come out, . . . I can assure you that trouble is the next best thing to enjoyment, and that there is no fate in this world so horrible as to have no share in either its joys or sorrows. For the last ten years, I have not lived, but only dreamed of living. . . . You cannot conceive how utterly devoid of satisfaction all my retrospects are. I have laid up no treasures of pleasant remembrances against old age.[8]

Elaborate proof is not required to demonstrate that the late romances and *Grimshawe* in particular were not fully under the author's control. His own biographical and psychological concerns diverted the work from the circular quest romance pattern that was clearly his model. His hero begins as the typical romance foundling with tokens indicating noble origins. These tokens, however, turn out to be illusory, because in the process of the book's development Ned becomes a victim of diabolic deceit, the instrument of his educator's vengeance, and not the true heir. The true heir is finally an aged pauper saint who has only contempt for such wordly vanities as estates and titles. Reinstatement into a noble place in the world is both denied to Etherege and devalued at the same time. If it is just as well to be an American with no past at one's back, there is no particular salvation in having the tokens that will prove one's claim to a noble title. Thus the democratic author fails to sustain the goal of his hero's quest. This quest is informed, then, not by religiously sanctioned fixed values, but by nostalgia for the age of fixed values. For such fixities Hawthorne was too skeptical, too disillusioned, and too late.

Etherege's quest becomes converted into an inner, psychic drive for reunion with the lost mother and a fruitless search for the true father. Unlike the romance hero, he finds not his true father but only a series of constantly mutating father-surrogates who, despite their differences, are all transformations of the first one. The characters refuse to remain fixed archetypes of good and evil; they split under the psychological pressure of disguised autobiography into complexities that cannot be contained by the format. Paradoxical figures like benevolent tyrants, infuriating saints, and compassionate poisoners are conceivable, and may even be treatable by literary techniques, but they burst apart the seams of a romance. Without quite knowing it, Hawthorne anticipated the modern novel of the inner quest. Had he been aware of the forces propelling him, he could have used the romance quest with conscious irony, as Browning did in "Childe Roland to the Dark Tower Came," showing that the quest of the modern hero may wind up in a wasteland. But Hawthorne did not keep up with the direction of Victorian letters. He attempted a traditional quest romance when it was too late in his own and in literary history, and too early for him to control what he really was trying to write, his personal, disguised version of the family romance.

Notes

PREFACE

1. Arlin Turner, *Nathaniel Hawthorne: A Biography* (New York: Oxford University Press, 1980), and James R. Mellow, *Nathaniel Hawthorne in His Time* (Boston: Houghton Mifflin, 1980).

2. Randall Stewart, *Nathaniel Hawthorne: A Biography* (New Haven: Yale University Press, 1948).

3. Frederick C. Crews, *The Sins of the Fathers: Hawthorne's Psychological Themes* (New York: Oxford University Press, 1966).

4. Eric J. Sundquist, *Home as Found: Authority and Genealogy in Nineteenth-Century American Literature* (Baltimore and London: Johns Hopkins University Press, 1979).

5. Gloria C. Erlich, "Who Wrote Hawthorne's First Diary?" *Nathaniel Hawthorne Journal* (1977): 37–70.

6. J. Donald Crowley, ed., *Hawthorne: The Critical Heritage* (London: Routledge & Kegan Paul, 1970).

CHAPTER ONE

1. John Franzosa ("Hawthorne's Separation from Salem," *ESQ: Journal of the American Renaissance* 24 [1978]: 57–71) makes connections between *The Scarlet Letter* and Hawthorne's maternal ties, separation anxieties, and dependency needs. I agree with Franzosa that Pearl's "maternal Umwelt includes not only a maternal presence but an absent father" (p. 59), but question his view that Hawthorne's mother or Hester suggest the "phallic mother." Other articles relevant to issues in this chapter are: Frank MacShane, "The House of the Dead: Hawthorne's 'The Custom-House' and *The Scarlet Letter*," *New England Quarterly* 35 (1962): 93–101; Dan McCall,

"The Design of Hawthorne's 'Custom-House,'" *Nineteenth-Century Fiction* 21 (1967): 349–358; Marshall Van Deusen, "Narrative Tone in 'The Custom-House' and *The Scarlet Letter*," *Nineteenth-Century Fiction* 21 (1967): 61–71; Harry C. West, "Hawthorne's Editorial Pose," *American Literature* 44 (1972): 208–221; James M. Cox, *"The Scarlet Letter:* Through the Old Manse and 'The Custom-House,'" *Virginia Quarterly Review* 51 (1975): 432–447; Thomas H. Pauly, "Hawthorne's Houses of Fiction," *American Literature* 48 (1976): 271–291. Paul John Eakin, in "Hawthorne's Imagination and the Structure of 'The Custom-House'" *(American Literature* 43 [1971]: 346–358), defines the death and resurrection theme of the preface, concluding that "the germinal moment of his communion with the dead, with the remains of Hester Prynne and Surveyor Pue, is an account of a decisive event in the creative process, the genesis of *The Scarlet Letter"* (p. 358). Nina Baym, in an essay published when the manuscript of the present book had been completed ("Nathaniel Hawthorne and His Mother: A Biographical Speculation," *American Literature* 54 [1982]: 1–27) chides biographers for neglecting Hawthorne's mother and connects composition of *The Scarlet Letter* to her death. I agree with Baym that Hawthorne's choice of a solitary mother as main character relates to Elizabeth Hawthorne's death and to her importance in his psychic life. I disagree, however, with Baym's idea that "Hawthorne probably never missed his dead father consciously" because the Manning men made adequate compensation for this loss (pp. 11–12) or that "the search for the lost *mother,* rather than the lost father, underlies much of the story patterning in his mature fiction" (p. 13). I think it unnecessary to pit mother against father or matriarchy against patriarchy in discussing Hawthorne's psychic needs. He longed for a complete parental *set* as the center of his family constellation—both parents present and functioning with respect to each other and to himself. Although I fully share Baym's view that young Hawthorne suffered from maternal deprivation, I question that "for him, Eden is a benign matriarchy" (p. 12). He had more than enough matriarchy with his strong-minded grandmother and Aunt Mary, from whose dominance the children tried to escape and had to protect their own mother. It seems to me that Hawthorne sought to avoid dominant women.

2. Julian Hawthorne, *Nathaniel Hawthorne and His Wife,* vols. 14 and 15 of *The Works of Nathaniel Hawthorne* (Boston: Houghton Mifflin, 1851–1884), 14: 353–354. Hereafter, vol. 14 will be referred to as Julian I and vol. 15 will be referred to as Julian II.

3. Daniel J. Levinson, Charlotte N. Darrow, Edward B. Klein, Maria H. Levinson, and Braxton McKee, *The Seasons of a Man's Life* (New York: Ballantine, 1978), p. 41. Although Levinson's methodology has been ques-

tioned by some critics, his study builds on a vast literature on the adult life cycle and provides a useful framework for structuring life histories.

4. "Settling down" is Levinson's term for relinquishing multiple possibilities for work and love and accepting a particular vocation and a particular life partner.

5. Erik H. Erikson, *Life History and the Historical Moment* (New York: Norton, 1975), pp. 72–73.

6. September 16, 1832, Nathaniel Hawthorne to his mother, written from Burlington, Vermont.

7. Throughout life Hawthorne was fascinated by aging and death, with morbid curiosity about postmortem decay and interest in elixirs of life. His expectation of dying before the age of twenty-five was reported by Ebe Hawthorne to James T. Fields in December 1870, Randall Stewart, "Recollections of Hawthorne by His Sister Elizabeth," *American Literature* 16 (1945): 320. His periods of depression are reported in notebook entries both early and late, and letters from Horatio Bridge try to cajole him out of despairing, if not suicidal, moods. Some notebook entries, such as that of July 27, 1838 *(American Notebooks*, ed. Claude M. Simpson, VIII, 85) imply sufficient necrophilia to lead him to peek into tombs.

8. *English Notebooks*, ed. Randall Stewart (New York: Modern Language Association, 1941), p. 98; December 28, 1854.

9. Levinson et al., *Seasons*, p. 213.

10. For a detailed study of this subject, see Nina Baym, *The Shape of Hawthorne's Career* (Ithaca and London: Cornell University Press, 1976).

11. Terence Martin, in *Nathaniel Hawthorne* (Boston: Twayne, 1965), p. 18 and *passim*, discusses the poet-bookkeeper typology and its literary manifestations throughout Hawthorne's work from early to late.

12. Ibid., pp. 63–65.

13. January 24, 1846. MS Duyckinck Collection, New York Public Library. Quoted by Donald Crowley, introduction to *Mosses from an Old Manse*, X, p. 517.

14. Levinson et al., *Seasons*, pp. 209ff.

15. Ibid., pp. 223–224.

16. Elliott Jaques, "Death and the Mid-Life Crisis," *International Journal of Psychoanalysis* 46 (1965): 502–514.

17. Levinson et al., *Seasons*, p. 30.

18. Hawthorne's generativity in the Eriksonian sense of helping to lead the next generation into its maturity is expressed in the role Hawthorne was soon to play in catalyzing the genius of Herman Melville shortly after they met in the Berkshires.

19. Levinson et al., *Seasons*, pp. 228ff.

20. Robert Jay Lifton, *The Life of the Self: Toward a New Psychology* (New York: Simon and Schuster, 1976), p. 115.

CHAPTER TWO

1. A version of this chapter appeared as "Hawthorne and the Mannings," *Studies in the American Renaissance* (1980): 97–117. A fortunate consequence of Richard Manning's move to Maine and of Elizabeth Hawthorne's sojourn there, is the wealth of family correspondence that makes it possible to reconstruct their personalities and relationships.

2. Vernon Loggins, *The Hawthornes: The Story of Seven Generations of an American Family* (New York: Columbia University Press, 1951). Loggins gives 1662 as the date of Nicholas Manning's arrival in Salem, 1630 or 1633 as the date of William Hathorne's arrival. Randall Stewart says that the Mannings emigrated from England in 1679.

3. Joseph B. Felt, *Annals of Salem*, 2d ed. (Salem: Ives, 1845), I: 459–460.

4. Loggins, *The Hawthornes*, p. 279. Further details on the trial of the Manning sisters can be found in *Records and Files of the Quarterly Courts of Massachusetts*.

5. Many authors state in effect that "the Manning influence should not be too much discounted," but usually treatment of the subject goes no farther than this recognition. Randall Stewart (*Nathaniel Hawthorne: A Biography*), whose words I have just quoted, covers ancestry and boyhood in twelve pages. The two most recent biographies, by Arlin Turner (New York: Oxford University Press, 1980) and James R. Mellow (Boston: Houghton Mifflin, 1980), use the Manning family correspondence and make some attempt to account for Hawthorne's maternal relatives. Turner recognizes that the move from Union Street to Herbert Street brought about a substitution of "the Mannings for the Hawthornes in [the] children's close relationships" (p. 12) and offers an eleven-page chapter on "The Manning Years." Mellow gives the youthful years with the Mannings a bit more attention and attempts to characterize the Manning aunts and uncles. In addition, Mellow occasionally observes the tension between Nathaniel and his Uncle Robert (pp. 16 and 610). Although Loggins's *The Hawthornes* (1951) is a family chronicle covering seven generations rather than a biography, the chapter "Herbert Street" depicts some of the tensions within the Manning and Hawthorne families.

6. Letter from Rebecca Manning to Gertrude Manning, December 16, 1923, Hawthorne-Manning Collection, Essex Institute, hereafter cited as MSaE.

7. July 26, 1819, *The Letters, 1813–1853*, Letter 5, Centenary Edition XV (Columbus: Ohio State University Press, 1984), edited by Thomas Woodson, L. Neal Smith, and Norman Holmes Pearson. Hereafter citations to this volume will be to volume and letter number.

8. Letter from Elizabeth M. Hawthorne to Richard Manning, March 30, 1826, Nathaniel Hawthorne Collection, Bowdoin College Library, hereafter cited as Bowdoin.

9. 1799, MSaE.

10. NH to mother, September 26, 1820, MSaE.

11. February 24, 1816, MSaE.

12. *Dictionary of American Biography*, ed. Dumas Malone (New York: Scribner's, 1933), 12: 252–253.

13. 1923, MSaE.

14. Robert Manning, *Book of Fruits* (Salem: Ives and Jewett, 1838), p. 10.

15. 1814, MSaE.

16. Randall Stewart, "Recollections of Hawthorne by His Sister Elizabeth," *American Literature* 16 (1945): 319–320. Elizabeth considered this injury a major event in her brother's early life. She attributed to it his habit of reading, his unsuitability for a life of business, and his expectation of an early death.

17. January 12, 1814, MSaE.

18. September 1816, MSaE.

19. MSaE.

20. September 9, 1814, MSaE.

21. December 1818 and November 1827, MSaE.

22. MSaE.

23. Pearson Transcript.

24. March 20, 1816, Pearson Transcript.

25. MSaE.

26. MSaE.

27. Even Julian Hawthorne acknowledges his father's lethargy. See, for example, Julian I, p. 122.

28. August 28, 1821, *The Letters* XV, Letter 26.

29. Bowdoin, printed in *Nathaniel Hawthorne Journal* (1975): 15.

30. *The Letters* XV, Letter 46.

31. *The Letters* XV, Letter 7.

32. NH to mother, June 19, 1821, *The Letters* XV, Letter 24.

33. Bowdoin.

34. MSaE.

35. Julian I, pp. 116–117; November 26, 1824.

36. MSaE.

37. September 14, 1859, MSaE.

38. December 21, 1855, Berg Collection, quoted here from photocopied transcript supplied by editors of the forthcoming *The Letters, 1853–1864*, Centenary Edition XVI (Columbus: Ohio State University Press), edited by Thomas Woodson, L. Neal Smith, and Norman Holmes Pearson. Hereafter citations to this volume will be identified by date alone.

39. May 16, 1814; January 28, 1823; March 31, 1824, MSaE.

40. MSaE.

41. 1828, 1829, MSaE.

42. MSaE.

43. MSaE.

44. September 29, 1841, *The Letters* XV, Letter 213.

CHAPTER THREE

1. James T. Fields, *Yesterdays with Authors* (Boston and New York: Houghton Mifflin, 1899), p. 43.

2. Norman Holmes Pearson, "Elizabeth Peabody on Hawthorne," *Essex Institute Historical Collections* 94 (1958): 256–276.

3. Baym, "Nathaniel Hawthorne and His Mother." Baym attributes Elizabeth Hawthorne's avoidance of her husband's family to embarrassment and possible snubs over the fact that Ebe was born only seven months after her parents' marriage. Because a seven-month birth can signify prematurity as well as a "bridal pregnancy," and because I am aware of no evidence that Madame Hawthorne was treated by her husband's family or anyone else as a sinful woman, I would hesitate to build too much on this speculation.

4. June 9, 1842, to Sophia; *The Letters* XV, Letter 239.

5. Bowdoin.

6. George Parsons Lathrop, *A Study of Hawthorne* (Boston: J. R. Osgood, 1876); reprint (New York: A & S Press, 1969), p. 112.

7. Bowdoin, August 9, 1820.

8. NH to Sophia, April 14, 1844; *The Letters* XV, Letter 286.

9. January 10, 1821, to Louisa, MSaE.

10. Erik H. Erikson, *Childhood and Society* (New York: Norton, 1950), p. 222.

11. Pearson, "Elizabeth Peabody on Hawthorne," pp. 256–276.

12. Manning Hawthorne, "The Youth of Hawthorne," M.A. thesis, University of North Carolina, 1937; Stewart, *Nathaniel Hawthorne: A Biography*; Crews, *Sins of the Fathers*; Jean Normand, *Nathaniel Hawthorne: An Approach to an Analysis of Artistic Creation*, trans. Derek Coltman (Cleveland and London: Case Western Reserve University Press, 1970); Baym, "Nathaniel Hawthorne and His Mother," pp. 1–27.

13. Baym, "Nathaniel Hawthorne and His Mother," pp. 4ff.
14. Horatio Bridge, *Personal Recollections of Nathaniel Hawthorne* (New York: Harpers, 1892), pp. 32ff.
15. Rose Hawthorne Lathrop, *Memories of Hawthorne* (Boston and New York: Houghton Mifflin, 1897), p. 78.
16. Julian I, p. 314.
17. Julian II, pp. 95–96.
18. Fields, *Yesterdays with Authors*, p. 113.
19. MSaE.
20. MSaE.
21. MSaE.
22. MSaE.
23. MSaE.
24. MSaE.
25. *The Letters* XV, Letter 18.
26. Ibid., Letter 8.
27. MSaE.
28. *The Letters* XV, Letter 10.
29. Ibid., Letter 19.
30. Ibid., Letter 11.
31. Ibid., Letter 16.
32. Ibid., Letter 24.
33. Edgar Dryden, *Nathaniel Hawthorne: The Poetics of Enchantment* (Ithaca and London: Cornell University Press, 1977); Eric J. Sundquist, *Home as Found.* Hawthorne's sense of dislocation has been noted by recent critics who relate his interest in "origins" to his personal rootlessness. Edgar Dryden, for example, observes nostalgia for home in Hawthorne's prefaces and traces the homeless characters in his fiction from the early stories to the late romances. Eric J. Sundquist builds from such ideas a reading of *The House of the Seven Gables* that draws elaborate psychoanalytic conclusions from Hawthorne's interest in thresholds and houses and relates this to his uncertain sense of self.
34. Julian I, p. 429.
35. Crews, *Sins of the Fathers*, p. 70.
36. Manning Hawthorne, "The Youth of Hawthorne," p. 150.
37. Julian I, pp. 96–97.
38. October 4, 1840, *The Letters* XV, Letter 173.
39. Manning Hawthorne prints a good number of her girlish and affectionate letters in "Maria Louisa Hawthorne," *Essex Institute Historical Collections* 75 (1939): 103–134.
40. Manning Hawthorne, "Aunt Ebe; Some Letters of Elizabeth M.

Hawthorne," *New England Quarterly* 20 (1947): 209–231, 210. This article contains a broad sampling of Ebe's letters, especially the late ones written from Montserrat to her many relatives, and gives a good idea of the extensive range of her reading.

41. Pearson, "Elizabeth Peabody on Hawthorne," pp. 256–276.

42. Bowdoin.

43. Richard's letter is in the Essex Institute collection. Sophia's is quoted in Manning Hawthorne, "Aunt Ebe," p. 215.

44. MSaE, March 22, 1836.

45. MSaE, May 5, 1836.

46. May 27, 1862; Berg Collection of the New York Public Library, *The Letters* XVI.

47. May 9, 1876, to Maria Manning, Manning Transcript. Ebe's letters from Montserrat were preserved in typed transcripts by Professor Richard Clarke Manning. One copy of these transcripts is held by the Beinecke Rare Book and Manuscript Library at Yale University; the other is divided between the Essex Institute and Bowdoin College. Since I have consulted both copies I cite these letters as "Manning Transcript." Professor Manning destroyed the originals of these letters.

48. November 23, 1875, Manning Transcript.

49. December 1876, Manning Transcript.

50. Stewart, *English Notebooks*, p. 556.

51. Ibid., p. 88.

52. Quoted by Edward Wagenknecht, *Nathaniel Hawthorne: Man and Writer* (New York: Oxford University Press, 1961), p. 150.

53. Stewart, *English Notebooks*, p. 88.

54. February 18, 1877, Manning Transcript.

55. April 17 [18, 19] 1839, *The Letters* XV, Letter 96.

56. Lathrop, *Memories of Hawthorne*, pp. 4, 21.

57. Julian I, pp. 191–193.

58. Ibid., 197–198. In dismissing Julian's and Rose Hawthorne's versions of Ebe's role in Hawthorne's delayed announcement to his mother of his engagement, Nina Baym not only overlooks Ebe's jealousy of Sophia, but asserts without providing her evidence that Sophia "later worked out a tale which made Ebe (conveniently) the culprit in the concealment. Obligingly . . . Julian transmitted her explanation." Baym, "Hawthorne and His Mother," p. 17.

59. Julian I, p. 189.

60. November 1851, to Louisa, Manning Transcript.

61. March 8, 1879, to cousin Robert Manning, Manning Transcript.

62. December 13, 1879, Manning Transcript.

63. Manning Hawthorne, "Aunt Ebe," 223–224.
64. *The Letters* XV, Letter 386.
65. As quoted in Julian I, p. 184; see *The Letters* XV, Letter 388 .
66. Stewart, *English Notebooks*, p. 321.
67. Sundquist, "Representation and Speculation in Hawthorne and *The House of the Seven Gables*," *Home as Found*, pp. 86–142.
68. Julian I, p. 181.
69. Ibid., p. 192.
70. Ibid., p. 181.
71. Levinson et al., *Seasons*, p. 109.

CHAPTER FOUR

1. This argument also appears in Louis B. Salomon, "Hawthorne and His Father: A Conjecture," *Literature and Psychology* 12 (1963): 12–17.
2. For the dating of the story and a useful summary of the critical controversy surrounding it, I am indebted to Lea Bertani Vozar Newman, *A Reader's Guide to the Short Stories of Nathaniel Hawthorne* (Boston: G. K. Hall, 1979), pp. 327–332.
3. Hyatt H. Waggoner, Introduction to 3d ed., *Nathaniel Hawthorne: Selected Tales and Sketches* (New York: Holt, Rinehart & Winston, 1970), p. viii.
4. Stewart, *English Notebooks*, p. 642, n. 298.
5. Ibid., p. 64, June 30, 1854.
6. George Parsons Lathrop, *A Study of Hawthorne*, pp. 64–65, first made this astute observation.
7. *The Letters* XV, Letter 253.
8. My discussion of the story is adapted from my fuller treatment of it in "Guilt and Expiation in 'Roger Malvin's Burial,'" *Nineteenth-Century Fiction* 26 (1972): 377–389.
9. See Crews, *Sins of the Fathers*, pp. 80–95. Crews is surely right in this ground-breaking chapter proving that the slaying of Cyrus was not a mere hunting accident and that Oedipal anxiety figures among Reuben's unconscious motives. However, Crews does not follow his own leads to ask *why* Roger Malvin's altruism should occasion resentment and what psychological motives of the author led him to find atonement in the slaying of a son. My answers to these and other questions can be found in my article cited above in n. 8.
10. James R. Mellow, *Nathaniel Hawthorne in His Times* (Boston: Houghton Mifflin, 1980), p. 610. Mellow, deliberately eschewing psychoanalytic interpretation in his biography, condenses into a long footnote a speculation that a "homosexual assault" generated an "animus toward Robert Manning" that

was probably the origin of Hawthorne's themes of initiation into sin and the "unpardonable sin," and the source of his horticulturally inclined villains. Apparently Mellow arrived independently at many facts and conclusions already adduced in my "Paradox of Benevolence: Hawthorne and the Mannings," a dissertation completed in 1977. In his footnote and occasionally at various points in his narrative, Mellow uses some of the evidence presented earlier in my dissertation, including Hawthorne's frequent linking of pear trees (Uncle Robert's favorite) to heavy villains reminiscent of this uncle. However, Mellow does not build on these insights or integrate them into a theory of life and literature.

11. Erikson, "Eight Stages of Man," *Childhood and Society*, pp. 223–224.

12. This issue is summed up in Wagenknecht, *Nathaniel Hawthorne*, pp. 17–18.

13. Ibid., pp. 109–110.

14. NH to Sophia from Liverpool, February 7, 1856, *The Letters* XVI.

15. Ibid., October 18, 1863, NH to J. T. Fields from Concord.

16. Stewart, *English Notebooks*, p. 642, n. 298.

17. Bowdoin.

18. Bowdoin.

19. Fields, *Yesterdays with Authors*, p. 113.

20. See especially Edwin Haviland Miller, *Melville* (New York: Braziller, 1975).

21. Stewart, *English Notebooks*, p. 8.

22. Crews, *Sins of the Fathers*, pp. 134–135.

23. Seymour Gross, ed., *The House of the Seven Gables* (New York: Norton, 1967), pp. 25–26. James Mellow hints parenthetically (p. 361) at the Robert Manning component in Judge Pyncheon, as well as noting elements of the late Senator Nathaniel Silsbee.

CHAPTER FIVE

1. An abbreviated version of this chapter was read at the Concord Conference: Hawthorne's Last Years, in October 1981, and printed in *Essex Institute Historical Collections* 118 (1982): 49–58. In *The Poetics of Enchantment*, pp. 162–172, Edgar A. Dryden presents an eloquent treatment of *Grimshawe* as a failed quest romance related to Hawthorne's own sense of rootlessness, but he discusses the book as if it were a unified work. I show that in the process of composing the drafts and fragments Hawthorne discovered the theme of psychological determinism and was virtually disabled by the powerful material that this process brought forth.

2. Stewart, *English Notebooks*, p. 92.

3. Letter to James T. Fields, date not given, but written during the Liverpool consulship. Quoted by Fields in *Yesterdays with Authors*, p. 74.

4. *Doctor Grimshawe's Secret*, ed. Edward H. Davidson (Cambridge, Mass.: Harvard University Press, 1954).

5. Entitled *The American Claimant Manuscripts*, vol. XII of the Centenary Edition also includes *The Ancestral Footstep*. This volume divides the two major drafts of the book Julian Hawthorne entitled *Doctor Grimshawe's Secret* into two sections, called "Etherege" and "Grimshawe," titled according to the name most frequently used in each draft for the Doctor. Since "Etherege" is also the name most often used for the young protagonist in both drafts (he is also called Redclyffe), I refer to these versions instead as the "first and second drafts."

6. Edward H. Davidson, *Hawthorne's Last Phase* (New Haven: Yale University Press, 1949), p. 60. The quotation is taken from Stewart, *The English Notebooks*, pp. 75–76.

7. Davidson edition of *Doctor Grimshawe's Secret*, p. 299, n. 22.

8. Quoted in George Parsons Lathrop, *A Study of Hawthorne*, pp. 175–176.

Bibliography

MANUSCRIPT MATERIALS

Nathaniel Hawthorne Collection. Bowdoin College Library. Brunswick, Maine.

Files of the late Norman Holmes Pearson, including letters to and from Nathaniel Hawthorne and transcripts of the Manning Family Intercorrespondence. Beinecke Rare Book and Manuscript Library, Collection of American Literature. Yale University, New Haven, Connecticut.

Hawthorne-Manning Collection. The Essex Institute. Salem, Massachusetts.

WORKS BY NATHANIEL HAWTHORNE

The Centenary Edition of the Works of Nathaniel Hawthorne. 16 vols. Edited by William Charvat et al. Columbus: Ohio State University Press, 1962–.

Doctor Grimshawe's Secret. Edited by Edward H. Davidson. Cambridge, Mass.: Harvard University Press, 1954.

The English Notebooks by Nathaniel Hawthorne: Based upon the Original Manuscripts in the Pierpont Morgan Library. Edited by Randall Stewart. New York: Modern Language Association of America, 1941.

Hawthorne as Editor: Selections from His Writings in the American Magazine of Useful and Entertaining Knowledge. Edited by Arlin Turner. Baton Rouge: Louisiana State University Press, 1941.

Hawthorne's Lost Notebook, 1835–1841. Transcript by Barbara S. Mouffe. University Park: Pennsylvania State University Press, 1978.

Letters of Hawthorne to William D. Ticknor: 1851–1864. 2 vols. Newark: Carteret Book Club, 1910. Reprinted in one volume with foreword by C. E. Frazer Clark, Jr. Washington, D.C.: NCR/Microcard Editions, 1972.

Love Letters of Nathaniel Hawthorne. 2 vols. Chicago: Society of the Dofobs, 1907. Reprinted in one volume with foreword by C. E. Frazer Clark, Jr. Washington, D.C.: NCR/Microcard Editions, 1972.

The Works of Nathaniel Hawthorne, with introductory notes by George Parsons Lathrop, Standard Library Edition. 13 vols. Boston: Houghton Mifflin, 1851–1884.

SECONDARY SOURCES

Adams, Timothy Dow. "To Prepare a Preface to Meet the Faces That You Meet: Autobiographical Rhetoric in Hawthorne's Prefaces." *ESQ: Journal of the American Renaissance* 23 (1977): 89–98.

Arac, Jonathan. "The House and the Railroad: *Dombey and Son* and *The House of the Seven Gables.*" *New England Quarterly* 51 (1978): 3–22.

Arvin, Newton. *Hawthorne.* New York: Russell & Russell, 1961.

Bassan, Maurice. *Hawthorne's Son: The Life and Literary Career of Julian Hawthorne.* Columbus: Ohio State University Press, 1970.

———. "Julian Hawthorne Edits Aunt Ebe." *Essex Institute Historical Collections* 100 (1964): 274–278.

Baym, Nina. "Hawthorne's Gothic Discards: *Fanshawe* and 'Alice Doane.'" *Nathaniel Hawthorne Journal* (1974): 105–115.

———. "Nathaniel Hawthorne and His Mother: A Biographical Speculation." *American Literature* 54 (1982): 1–27.

———. *The Shape of Hawthorne's Career.* Ithaca and London: Cornell University Press, 1976.

Bell, Michael. *Hawthorne and the Historical Romance of New England.* Princeton: Princeton University Press, 1971.

Bell, Millicent. *Hawthorne's View of the Artist.* New York: New York State University Press, 1962.

Bercovitch, Sacvan. "Of Wise and Foolish Virgins: Hilda versus Miriam in Hawthorne's *Marble Faun.*" *New England Quarterly* 41 (1968): 281–286.

Berthold, Dennis. "From Freud to Marx: Recent Directions in Hawthorne Criticism." *ESQ: Journal of the American Renaissance* (1976): 107–119.

Bridge, Horatio. *Personal Recollections of Nathaniel Hawthorne.* New York: Harpers, 1893.

Brodhead, Richard. *Hawthorne, Melville, and the Novel.* Chicago and London: University of Chicago Press, 1976.

Brodwin, Stanley. "Hawthorne and the Function of History: A Reading of 'Alice Doane's Appeal.'" *Nathaniel Hawthorne Journal* (1974): 116–128.

Cameron, Sharon. *The Corporeal Self: Allegories of the Body in Melville and Hawthorne*. Baltimore and London: Johns Hopkins University Press, 1981.

Cantwell, Robert. *Nathaniel Hawthorne: The American Years*. New York and Toronto: Rinehart, 1948.

Clark, C. E. Frazer, Jr. "Census of Nathaniel Hawthorne Letters, 1813–1849." *Nathaniel Hawthorne Journal* (1972): 257–282.

———. "Census of Nathaniel Hawthorne Letters, 1850–1864." *Nathaniel Hawthorne Journal* (1973): 202–252.

Coffey, Dennis G. "Hawthorne's 'Alice Doane's Appeal': The Artist Absolved." *ESQ: Journal of the American Renaissance* 21 (1974): 230–240.

Cohen, B. Bernard. "*Paradise Lost* and 'Young Goodman Brown.'" *Essex Institute Historical Collections* 94 (1958): 282–296.

Colacurcio, Michael J. "The Sense of an Author: The Familiar Life and Strange Imaginings of Nathaniel Hawthorne." *ESQ: Journal of the American Renaissance* 27 (1981): 108–133.

Conway, Moncure D. *Life of Nathaniel Hawthorne*. New York: Scribner's, 1890.

Cox, James M. "*The Scarlet Letter*: Through the Old Manse and 'The Custom-House.'" *Virginia Quarterly Review* 51 (1975): 432–447.

Crews, Frederick C. *The Sins of the Fathers: Hawthorne's Psychological Themes*. New York: Oxford University Press, 1966.

Crowley, J. Donald, ed. *Hawthorne: The Critical Heritage*. London: Routledge & Kegan Paul, 1970.

Davidson, Edward H. *Hawthorne's Last Phase*. New Haven: Yale University Press, 1949.

Dauber, Kenneth. *Rediscovering Hawthorne*. Princeton: Princeton University Press, 1977.

Doubleday, Neal Frank. *Hawthorne's Early Tales: A Critical Study*. Durham: Duke University Press, 1972.

Duncan, Jeffrey L. "The Design of Hawthorne's Fabrications." *Yale Review* 70 (1981): 51–71.

Dryden, Edgar A. *Nathaniel Hawthorne: The Poetics of Enchantment*. Ithaca and London: Cornell University Press, 1977.

Eakin, Paul John. "Hawthorne's Imagination and the Structure of 'The Custom-House.'" *American Literature* 43 (1971): 346–358.

Erikson, Erik H. *Childhood and Society*. New York: Norton, 1950.

———. *Identity: Youth and Crisis*. New York: Norton, 1968.

———. *The Life Cycle Completed: A Review*. New York and London: Norton, 1982.

———. *Life History and the Historical Moment*. New York: Norton, 1975.

Erlich, Gloria C. "Deadly Innocence: Hawthorne's Dark Women." *New England Quarterly* 41 (1968): 163–179.

———. "Doctor Grimshawe and Other Secrets." *Essex Institute Historical Collections* 118 (1982): 49–58.

———. "Guilt and Expiation in 'Roger Malvin's Burial.'" *Nineteenth-Century Fiction* 26 (1972): 377–389.

———. "Hawthorne and the Mannings." *Studies in the American Renaissance* (1980): 97–117.

———. "The Paradox of Benevolence: Hawthorne and the Mannings." Ph.D. diss., Princeton University, 1977.

———. "Who Wrote Hawthorne's First Diary?" *Nathaniel Hawthorne Journal* (1977): 37–70.

Fairbanks, Henry George. *The Lasting Loneliness of Nathaniel Hawthorne.* Albany: Magi Books, 1965.

Felt, Joseph B. *Annals of Salem.* 2d ed. 2 vols. Salem: Ives, 1845.

Fields, Annie. *Nathaniel Hawthorne.* Boston: Small, Maynard, 1899.

Fields, James T. *Hawthorne.* Boston: Osgood, 1876.

———. *Yesterdays with Authors.* Boston: Houghton Mifflin, 1899.

Fogle, Richard Harter. *Hawthorne's Fiction: The Light and the Dark.* Norman: University of Oklahoma Press, 1952. Reprint, 1963.

———. "Priscilla's Veil: A Study of the Veil-Imagery in *The Blithedale Romance.*" *Nathaniel Hawthorne Journal* (1972): 59–68.

Franzosa, John. "Hawthorne's Separation from Salem." *ESQ: Journal of the American Renaissance* 24 (1978): 57–71.

———. "A Psychoanalysis of Hawthorne's Style." *Genre* 14 (1981): 383–409.

Gollin, Rita. *Nathaniel Hawthorne and the Truth of Dreams.* Baton Rouge: Louisiana State University Press, 1979.

Gorman, Herbert. *Hawthorne.* New York: Doran, 1927.

Gross, Seymour, ed. *Nathaniel Hawthorne: The House of the Seven Gables.* New York: Norton, 1967.

Gross, Seymour, and Rosalie Murphy, eds. *Nathaniel Hawthorne: The Blithedale Romance.* New York: Norton, 1978.

Hall, Spencer. "Beatrice Cenci: Symbol and Vision in *The Marble Faun.*" *Nineteenth-Century Fiction* 25 (1970): 85–95.

Hawthorne, Hildegarde. *Romantic Rebel: The Story of Nathaniel Hawthorne.* New York and London: Century, 1932.

Hawthorne, Julian. *Hawthorne and His Circle.* New York and London: Harper, 1903.

———. *Nathaniel Hawthorne and His Wife.* Vols. 14 and 15 of *The Works of Nathaniel Hawthorne.* Boston and New York: Houghton Mifflin, 1851–1884.

Hawthorne, Manning. "Aunt Ebe: Some Letters of Elizabeth M. Hawthorne." *New England Quarterly* 20 (1947): 209–231.

––––––. "A Glimpse of Hawthorne's Boyhood." *Essex Institute Historical Collections* 83 (1947): 178–184.

––––––. "Hawthorne's Early Years." *Essex Institute Historical Collections* 74 (1938): 1–21.

––––––. "Maria Louisa Hawthorne." *Essex Institute Historical Collections,* 75 (1939): 103–134.

––––––. "Parental and Family Influences on Hawthorne." *Essex Institute Historical Collections* 76 (1940): 1–12.

––––––. "Review of Edward Mather's *Nathaniel Hawthorne: A Modest Man.*" *New England Quarterly* 14 (1941): 380–391.

––––––. "The Youth of Hawthorne." M.A. thesis, University of North Carolina, 1937.

Hennelly, Mark. "Hawthorne's Opus Alchymicum: 'Ethan Brand.'" *ESQ: Journal of the American Renaissance* 22 (1976): 96–106.

Hoeltje, Hubert H. "Hawthorne as a Senior at Bowdoin." *Essex Institute Historical Collections* 94 (1958): 205–228.

Holland, Norman N. *5 Readers Reading.* New Haven and London: Yale University Press, 1975.

––––––. *Poems in Persons: An Introduction to the Psychoanalysis of Literature.* New York: Norton, 1973.

Hull, Raymona E. *Nathaniel Hawthorne: The English Experience, 1853–1864.* Pittsburgh: University of Pittsburgh Press, 1980.

Jaques, Elliott. "Death and the Mid-Life Crisis." *International Journal of Psychoanalysis* 46 (1965): 502–514.

James, Henry. *Hawthorne.* New York: Harpers, 1879.

Jones, Buford. "Hawthorne and Spenser: From Allusion to Allegory." *Nathaniel Hawthorne Journal* (1975): 71–90.

Jones, Wayne Allen. "Hawthorne's Slender Means." *Nathaniel Hawthorne Journal* (1977): 1–34.

––––––. "Sometimes Things Just Don't Work Out: Hawthorne's Income from *Twice-Told Tales* (1837), and Another 'Good Thing' for Hawthorne." *Nathaniel Hawthorne Journal* (1975): 11–26.

Kesselring, Marion L. *Hawthorne's Reading: 1828–1850.* New York: New York Public Library, 1949.

Labaree, Benjamin W., and B. Bernard Cohen. "Hawthorne at the Essex Institute." *Essex Institute Historical Collections* 94 (1958): 297–308.

Lamont, John H. "Hawthorne's Unfinished Works." *Harvard Medical Alumni Bulletin* 36, no. 5 (1962): 13–20.

Lathrop, George Parsons. *A Study of Hawthorne.* Boston: J. R. Osgood, 1876. Reprint. New York: A & S Press, 1969.

Lathrop, Rose Hawthorne. *Memories of Hawthorne*. Boston and New York: Houghton Mifflin, 1897.

Lesser, Simon. *Fiction and the Unconscious*. Boston: Beacon Hill Press, 1957.

Levinson, Daniel J., Charlotte N. Darrow, Edward B. Klein, Maria H. Levinson, and Braxton McKee. *The Seasons of a Man's Life*. New York: Ballantine, 1978.

Levy, Leon B. "'Lifelikeness' in Hawthorne's Fiction." *Nathaniel Hawthorne Journal* (1975): 141–145.

Lichtenstein, Heinz. "The Dilemma of Human Identity: Notes on Self-Transformation, Self-Objectivation, and Metamorphosis." *Journal of the American Psychoanalytic Association* 11 (1963): 173–223.

———. "Identity and Sexuality: A Study of Their Interrelationship in Man." *Journal of the American Psychoanalytic Association* 9 (1961): 179–260.

Liebman, Sheldon. "Hawthorne's Romanticism: 'The Artist of the Beautiful.'" *ESQ: Journal of the American Renaissance* 22 (1976): 85–95.

Lifton, Robert Jay. *The Life of the Self: Toward a New Psychology*. New York: Simon and Schuster, 1976.

Loggins, Vernon. *The Hawthornes: The Story of Seven Generations of an American Family*. New York: Columbia University Press, 1951.

Lueders, Edward G. "The Melville-Hawthorne Relationship in *Pierre* and *The Blithedale Romance*." *Western Humanities Review* 4 (1950): 323–334.

Lundblad, Jane. *Nathaniel Hawthorne and the Tradition of Gothic Romance*. Cambridge, Mass.: Harvard University Press, 1946.

MacShane, Frank. "The House of the Dead: Hawthorne's 'The Custom-House' and *The Scarlet Letter*." *New England Quarterly* 35 (1962): 93–101.

Male, Roy R. *Hawthorne's Tragic Vision*. Austin: University of Texas Press, 1957.

Manning, E. "The Boyhood of Hawthorne." *Wide Awake*, November 1891.

Manning, Robert. *Book of Fruits*. Salem: Ives and Jewett, 1838.

Manning, William H. *The Genealogical and Biographical History of the Manning Families of New England and Descendants from the Settlement in America to the Present Time*. Salem: Salem Press, 1902.

Marks, Alfred H. "Who Killed Judge Pyncheon? The Role of the Imagination in *The House of the Seven Gables*." *Publications of the Modern Language Association of America* 71 (1956): 355–369.

Martin, Terence. *Nathaniel Hawthorne*. New York: Twayne, 1965.

Mather, Edward. *Nathaniel Hawthorne: A Modest Man*. New York: Crowell, 1940.

McCall, Dan. "The Design of Hawthorne's 'Custom House.'" *Nineteenth-Century Fiction* 21 (1967): 349–358.

McDonald, John Joseph. "Hawthorne at the Old Manse." Ph.D. diss., Princeton University, 1971.

————. "The Old Manse Period Canon." *Nathaniel Hawthorne Journal* (1972): 13–40.

Mellow, James R. *Nathaniel Hawthorne in His Time.* Boston: Houghton Mifflin, 1980.

Miller, Edwin Haviland. *Melville.* New York: Braziller, 1975.

Miller, J. E. "Hawthorne and Melville: The Unpardonable Sin." *Publications of the Modern Language Association of America* 70 (1955): 91–114.

Mollinger, Shernaz. "The Divided Self in Nathaniel Hawthorne and D. H. Lawrence." *The Psychoanalytic Review* 66 (1979): 79–102.

Morris, Lloyd. *The Rebellious Puritan: Portrait of Mr. Hawthorne.* New York: Harcourt Brace, 1927.

Mottram, Richard Allen. "Hawthorne's Men: Their Dominant Influence." *Dissertation Abstracts International,* 35, 5419-A (Tulane).

Newman, Lea Bertani Vozar. *A Reader's Guide to the Short Stories of Nathaniel Hawthorne.* Boston: G. K. Hall, 1979.

Normand, Jean. *Nathaniel Hawthorne: An Approach to an Analysis of Artistic Creation.* Translated by Derck Coltman. Cleveland and London: Case Western Reserve University Press, 1970.

Paul, Louis. "A Psychoanalytic Reading of Hawthorne's 'Major Molineaux': The Father Manqué and the Protegé Manqué." *American Imago* 18 (1961): 279–288.

Pauly, Thomas H. "Hawthorne's Houses of Fiction." *American Literature* 48 (1976): 271–291.

Pearce, Roy Harvey, ed. *Hawthorne Centenary Essays.* Columbus: Ohio State University Press, 1964.

Pearson, Norman Holmes. "Elizabeth Peabody on Hawthorne." *Essex Institute Historical Collections* 94 (1958): 256–276.

————. "A 'Good Thing' for Hawthorne." *Essex Institute Historical Collections* 100 (1964): 300–305.

————. "Hawthorne and the Mannings." *Essex Institute Historical Collections* 94 (1958): 170–193.

————. "Hawthorne's Duel." *Essex Institute Historical Collections* 94 (1958): 249–252.

————. "Hawthorne's Two 'Engagements.'" Northampton: Smith College, 1963.

————. "The Pyncheons and Judge Pyncheon." *Essex Institute Historical Collections* 100 (1964): 235–255.

Pickard, Samuel T. *Hawthorne's First Diary.* Boston and New York: Houghton, Mifflin, 1897.

Ricoeur, Paul. "Psychoanalysis and the Work of Art." *Psychiatry and the Humanities.* Vol. 1. New Haven: Yale University Press, 1976.

Ryan, Pat M., Jr. "Young Hawthorne at the Theatre." *Essex Institute Historical Collections* 94 (1958): 243–255.

Salomon, Louis B. "Hawthorne and His Father: A Conjecture." *Literature and Psychology* 12 (1963): 12–17.

Sampson, Edward W. "The 'W' in Hawthorne's Name." *Essex Institute Historical Collections* 100 (1964): 297–299.

Sanborn, F. B. *Hawthorne and His Friends.* Cedar Rapids, Iowa: Torch Press, 1908.

Savarese, John. "Some Theories of Short Fiction in America in the Nineteenth Century." Ph.D. diss., Princeton University, 1975.

Shaw, Peter. "Fathers, Sons, and the Ambiguities of Revolution in 'My Kinsman, Major Molineux.'" *New England Quarterly* 49 (1976): 559–576.

Smelser, Neil J., and Erik H. Erikson, eds. *Themes of Work and Love in Adulthood.* Cambridge, Mass.: Harvard University Press, 1980.

Spengemann, William C. *The Forms of Autobiography: Episodes in the History of a Literary Genre.* New Haven: Yale University Press, 1980.

Spitzer, Michael. "Hawthorne's Women: Female Influences on the Life and Fiction of Nathaniel Hawthorne." *Dissertation Abstracts International*, 35, 4561-A (New York).

Stearns, Frank Preston. *The Life and Genius of Nathaniel Hawthorne.* Philadelphia and London: Lippincott, 1906.

Stewart, Randall. "Editing *The American Notebooks.*" *Essex Institute Historical Collections* 94 (1958): 277–281.

———. "Hawthorne and *The Faerie Queene.*" *Philological Quarterly* 12 (1933): 196–206.

———. *Nathaniel Hawthorne: A Biography.* New Haven: Yale University Press, 1948.

———. "Recollections of Hawthorne by His Sister Elizabeth." *American Literature* 16 (1945): 316–331.

Stock, Ely. "History and the Bible in Hawthorne's 'Roger Malvin's Burial.'" *Essex Institute Historical Collections* 100 (1960): 279–298.

Stone, Edward. "More on Hawthorne and Melville." *Nathaniel Hawthorne Journal* (1975): 59–69.

Stubbs, John Caldwell. *The Pursuit of Form: A Study of Hawthorne and the Romance.* Urbana: University of Illinois Press, 1970.

Sundquist, Eric J. *Home as Found: Authority and Genealogy in Nineteenth-Century American Literature.* Baltimore: Johns Hopkins University Press, 1979.

Tharp, Louise Hall. *The Peabody Sisters of Salem.* Boston: Little Brown, 1950.

Thompson, G. R., and Virgil Z. Lokke, eds. *Ruined Eden of the Present: Hawthorne, Melville, and Poe.* West Lafayette, Ind.: Purdue University Press, 1981.

Turner, Arlin. *Nathaniel Hawthorne: A Biography*. New York: Oxford University Press, 1980.

———. *Nathaniel Hawthorne: An Introduction and Interpretation*. New York: Barnes and Noble, 1961.

———. "Needs in Hawthorne Biography." *Nathaniel Hawthorne Journal* (1972): 43–46.

Van Deusen, Marshall. "Narrative Tone in 'The Custom-House' and *The Scarlet Letter*." *Nineteenth-Century Fiction* 21 (1967): 61–71.

Van Doren, Mark. *Nathaniel Hawthorne*. New York: William Sloane Associates, 1949.

Von Abele, Rudolph. *The Death of the Artist: A Study of Hawthorne's Disintegration*. The Hague: Martinus Nijhoff, 1957.

Wagenknecht, Edward. *Nathaniel Hawthorne: Man and Writer*. New York: Oxford University Press, 1961.

Waggoner, Hyatt H. *Hawthorne*. Cambridge, Mass.: Harvard University Press, 1955.

———. "A Hawthorne Discovery: The Lost Notebook, 1825–1841." *New England Quarterly* 49 (1976): 618–626.

———. Introduction. *Nathaniel Hawthorne: Selected Tales and Sketches*. 3d ed. New York: Rinehart, 1956.

———. *The Presence of Hawthorne*. Baton Rouge: Louisiana State University Press, 1979.

Welsh, Alexander. "Lives of Hawthorne." *Yale Review* 70 (1981): 421–430.

West, Harry C. "Hawthorne's Editorial Pose." *American Literature* 44 (1972): 208–221.

Wilson, James D. "Incest and American Romantic Fiction." *Studies in the Literary Imagination* 7 (1974): 31–50.

Winters, Yvor. *In Defense of Reason*. New York: Swallow Press and William Morrow, 1947.

Woodberry, George. *Nathaniel Hawthorne*. Boston and New York: Houghton, Mifflin, 1902.

Index

of contact with, 32–33; life structure and, 4–5; of Manning grandfather, 41, 42; of Manning grandmother, 79; *The Marble Faun* and, 33–34; of Maria Miriam (Aunt), 40, 41, 57; real and symbolic forms of, 2; rebirth into past and, 162; *Seven Gables* and ancestral line and, 138–145; of sister, Maria Louisa, 64; of Ticknor, 126; unburied bodies and, 109, 110, 111, 113–116; of Uncle Robert (Manning), 44, 110, 112–113, 135; of Uncle Samuel (Manning), 13, 41

Dependency, 24, 30, 31, 37, 71–72, 118

Development, Erikson's theory of, 34, 119

"The Devil in Manuscript," 16

Dickinson, Emily, 143 n

The Dictionary of American Biography (article on Uncle Robert Manning in), 42

Dike, John (husband of Aunt Priscilla Manning), 40, 50, 55

Dike, Priscilla Manning (aunt). *See* Manning, Priscilla (aunt, Mrs. John Dike)

Dimmesdale (*The Scarlet Letter*), 28, 29, 122–123, 128, 148

Dingley, Susannah (later wife of Uncle Richard Manning), 40

Dislocation. *See* Sense of dislocation

Doctor Gibben (*Doctor Grimshawe's Secret*), 160

Doctor Grimshawe's Secret (unfinished romance): ambivalence toward guardian figures and, 152–160; ambivalence toward Palmer-Pensioner's benevolence and,

162–167; autobiographical nature of quest theme and, 146–152, 157, 161, 180, 181; bifurcated father-surrogate figures and, 160–162, 173–176; Bloody Footstep symbolism and, 167–172; enthrallment and, 148, 157–159; Hawthorne and guardians and, 117; past and future tension and, 150–152; psychic self-enthrallment and, 176–181; true feelings toward guardians and, 155–157

Doctor Portsoaken (*Septimius Felton*), 148

Donatello (*The Marble Faun*), 129

Dorcas Malvin ("Roger Malvin's Burial"), 114, 115, 128

Doubt (in Erikson's life cycle theory), 119, 120

Dream fantasies, 110

Dreams: as instinctive perception of the soul, 120–121; recurrent, 7; Sophia's displacement in, 91–92, 93

Dryden, Edgar A., 192 n. 1

Duyckinck, Evert, 19

Eakin, Paul John, 184 n. 1

Ebe. *See* Hawthorne, Elizabeth (sister, Ebe)

Edith ("The White Old Maid"), 95

Education: in *Doctor Grimshawe's Secret*, 154–155; of Hawthorne, 13, 44–45, 48–50, 51, 69, 70–71, 74–75, 79

Elsie (*Doctor Grimshawe's Secret*), 150, 151, 153, 154, 167, 168, 172, 173

Emerson, Ralph Waldo, 124, 125, 163, 166

English Notebooks, 163

43,391